X

THE
GREENPEACE
BOOK OF
DOLPHINS

EDITED BY
JOHN MAY

CENTURY
LONDON · SYDNEY · AUCKLAND · JOHANNESBURG

Previous page: **The dramatic profile of a leaping common dolphin.**
(Eric Martin)
Opposite: **Like symmetrical emblems on a Greek medallion, these
two bottlenose dolphins, photographed off the Azores, display
their natural grace and beauty.**
(Jonathan Gordon/IFAW)

Text copyright © Greenpeace Communications Ltd. 1990

First published in 1990 by Century Editions, an imprint of The Random
Century Group Ltd, 20 Vauxhall Bridge Road, London SW1V 2SA

Random Century (Pty) Ltd, 20 Alfred Street, Milsons Point, Sydney,
New South Wales 2061, Australia

Random Century New Zealand Ltd, Glenfield, Auckland 10, New Zealand

Random Century South Africa (Pty) Ltd, PO Box 337, Bergvlei,
2012 South Africa

British Library Cataloguing in Publication Data

May, John, 1950 –
     The Greenpeace book of dolphins
     1. Dolphins
     I. Title II. Mulvaney, Kieran
     599.53
     ISBN 0-7126-3051-1

GREENPEACE BOOKS

Editor/Picture Research/Additional Text: John May
Design/Maps: Andy Gammon
Production Manager/Additional Text: Ian Whitelaw
Manuscript Production: Tanya Seton

Typeset by Brenda Mason
Index by Richard Raper et al/Indexing Specialists, Hove

Martin Camm's illustrations © of the Artist. Courtesy of Bernard Thornton
Artists, London

Colour origination by Hong Kong Graphic Art Ltd
Printed and bound in West Germany by Mohndruck

Main Text
Kieran Mulvaney

Principal Text Contributors
Kenneth Brower
Mark Carwardine
Dwight Holing
Erich Hoyt

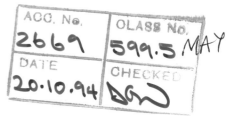
Principal Photographic Contributors
EarthViews
Marine Mammal Images
Eric Martin

Illustrations
Ian Andrew
Martin Camm
Pieter Arend Folkens

Principal Consultants
Lawrence G. Barnes
Hannah Bernard
Margaret Klinowska
Stephen Leatherwood
Randall R. Reeves

PREFACE

by Lyall Watson

We need a metaphor for the new age. Too much of our thinking is still based on views inherited from the nineteenth century and a model of nature that is red in tooth and claw. Naive observation of animal behaviour in the days of Darwin led to a description of evolution as a ruthless struggle in which the winners take all. The truth is that there is no such war in nature. Co-operation, not competition, is the secret of survival. Fitness means just that. It is a measure of ability to fit in, not fight back. And growing awareness of the power of such community makes it necessary for us to look for a new symbol – or, better still, to revive a very old one.

Creation myths in every culture portray the sea as the source of life. They tell of watery origins, but they deal also with relationships. Flowing through them all is the shape-shifting, life-enhancing image of a genesis in which both humans and animals are intimately involved. A symbiosis most vividly represented by a child riding so closely on a dolphin that their bodies blend into a single liquid concert of birth and renewal.

Even the word 'dolphin' is hedged with the same creative magic. It derives from the Indo-European root *gwelbh* that gave rise to both the Greek *delphis*, for the marine mammal, and *delphys*, meaning 'womb'.

There is something about dolphins, something to do perhaps with their ecstatic reunion with the ocean, that makes us envious – and prone, on occasion, to exaggerate their spirituality. But there is nothing imaginary about their musicality, their social skills, their easy sensuality and evident intelligence. More than any other creatures on the planet, they call our assumed dominion over nature into question. With every contact, they promise both to satisfy our craving for communication with another species, and to intensify our sense of inadequacy.

I know from my own experience of dolphins in every part of the world ocean, how sweet and strange such contacts can be. While they last, they produce a kind of euphoria – the sort of well-being and sense of belonging that comes sometimes from great music or an extraordinary sunset. But these encounters with another mind are also very troubling. I find myself, each time one ends, feeling that I must have missed a cue, wondering what it was I could have thought or done to respond more meaningfully to yet another of their exuberant overtures.

I haven't found an answer to that dilemma yet. I don't really expect to do so until we learn more about the community to which we both belong. Which is why I welcome this initiative by Greenpeace. This seems to me to be a very proper response to the problem. A celebration of what we already know about dolphins, coupled with a plea for the sort of restraint and responsibility that will make it possible for us to learn a great deal more.

This is more than just a book about dolphins. It is a powerful presentation of the most appropriate and revealing metaphor for our time.

CONTENTS

This powerful action shot of a bottlenose dolphin breaking the surface of the water shows clearly the array of toothmarks made by other dolphins on its skin.
(Eric Martin)

THE HUMAN THREAT:
Hunting and Fishing
    86-107

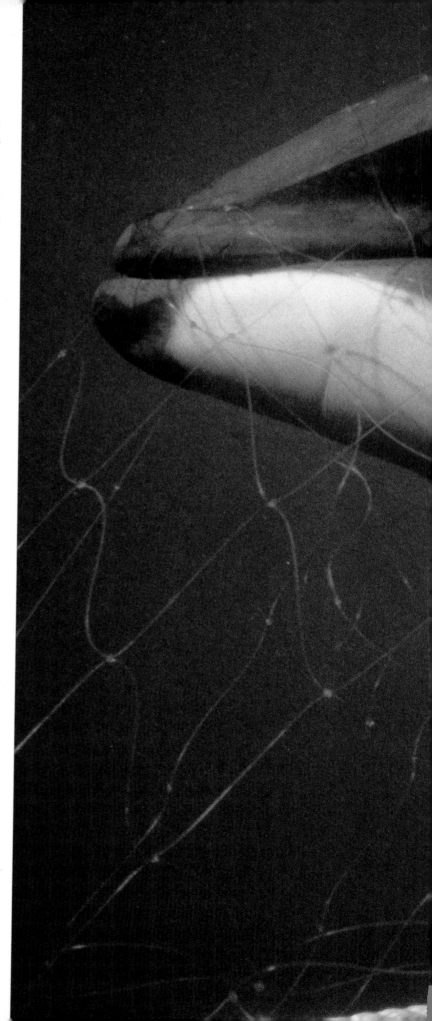

A dead Hector's dolphin calf, one of the rarest of all cetacean species, drifts in the net that drowned it.
(Steve Dawson/Hedgehog House New Zealand)

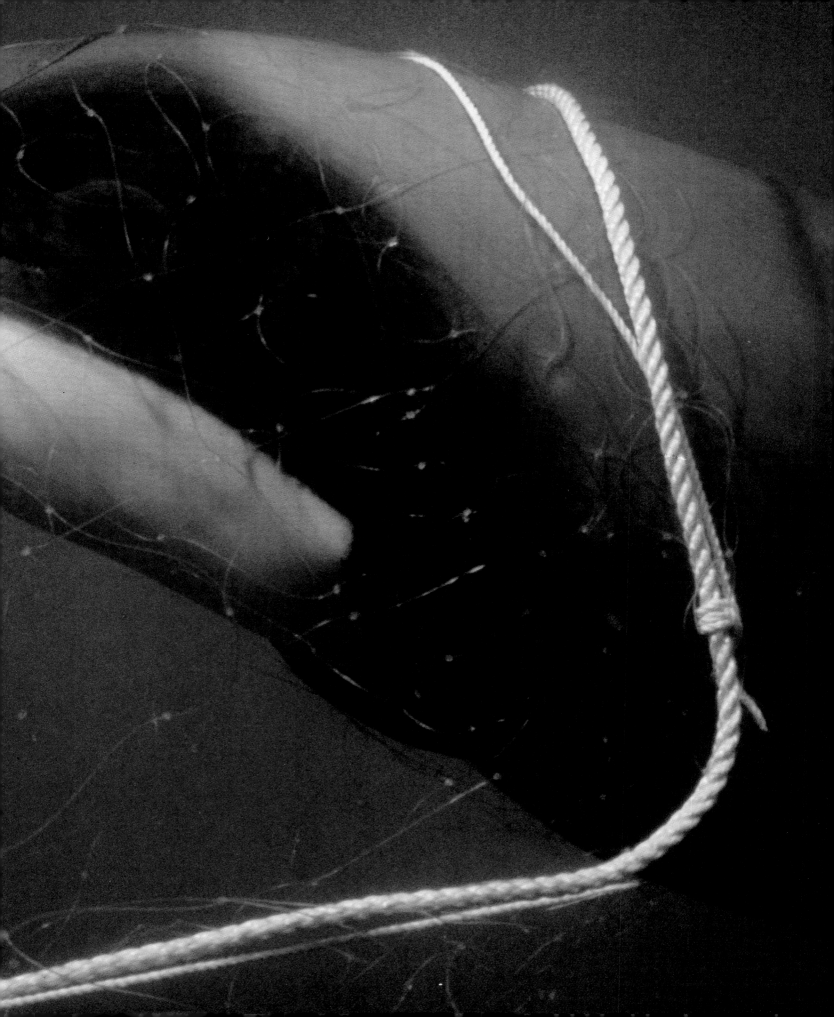

One of the hundreds of dead bottlenose dolphins that were washed up on the east coast of the USA in the summer of 1987 being stretchered away for post-mortem examination.
(Michael Baytoff)

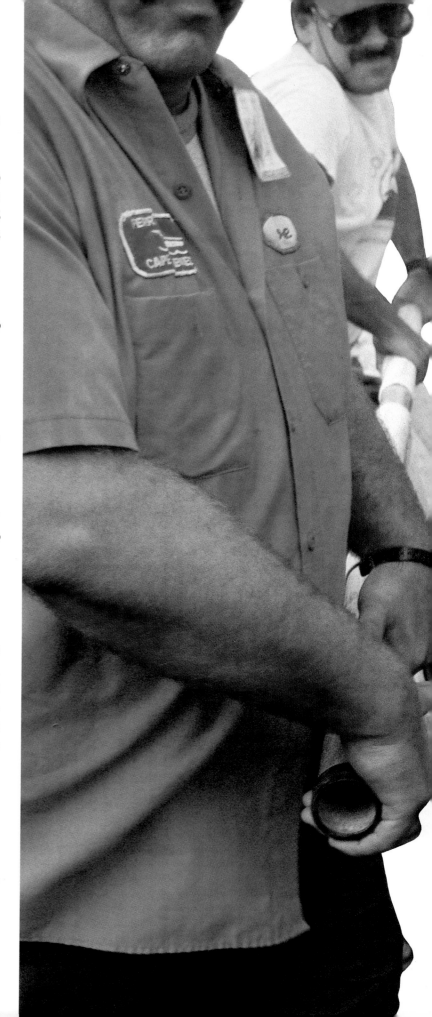

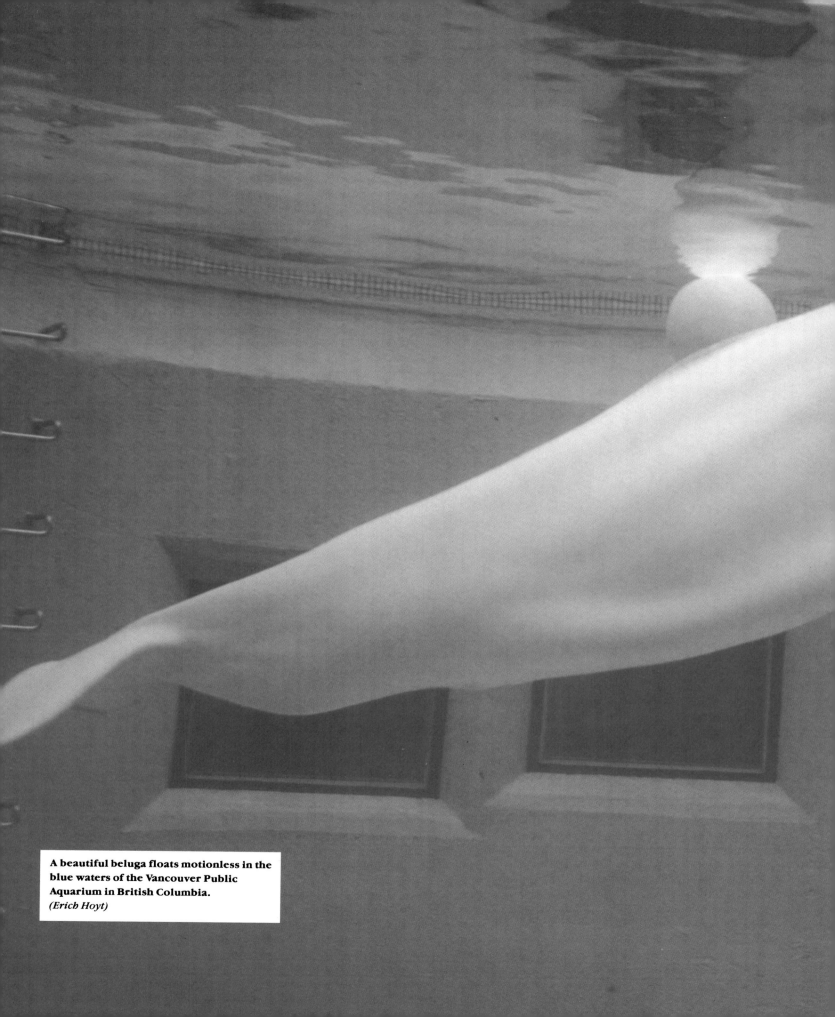

A beautiful beluga floats motionless in the blue waters of the Vancouver Public Aquarium in British Columbia.
(Erich Hoyt)

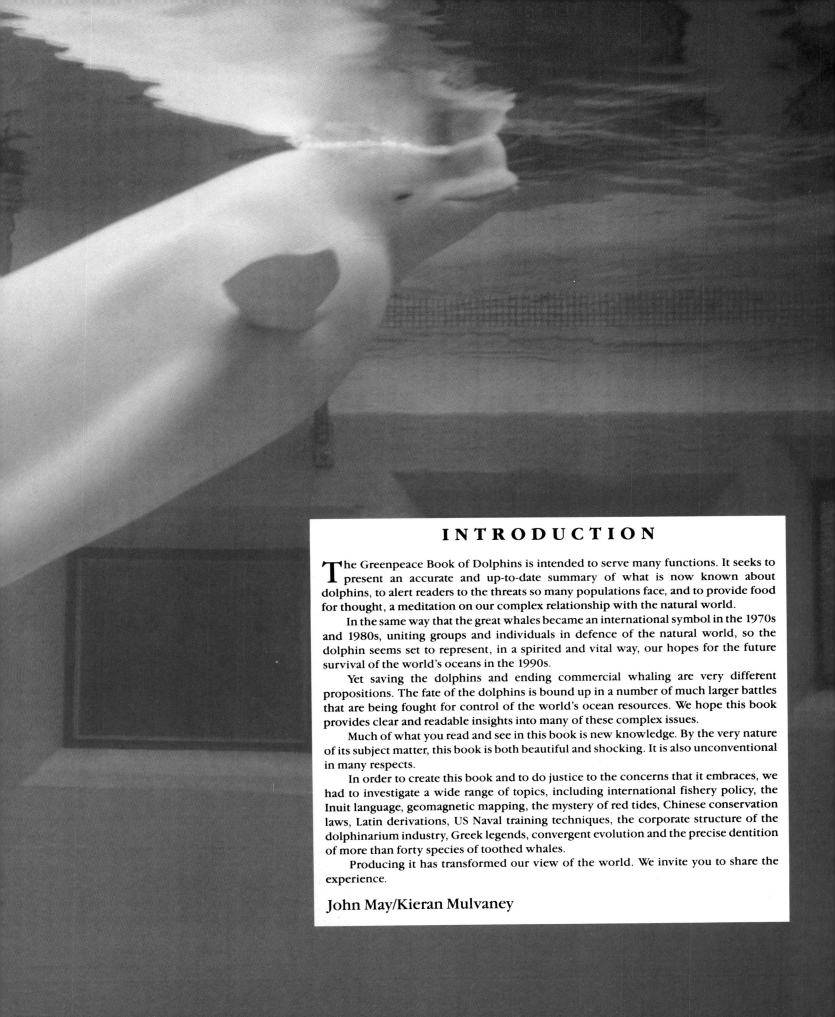

INTRODUCTION

The Greenpeace Book of Dolphins is intended to serve many functions. It seeks to present an accurate and up-to-date summary of what is now known about dolphins, to alert readers to the threats so many populations face, and to provide food for thought, a meditation on our complex relationship with the natural world.

In the same way that the great whales became an international symbol in the 1970s and 1980s, uniting groups and individuals in defence of the natural world, so the dolphin seems set to represent, in a spirited and vital way, our hopes for the future survival of the world's oceans in the 1990s.

Yet saving the dolphins and ending commercial whaling are very different propositions. The fate of the dolphins is bound up in a number of much larger battles that are being fought for control of the world's ocean resources. We hope this book provides clear and readable insights into many of these complex issues.

Much of what you read and see in this book is new knowledge. By the very nature of its subject matter, this book is both beautiful and shocking. It is also unconventional in many respects.

In order to create this book and to do justice to the concerns that it embraces, we had to investigate a wide range of topics, including international fishery policy, the Inuit language, geomagnetic mapping, the mystery of red tides, Chinese conservation laws, Latin derivations, US Naval training techniques, the corporate structure of the dolphinarium industry, Greek legends, convergent evolution and the precise dentition of more than forty species of toothed whales.

Producing it has transformed our view of the world. We invite you to share the experience.

John May/Kieran Mulvaney

THE
NATURE
OF
DOLPHINS

'From an evolutionary standpoint, humans have a generalized body. Dolphins do not. We can put on a wet suit and go diving among the cetaceans to study them. They cannot put on a "dry suit" and come on to land to observe us. We must go to them. We must take the initiative if we want to understand cetaceans.'

Lawrence G. Barnes

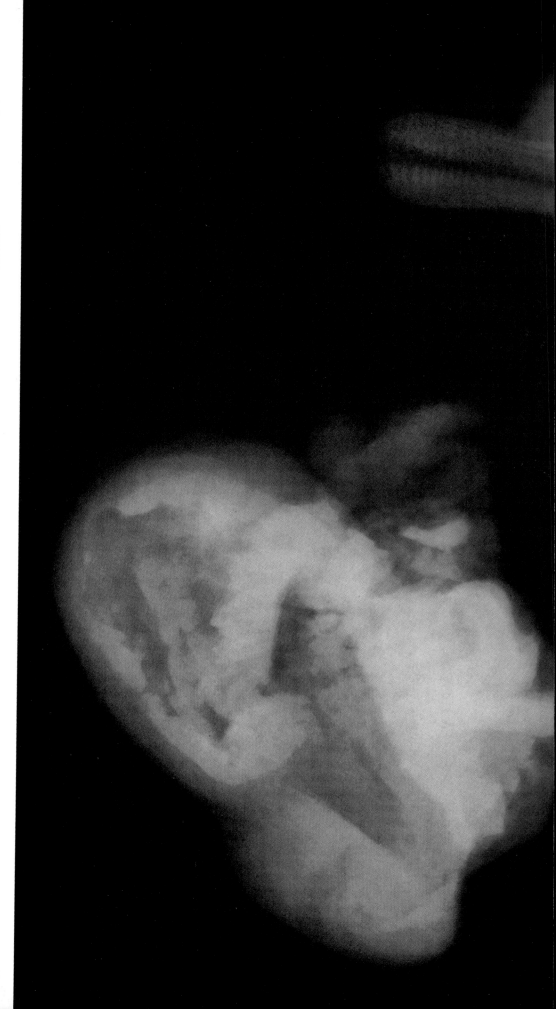

An extraordinary X-ray photograph of the embryo of a Ganges susu *(Platanista gangetica)* showing the umbilical cord and placenta.
(Giorgio Pilleri)

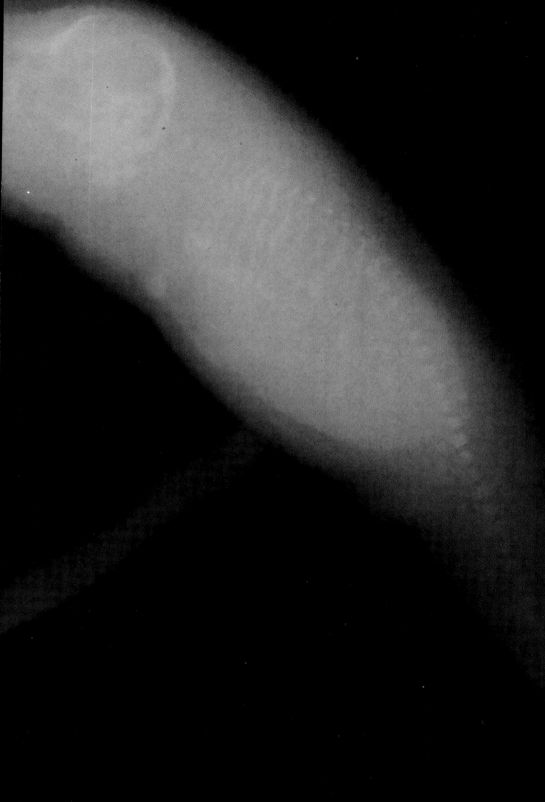

WHAT IS A DOLPHIN?

By most accounts, there are about 80 species of whales, dolphins and porpoises known to exist in the world today. They all belong to the order of mammals known as cetaceans, in the same way that apes (including humans), monkeys and lemurs all belong to the order of mammals called primates.

Cetacean species are assigned by scientists to two suborders - the Mysticeti or baleen whales and the Odontoceti or toothed whales. These suborders, and the smaller sub-groups into which each is divided, are based on a logical, well-defined system of classifying animals by commonly held characteristics. However, the popular names given to cetaceans are less consistent and often confusing.

For example, the term whale conjures up the image of a huge animal. In fact some of the smaller cetaceans are also called whales. Most of the mysticetes are referred to as great whales, as is the sperm whale (an odontocete), because of their size.

Both the killer whale and pilot whale are members of the family Delphinidae, which includes all the oceanic, or 'true' dolphins, as well as some coastal and riverine species. The narwhal is in a different family - the Monodontidae - which also includes the beluga, or white whale. However it is appropriate to refer to them as dolphins as they are members of the superfamily Delphinoidea.

The term porpoise is flexible, and the words dolphin and porpoise are used interchangeably in most countries. Strictly speaking, porpoise should be used only to refer to the six members of the family Phocoenidae which are all small, robust species.

In this book, a dolphin is considered as any member of the Delphinoidea (currently considered to contain three familes - the Delphinidae, the Monodontidae and the Phocoenidae) and the five species of 'river' dolphins which compose the superfamily Platanistoidea. All are toothed whales (Odontoceti) and they are sometimes referred to as 'small' cetaceans even though some are large.

This confusion of terms and descriptions is further clarified in an appendix at the back of this book.

Evolution

A ny discussion about the evolution of cetaceans needs to be approached with caution, due to the incompleteness of the available fossil records. There are large gaps, but new intermediate forms are consistently being discovered which explain or illuminate the transitional stages between successive groups of cetaceans.

Below: **Zygohriza was a typical doruntid, an oceanic archaeocete of the late Eocene, which had almost completely lost the hind limbs of its land-based ancestors. Probably the dominant predator of the time, it was a generalized eater with a wide variety of prey.**

Right: **Squalodont was a primitive dolphin-like animal from the early Miocene, with a very long rostrum, flexible neck and a primitive echolocation system. Its sharp teeth, which protruded beyond the rostrum, were used to grasp its prey of small to medium-size fish.**

Illustrations: Pieter Arend Folkens

CETACEAN PRECURSORS

All life on this planet began, billions of years ago, in the ocean. Here vertebrates (animals with backbones) developed and, many hundreds of millions of years later, spread to the land. Some groups subsequently returned to the ocean, amongst them the suspected ancestors of cetaceans, the Mesonychidae. These were once a widely-distributed group of now extinct mammals that ranged in size from a small dog to a large bear; they are also believed to be the forerunners of the modern ungulates or hoofed mammals.

More than 50 million years ago, probably during the early part of the Eocene Epoch, some type of Mesonychidae may have begun spending progressively more time foraging for fish and other aquatic organisms in the warm, shallow waters of the Tethys Sea. This vast sea subsequently divided, as the continents shifted, to form the present-day Mediterranean Sea and the north-western Indian Ocean.

Their return to the water may have brought significant benefits to these terrestrial carnivores. Animals in the sea provided a new and unexploited food resource. The adaptation and selection processes, which we collectively call evolution, might have proceeded at a relatively rapid rate. Nonetheless, it took millions of years before species which could be considered true cetaceans appeared on the scene.

EARLY CETACEANS

Protocetidae, the oldest and most primitive cetaceans, arose and diversified during the Eocene Epoch, some 45-50 million years ago. We know little about them, except that they already had a number of characteristics which made them recognizable as cetaceans: inflated earbones, which probably facilitated underwater hearing, and an elongated snout, with nostrils near its tip. At least some of them appear to have retained hind limbs and their lifestyle may have been amphibious rather than fully

aquatic. The only known fossil remains, which have been found in the Himalayan region of Pakistan and India, as well as in Eygpt and Nigeria, suggest that most Protocetidae were small-bodied animals less than 3m (10ft) long.

By about 40 million years ago, more advanced groups of Archaeoceti, or ancient whales, had developed. The Dorudontinae were dolphin-like cetaceans which grew to lengths of about 5m (16ft), had nostrils further back on the snout than the Protocetidae and bodies that were more streamlined. They were closely related to the Basilosaurinae, the largest known archaeocetes, which were more than 20m (65ft) in length.

During the Oligocene Epoch, between 24 and 34 million years ago, the Archaeoceti apparently gave rise to the two major groups, or suborders, of modern cetaceans, the Odontoceti (toothed whales) and Mysticeti (baleen whales).

Among the many diverse forms of primitive Odontoceti, the Squalodontae were like modern dolphins in many respects and are probably the group from which most later odontocetes ultimately derived. However, these relatively large cetaceans, 3m (10ft) or more in length, retained one primitive feature: they had a heterodont dentition i.e. they had more than one kind of tooth. Modern dolphins have homodont dentition, i.e. all their teeth are essentially alike.

SELECTIVE FORCES

The primary factors which shaped the early cetaceans were a consequence of their new ocean environment.

Water is an efficient conductor of heat and any warm-blooded creature which has to spend long periods immersed in it needs to find a way of conserving body heat. While certain mammals, like otters, have evolved a coat of hair or fur, the cetaceans acquired an insulating layer of blubber under the skin. This oily tissue also functions as a fat deposit, providing the animal with an important reservoir of energy to sustain it during lean periods when food is in short supply.

While the sea presented some daunting challenges to the early cetaceans and their ancestors, it also offered immense opportunities. Fish and invertebrates were probably available in abundance and, initially at least, there may have been little competition for these food resources.

Freed from the constraints of gravity, the cetaceans grew larger. Their increased body size was useful for overtaking and intimidating prey, discouraging predators, storing energy and conserving heat.

These successful adaptations allowed cetaceans to diversify and exploit a wide range of habitats, from lakes and rivers to shallow seas and the depths of the ocean. They have not only survived their transition from land to water but have thrived there. They remain to this day the sea's most magnificent inhabitants.

The smaller Kentriodontidae, approximately 2m (6ft 6in) or less in length, were a relatively diverse family that lived in both the Atlantic and Pacific Oceans in the Miocene Epoch (24-5 million years ago). The superfamily Delphinoidea, which includes the modern families Delphinidae, Phocoenidae and Monodontidae, may have arisen from the Kentriodontidae about ten million years ago.

The 'river' dolphins, the Platanistoidea, have a different skull structure from the other modern dolphins, raising the possibility that they evolved from different Oligocene ancestors.

Water is a denser medium than air and therefore offers greater resistance to movement through it, a fact that dictated not only the evolution of the cetaceans' overall shape but also the development of flukes, flippers and the specific alignment and formation of muscles.

Dramatic changes were necessary for these animals to survive in an environment that was basically hostile to mammalian life, and the evidence of the fossil record shows that the speed and magnitude of these transformations were nothing short of remarkable.

Above: **The appearance of Kentriodon in the late Miocene marks the point in evolutionary history at which delphinidae established themselves in the ocean. Although still primitive, it is not unlike modern dolphins in shape, with a fairly sophisticated echolocation system. All dolphins since Kentriodon have been variations on this basic theme.**

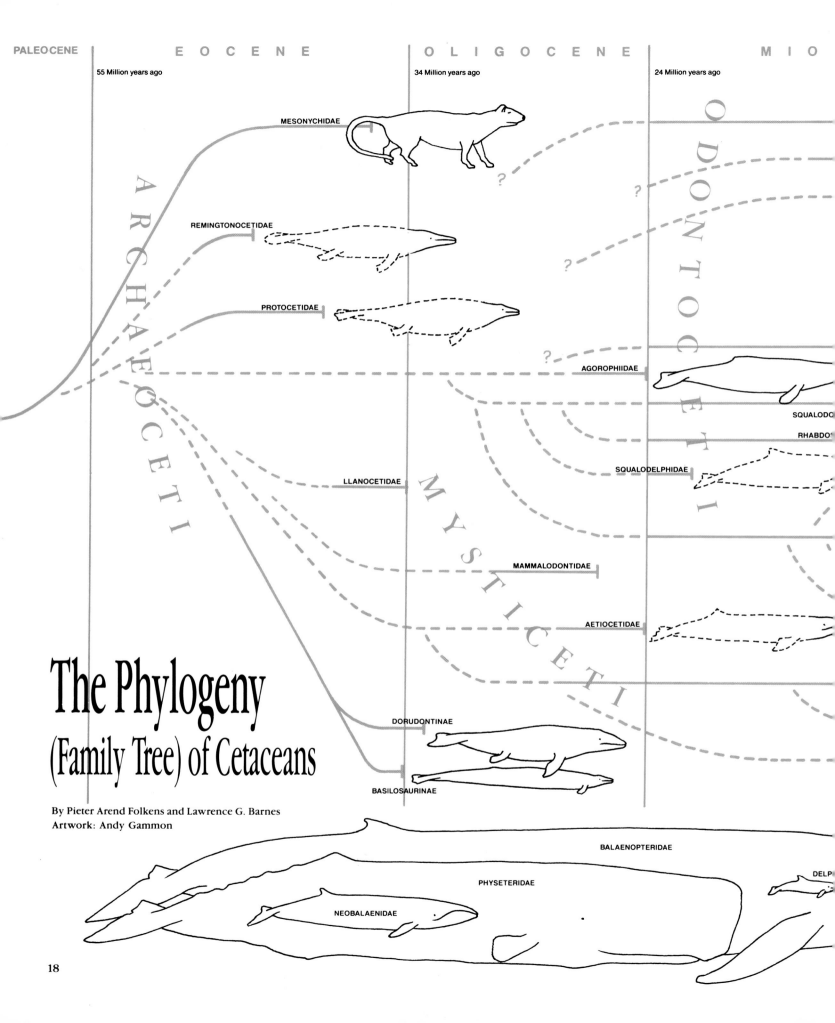

55 Million years ago

34 Million years ago

24 Million years ago

MESONYCHIDAE

REMINGTONOCETIDAE

PROTOCETIDAE

AGOROPHIIDAE

SQUALODO

RHABDO

SQUALODELPHIDAE

LLANOCETIDAE

MAMMALODONTIDAE

AETIOCETIDAE

DORUDONTINAE

BASILOSAURINAE

A R C H A E O C E T I

M Y S T I C E T I

O D O N T O C E T I

The Phylogeny
(Family Tree) of Cetaceans

By Pieter Arend Folkens and Lawrence G. Barnes
Artwork: Andy Gammon

BALAENOPTERIDAE

PHYSETERIDAE

DELP

NEOBALAENIDAE

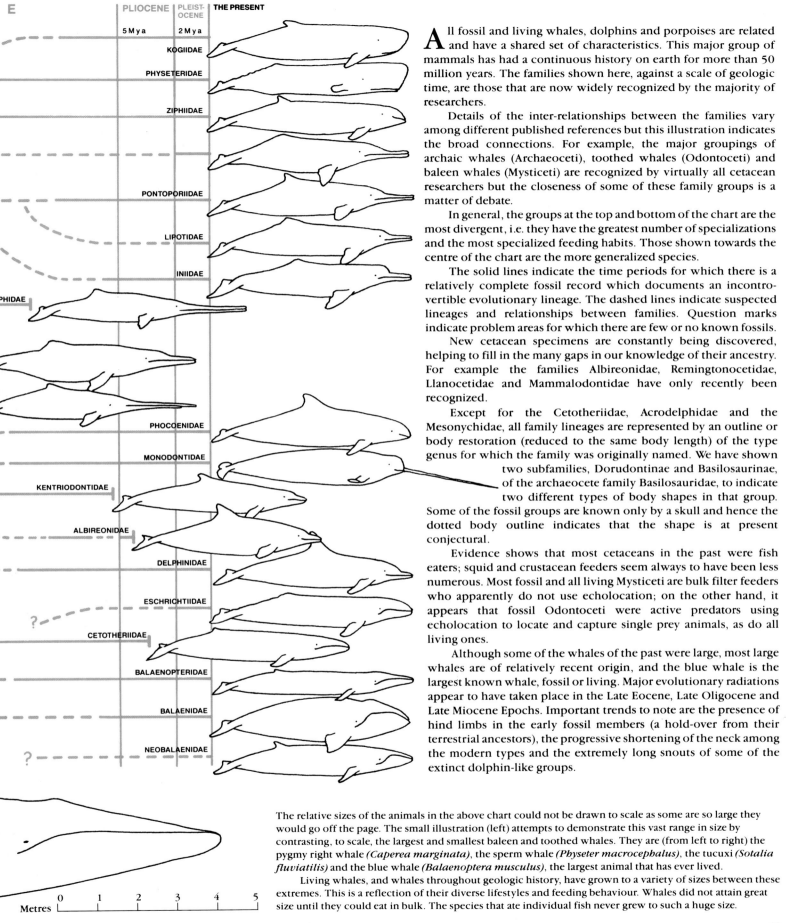

All fossil and living whales, dolphins and porpoises are related and have a shared set of characteristics. This major group of mammals has had a continuous history on earth for more than 50 million years. The families shown here, against a scale of geologic time, are those that are now widely recognized by the majority of researchers.

Details of the inter-relationships between the families vary among different published references but this illustration indicates the broad connections. For example, the major groupings of archaic whales (Archaeoceti), toothed whales (Odontoceti) and baleen whales (Mysticeti) are recognized by virtually all cetacean researchers but the closeness of some of these family groups is a matter of debate.

In general, the groups at the top and bottom of the chart are the most divergent, i.e. they have the greatest number of specializations and the most specialized feeding habits. Those shown towards the centre of the chart are the more generalized species.

The solid lines indicate the time periods for which there is a relatively complete fossil record which documents an incontrovertible evolutionary lineage. The dashed lines indicate suspected lineages and relationships between families. Question marks indicate problem areas for which there are few or no known fossils.

New cetacean specimens are constantly being discovered, helping to fill in the many gaps in our knowledge of their ancestry. For example the families Albireonidae, Remingtonocetidae, Llanocetidae and Mammalodontidae have only recently been recognized.

Except for the Cetotheriidae, Acrodelphidae and the Mesonychidae, all family lineages are represented by an outline or body restoration (reduced to the same body length) of the type genus for which the family was originally named. We have shown two subfamilies, Dorudontinae and Basilosaurinae, of the archaeocete family Basilosauridae, to indicate two different types of body shapes in that group. Some of the fossil groups are known only by a skull and hence the dotted body outline indicates that the shape is at present conjectural.

Evidence shows that most cetaceans in the past were fish eaters; squid and crustacean feeders seem always to have been less numerous. Most fossil and all living Mysticeti are bulk filter feeders who apparently do not use echolocation; on the other hand, it appears that fossil Odontoceti were active predators using echolocation to locate and capture single prey animals, as do all living ones.

Although some of the whales of the past were large, most large whales are of relatively recent origin, and the blue whale is the largest known whale, fossil or living. Major evolutionary radiations appear to have taken place in the Late Eocene, Late Oligocene and Late Miocene Epochs. Important trends to note are the presence of hind limbs in the early fossil members (a hold-over from their terrestrial ancestors), the progressive shortening of the neck among the modern types and the extremely long snouts of some of the extinct dolphin-like groups.

The relative sizes of the animals in the above chart could not be drawn to scale as some are so large they would go off the page. The small illustration (left) attempts to demonstrate this vast range in size by contrasting, to scale, the largest and smallest baleen and toothed whales. They are (from left to right) the pygmy right whale *(Caperea marginata)*, the sperm whale *(Physeter macrocephalus)*, the tucuxi *(Sotalia fluviatilis)* and the blue whale *(Balaenoptera musculus)*, the largest animal that has ever lived.

Living whales, and whales throughout geologic history, have grown to a variety of sizes between these extremes. This is a reflection of their diverse lifestyles and feeding behaviour. Whales did not attain great size until they could eat in bulk. The species that ate individual fish never grew to such a huge size.

19

Anatomy

Illustration: Andy Gammon/Margaret Klinowska

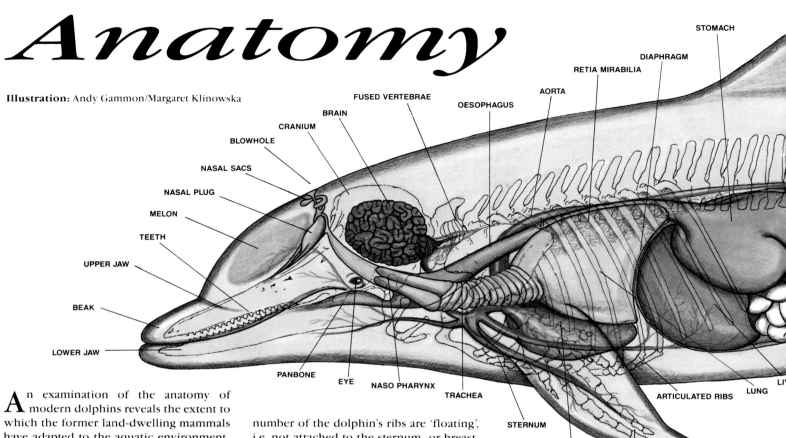

An examination of the anatomy of modern dolphins reveals the extent to which the former land-dwelling mammals have adapted to the aquatic environment.

Overall, the body shape has become streamlined to improve hydrodynamic efficiency. The hind limbs have disappeared, the forelimbs have developed into flippers and a powerful tail provides the means of propulsion. The dolphin has developed an insulating layer of blubber and a range of other adaptations to minimize heat loss.

SKIN
The dolphin's smooth skin is constantly being sloughed off and replaced. It is sensitive to touch and easily scarred. Virtually all adult dolphins carry at least a partial record of their interactions with companions, enemies and the environment, encoded in an array of scars, nicks and notches on their skin. This has been very useful to researchers as an aid to identifying individual animals.

SKELETON
The basic mammalian skeleton has undergone a number of specialized changes. The forelimbs have been modified into flippers and the bones of the hind limbs have disappeared altogether. The pelvic girdle remains as a mere vestige buried in the ventral musculature. A large number of the dolphin's ribs are 'floating', i.e. not attached to the sternum, or breastbone; ribs that are attached are often jointed, enabling the rib-cage to collapse under the pressure of a deep dive without being damaged. The skull has become tilted upwards in line with the spinal column and the cervical (or neck) vertebrae have become fused together in almost all species.

HEAD
The face of the dolphin is essentially unexpressive. Although the eyes may widen and dart about with excitement or narrow abruptly in anger, the perpetual smile of most species tells us nothing about their emotional state.

Some dolphins have a well-defined beak and others have none. There is no external ear, only a pinhole opening on either side of the head, which is vestigial and is not used for hearing. Set in front of these the eyes function independently of each other.

The asymmetrical skull of the dolphin has many interesting features. The jaws are straight, elongated and narrow in most species. Towards the back of the upper jaw, on what is effectively the animal's top lip, is an area of fatty, tissue called the 'melon'. The braincase lies at the very rear of the skull. The hollow lower jaw is filled with fatty tissue and has a thin area, known as the 'panbone', situated at the rear.

Most dolphin species have large numbers of teeth, some more than 200. The two most notable exceptions to this are: the adult Risso's dolphin, which has no teeth in the upper jaw and no more than 14 in the lower; and the male narwhal, whose tusk is almost always its only visible tooth. Unlike many mammals, toothed whales do not have milk teeth but develop a single set, none of which are replaced.

Situated behind the melon is the 'blowhole', the external opening to the animal's nasal passages. In most dolphins the blowhole is crescent-shaped, with the curve towards the back. In all species the blowhole is naturally closed and must be opened by muscular action. The two nasal passages in the animal's skull join together into a single tube, which fits over the end of the trachea, which then passes through the oesophagus. The fact that the trachea and the oesophagus are completely separate enables the animal to feed underwater without drowning.

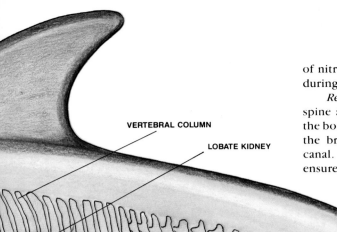

VERTEBRAL COLUMN

LOBATE KIDNEY

PENIS
TESTES
UROGENITAL OPENING
BLADDER
ANUS
INTESTINES
FLUKES

of nitrogen which may form in the blood during ascents from deep dives.

Retia in the thorax and around the spine are fed with blood from arteries in the body wall and supply blood directly to the brain through arteries in the spinal canal. It is thought that this arrangement ensures a constant blood supply to the brain even during deep dives. Water pressure could interrupt the supply of blood if it passed through an unprotected internal carotid artery, as it does in most other mammals.

Another specialized feature of the dolphin's circulatory system is designed to conserve body heat. In the dorsal fin and the flukes, warm blood flowing towards the extremities passes through arteries which are surrounded by bundles of veins carrying the returning blood. Heat from the outgoing blood is largely absorbed by the cooler returning blood, thereby minimizing the loss of heat to the environment. This system is known as 'countercurrent heat exchange' and it carries the additional advantage of helping the animal to lose heat during periods of intense activity. An increase in the flow of outgoing blood has the effect of expanding the arteries and thereby constricting the surrounding veins. This forces the returning blood to flow through other veins, closer to the skin, and thereby increases heat loss.

REPRODUCTIVE ORGANS

In males, the urogenital opening is in front of, and separate from, the anus. The long retractible penis, which is normally wholly inside the body, is almost prehensile and emerges when erect. The paired testes are hidden deep within the abdominal cavity near the kidneys. Females also have a urogenital slit on the belly, within which the reproductive and excretory organs are situated. The two mammary glands are located on either side of the urogenital opening and the nipples are recessed within longitudinal slits. The shape of the baby dolphin's mouth prevents it from suckling directly underwater; the mother's rich milk is therefore squirted from the nipples into the baby's mouth.

DORSAL FIN

Most dolphins have a dorsal fin, the size and shape of which varies between species, but it is unclear why this structure evolved. As far as we know it has no analogue in the terrestrial ancestors of cetaceans. As the dorsal fin has no bony support, it is not surprising that it is absent from the fossil record. Some modern species (the beluga, narwhal, finless porpoise and right whale dolphin) lack the fin entirely, and several of the river dolphins have what can only be regarded as a rudimentary ridge or hump-like fin. This indicates that a well-developed fin on the back is not essential for cetacean survival.

FLUKES

The two flukes of the dolphin's tail are flat and horizontal, and are held rigid not by bones but by tendons and fibrous tissue. The flukes function as powerful paddles and are driven up and down by the well-muscled tail stock or 'peduncle', rather than from side to side as is the case in fish. The long powerful muscles of the peduncle, some of which originate far forward on the back, need to be firmly attached to the skeleton; the dolphin's vertebrae therefore have specially adapted long spines to which they are anchored.

KIDNEY

The kidneys are large and consist of many inter-connected, closely-packed lobes called 'renculi'. Such lobate kidneys are also found in seals, otters and bears, so it is not clear what adaptive value these may have for life in the water. The dolphin's kidneys also contain special structures which may help with filtration during diving.

One might expect that dolphins would have a problem obtaining enough water to keep them alive, living as most of them do in a saline environment, and that the kidneys would have a vital role to play. In fact, dolphins get most of the water they need from eating fish and furthermore the dolphin's skin would appear to act as an osmotic membrane, allowing water, but not salt, to enter its system. This explains why the kidneys do not appear to be very specialized.

BLOOD CIRCULATION

The circulatory system of the dolphin is remarkable in several ways. One of its most extraordinary features is the presence of several *retia mirabilia* or 'wonderful nets'. (These are not exclusive to cetaceans but are also found in dugongs and manatees, seals, sloths, armadillos, anteaters and some rodents.) It is thought that these 'nets' of tiny blood vessels serve to protect vital organs from the effects of water pressure, and possibly to trap any bubbles

Behaviour/Adaptation

SIZE OF GROUPINGS

Although the popular impression of dolphins is that they are highly sociable and gregarious, their social structures and group sizes vary considerably between species and sometimes within the same species in different areas or circumstances.

Bottlenose and spotted dolphins, for example, occur in small groups everywhere but only form large groups offshore. In general, the riverine and coastal species occur alone, in pairs or in small groups of perhaps half a dozen. Some continental-shelf, shelf-edge and pelagic dolphins, by contrast, live in huge herds of hundreds or thousands.

Such herds may be structured internally, so that discrete bands of males, or of females with young, keep together and interact collectively with other social units in the herd. Some of these alliances are permanent, or at least last for several years, whilst others are temporary and fluid, lasting only for hours or days.

The scale on which one assesses such group structures makes a great difference. For example, separate groups of juveniles which, to a human observer, appear to be isolated may prove in fact to be just some of a number of segregated social units whose behaviour and distribution are in fact co-ordinated within a larger community. Furthermore, observations made in only one season or time of day may be biased and fail to reflect daily or seasonal differences.

To complicate the picture further, mixed-species herds are common: herds of pilot whales in many parts of the world may be attended by small groups of bottlenose dolphins; northern right whale dolphins and Pacific white-sided dolphins are often found together as are spotted and spinner dolphins. At times, up to six species may travel and feed in the same small area. Close study of such associations has revealed that the different species partition food resources and thereby avoid outright competition. In the mixed herds of spotted and spinner dolphins in the Eastern Tropical Pacific, for example, the spotted dolphins feed mainly on larger prey living near the surface while the spinners feed on smaller, deep-living prey.

Unlike the large baleen whales, which produce low-frequency underwater sounds that can travel hundreds of kilometres under ideal ocean conditions, the high-frequency sounds dolphins produce attenuate fairly rapidly, so their range is probably no more than a few kilometres. However, groups of dolphins can maintain loose contact over much greater distances through a range of auditory and visual signals generated as a result of their behaviour.

Dolphin groups, like schools of fish, flocks of birds and herds of ungulates, appear to have a cumulative sensory awareness which undoubtedly enhances their ability to find and exploit patchy food resources and possibly to detect, and respond to, threats from predators.

MIGRATION AND DISTRIBUTION PATTERNS

The migratory habits of dolphins are conditioned by their apparent inability to fast for long which means that they need to live in a region where the availability of adequate food is fairly constant throughout the year, or to move seasonally in response to the changing availability of prey.

The great mobility of free-ranging dolphins makes it difficult to study their behaviour, although recent advances in radio- and satellite-telemetry are rapidly making such studies feasible and affordable.

Although less thoroughly documented than the well-known migrations of certain populations of great whales, particularly humpbacks and gray whales, the migrations of some dolphin populations appear equally regular.

Bottlenose dolphins, for example, migrate each year along the coast of North Carolina, often within 100m (330ft) of the shore, moving south in autumn and north in spring. Fishermen and scientists were able to track these movements because, during their journey north, many of the dolphins carried stalked barnacles on the trailing edges of their flippers, dorsal fin or flukes, earning them the nickname 'tassel-fins'; in autumn and winter, southbound animals were free of such hitch-hikers.

The seasonal migration of harbor porpoises in and out of the Baltic Sea, through the Lille Belt in Denmark, used to be so large and predictable that a major fishery took advantage of it. However, this migration no longer occurs because this population has been severely depleted by over-fishing, pollution and the effects of coastal development.

The black outlines of a small section of a 2,000-strong herd of common dolphins in a grey sea at Arrow Point, some five miles south of Catalina, off the Californian coast.
(Eric Martin)

MIGRATION AND DISTRIBUTION PATTERNS

Dolphin migrations along the Pacific coast of Japan, on the other hand, are still large and regular enough to support a fairly extensive drive fishery. For example, southbound herds of striped dolphins migrate into Sagami Bay, along the east coast of Izu Peninsula, in autumn and winter; northbound herds move along the west coast of Izu Peninsula in spring.

The changing patterns of ocean currents may also affect dolphin migrations. Japanese investigators believe the precise position of the warm Kuro Shio current, which runs northwards along the western coast of Japan, is an important determinant of whether particular types of striped dolphin herds will appear near to the shore in any given year. Since the early 1980s, bottlenose dolphins off the coast of California appear to have extended their normal range some 600km (370mls) north, due initially to a change in current patterns associated with the El Niño of 1982-1983.

CHANGING CONDITIONS

Profound changes are now believed to be taking place in the global ocean-atmosphere system.

The impact of increased levels of ultra-violet radiation, as a result of the depletion of the ozone layer, will affect marine food production in a major way. More UV radiation means far less plankton, at least in the short term until resistant strains evolve. Hence the whole base of the marine food chain will be reduced.

Water temperature too has a profound influence on the availability of food in the oceans. The colder waters, and areas of upwelling where currents meet, are highly productive. Many cetacean species either live in such areas or migrate there seasonally.

Global warming – the so-called 'green-house effect' – will mean warmer oceans and the possible loss or shift in the location of these productive areas which, in turn, will radically affect the distribution of many cetacean species. This may benefit some specific populations and others may be able to adapt; some species or populations may simply perish.

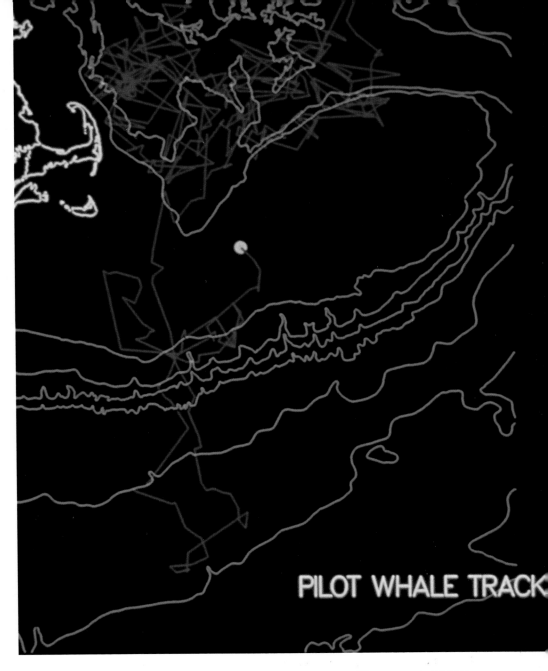

PILOT WHALE TRACK

The path (in red) of a pilot whale, as monitored by the Argos satellite system in 1987. It travelled nearly 7,600km (5,000mls) in 95 days, from a release point (yellow dot) 100km (60mls) off Cape Cod (yellow) in the eastern United States. Water depths are shown in blue. The transmissions revealed that the pilot whale covered 80km (50mls) every day, at an average speed of 3.3km per hour (2mph); its dives lasted from six seconds to more than nine minutes throughout the day and night. It slept at the surface every four to seven days and would, most typically, rest there immediately after sunrise.

First deployed in the 1970s, Argos is the only satellite-based location system presently available to civilians that can locate specialized transmitters anywhere in the world. Four Argos receivers are mounted on board each NOAA TIROS-N weather satellite.

Small radio transmitters that broadcast a one-watt signal on an extremely stable ultra-high frequency for three months are humanely attached to the whale. Unable to transmit through seawater, the whale transmitters use a saltwater switch to initiate transmissions only when the whale is at the surface. In order to save power, the transmitters are programmed to transmit only during times when the satellites are overhead.

Such satellite monitoring of whales and dolphins in the open ocean may soon transform our knowledge of these remarkable sea mammals.

(Bruce R. Mate)

Swimming

<big>M</big>any claims have been made about the swimming speeds and diving abilities of dolphins and whales but there are surprisingly few valid measurements of either.

SWIMMING

In general, the many pelagic dolphin species that feed on fast-moving fish and muscular squid can attain speeds of more than 24km per hour (15mph); coastal species, which tend to feed on slower-moving prey, can rarely exceed 16km per hour (10mph).

Bursts of speed up to 27km per hour (17mph) have been measured for bottle-nose dolphins and 40km per hour (25mph) for spotted dolphins, but this is an exception and few species are able to exceed 35km per hour (22mph).

Dolphins are only able to achieve such high speeds by leaping from the water in a series of curves and spending as little time as possible under the water. This is known as 'running'. Dolphins can attain much greater speeds by riding the bow wave of a fast-moving vessel than they could manage unassisted.

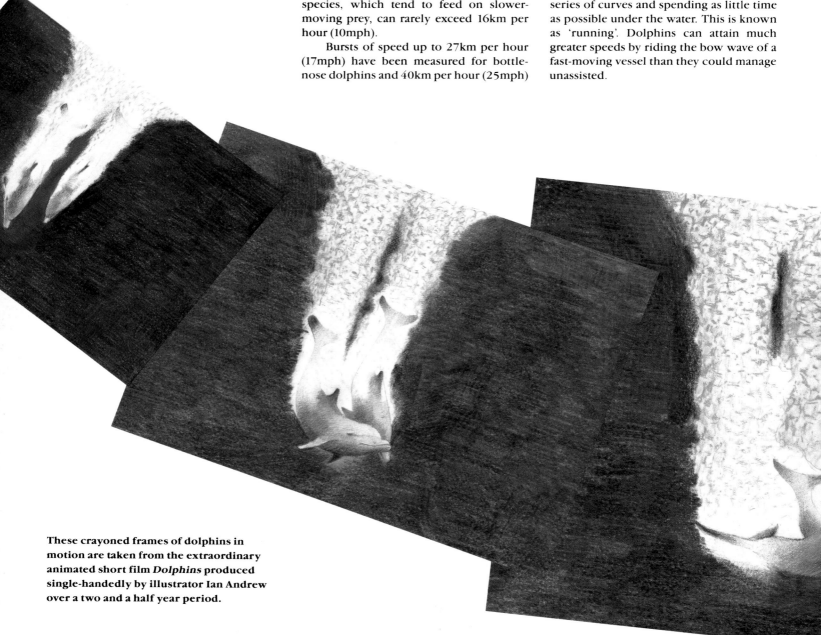

These crayoned frames of dolphins in motion are taken from the extraordinary animated short film *Dolphins* produced single-handedly by illustrator Ian Andrew over a two and a half year period.

and Diving

DIVING

Although they cannot compete with the diving abilities of the sperm whale, the deepest diver of all cetacean species, dolphins and porpoises can nevertheless reach impressive depths. Bottlenose dolphins, not commonly thought of as deep divers, can repeatedly reach depths of 300m (1,000ft) and can hold their breath for as long as six or seven minutes. Analyses of the stomach contents of Fraser's dolphins and Dall's porpoises indicate that they routinely forage at depths of at least 500m (1,640ft). Belugas are capable of making prolonged dives to depths of 650m (2,130ft), and a killer whale has been recorded at a depth of 1km (3,300ft).

Survival at such depths poses particular problems for an air-breathing mammal and these have been overcome in a variety of ways.

In order to obtain and retain enough oxygen, the dolphin has two useful adaptations. Firstly, it can exchange up to 80 per cent of the gases in its lungs at each breath (the human exchange rate is 30 per cent) and it dives with full lungs. Secondly, its circulatory system and muscles have been modified to increase the dolphin's capacity to store oxygen.

In adapting to the crushing effects of pressure, dolphins have evolved a collapsible rib cage and, as the animal dives, air in the lungs is forced into the passages leading to its blowhole. At the same time, the lining of the lungs thickens, which may have the effect of reducing the absorption of nitrogen into the blood - the major cause of 'the bends', which can cripple and even kill human divers returning from such depths.

The animal's heartbeat also responds to the changing availability of oxygen by slowing down while it is diving and speeding up rapidly when it takes a breath so that oxygen can be quickly supplied to the bloodstream and waste products rapidly removed.

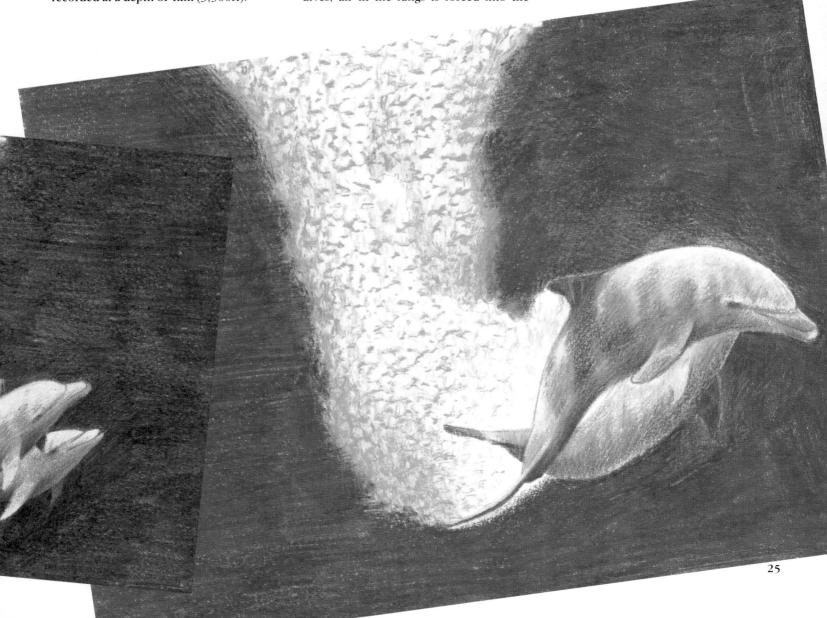

Social Relations

There are many well-documented cases of co-operative behaviour between dolphins. Perhaps the best-known are those in which pod-mates come to the aid of injured or restrained companions, placing themselves between a capture vessel and its target animal, attempting to remove holding lines or support a distressed comrade by actually lifting it above the surface of the water at regular intervals.

Care must be taken in interpreting such observations. Some scientists argue, for example, that this lifting behaviour is instinctive and may have a survival value but is not an act of compassion. Such behaviour appears to be indiscriminate and may sometimes be merely playful. It is indeed difficult to establish intentionality in much of animal behaviour.

Evidence that some dolphins co-operate in capturing and consuming prey is perhaps less equivocal. Bottlenose dolphins demonstrate a variety of co-operative feeding tactics, including one in which a pod collectively drives fish into shallow waters. Dusky dolphins work together to herd schools of anchovies, trapping them at the surface, then taking turns at making feeding passes through the ball of fish.

Two divers reported watching small groups of rough-toothed dolphins off Hawaii eat large dolphin-fish (dorado or mahi-mahi). In each case, one member of the group appeared to be the keeper of the fish. Its companions swam close alongside and bit off chunks, again taking turns and showing no signs of a 'feeding frenzy'. Although the observers did not see the dolphins catch the mahi-mahi, the high bursts of speed of which mahi-mahi are capable suggest that some kind of co-operative effort must have been involved.

However the relationships between dolphins of different species are not always amicable or mutually beneficial. Killer whales certainly attack and eat other dolphins. Pygmy killer whales act aggressively toward, and may even kill, other dolphins in captive situations. Observers aboard tuna-seining vessels in the Eastern Tropical Pacific reported numerous instances of false killer whales, and possibly even pygmy killer whales, pilot whales and melon-headed whales chasing and attacking dolphins during fishing operations. Bow-riding dolphins appear to establish a pecking order. For example, in the eastern North Pacific, white-sided dolphins may displace common dolphins from the best positions; they, in turn, are displaced by bottlenose dolphins.

Bottlenose dolphins following prawn trawl nets in Moreton Bay, Australia, show some evidence of a feeding hierarchy. Adult males tend to position themselves nearest the boat, giving them first choice of the fish spilled from the net as it is hauled in and as 'trash' fish are discarded at the end of a trawl. Females and juveniles remain some

distance away and must make do with leftovers.

Adult male spinner and spotted dolphins patrol throughout the herd in small sub-groups, often intimidating other individuals or sub-groups. Adult male spinners may mimic the behaviour of the gray reef shark, a dolphin predator, by facing their opponent, arching the back, bending their tail upwards and tipping their beak downwards in a so-called 'S-shaped' threat posture. Ramming, clapping their jaws and biting are other aggressive gestures used by adult dolphins, sometimes against members of their own pod.

STRUCTURE OF DOLPHIN SOCIETIES

Much of what we know about the structure of dolphin societies comes from a long-term research programme by Randall Wells, Michael Scott and Blair Irvine who, for 20 years, have closely studied the biology and behaviour of the bottlenose dolphin community in Sarasota Bay, western Florida. They are able to recognize (from photographs if not at first-hand in the wild) most of the population of about 100 animals.

In broad terms, this community appears to be matrilineal, and essentially resident within the bay. Mothers with calves of similar ages tend to stay together. The calves therefore develop stable associations with each other over a period of years. When sub-adult males leave the female band they often form groups which remain together into adulthood. Juvenile females sometimes join bachelor groups, but return to the female band upon reaching sexual maturity. Gene flow from adjacent dolphin communities is sustained through the more vagrant behaviour of adult males, which tend to roam well beyond the community's home range.

A community of about a thousand spinner dolphins along the Kona coast of Hawaii was studied during 1979 and 1980 by Kenneth Norris and several associates. Sub-groups were not obviously stable; alliances were fluid. Although some individual dolphins seemed rooted in overlapping 'core areas', others appeared in the study area only briefly, apparently passing through. The apparent openness of this society may be nothing more than a problem of scale; the researchers were probably sampling only one corner of a region inhabited by the aggregate dolphin population. Norris and his colleagues have argued that pelagic dolphins such as spinners live entirely within what they call a large school 'envelope', the school often consisting of hundreds or thousands of individuals. Sub-groups obviously form and interact within the broader community, but they are all ultimately interdependent.

Intelligence and

Nothing about dolphins has been more widely or passionately discussed over the centuries than their supposed intelligence and communication abilities. In fact, a persistent dogma holds that dolphins are among the most intelligent of animals and that they communicate with one another in complex ways. Implicit in this argument is the belief that dolphin cultures are at least as ancient and rich as our own.

To support the claim of high intelligence amongst dolphins, proponents note that they have large brains, live in societies marked as much by co-operative as by competitive interactions and rapidly learn the artificial tasks given to them in captivity. Indeed, dolphins are clearly capable of learning through observation and have good memories. People who spend time with captive dolphins are invariably impressed by their sense of humour, playfulness, quick comprehension of body language, command of situations, mental agility and emotional resilience. Individual dolphins have distinctive personalities and trainers often speak of being trained by their subjects, rather than the other way round.

It is misleading to speak of 'the dolphin brain'. Among the different species of toothed cetacean discussed in this book, there is great variation in brain size and brain anatomy. Adult franciscanas and Ganges river dolphins have relatively simple-looking brains weighing only about 200g (7oz), while those of several delphinid species are highly convoluted and weigh well over 1.5kg (3lbs 5oz). Absolute brain size is not necessarily a measure of intelligence, since there is a trend for brain size to increase with body size. Scientists have adopted the concept of an 'encephalization quotient' (EQ) which takes this trend into account.

The EQ, simply stated, is the ratio of brain mass to body mass. Most odontocete cetaceans have EQs similar to those of anthropoid primates such as gorillas, orang-utans and chimpanzees. In addition to their large size (both absolute and relative to body size), dolphins' brains have extremely convoluted cerebral hemispheres.

The EQ rating and the convolutions of the brain however still do not provide us with a direct measure of intelligence. In fact the latest studies of dolphins' brains show that they seem to be stuck at an early evolutionary stage of development, - the most primitive stage in land mammals - with a cortex that appears to lack even some features that are characteristic of hedgehogs.

The extremely varied repertoires of sounds made by dolphins are often invoked as *prima facie* evidence of advanced communication abilities. In addition, some 'scientific' experiments done by John Lilly and his associates during the 1950s and 1960s were claimed to show that dolphins communicate not only with one another but also with humans, mimicking human speech and reaching out across the boundaries that divide us.

These conclusions about dolphin intelligence and communication have not withstood critical scrutiny. While they have fuelled romantic speculation, their net impact has been to mislead. Rather than allowing dolphins to be discovered and appreciated for what they are, Lilly's vision has forced us to measure these animals' value according to how close they come to equalling or exceeding our own intelligence, virtue, and spiritual development.

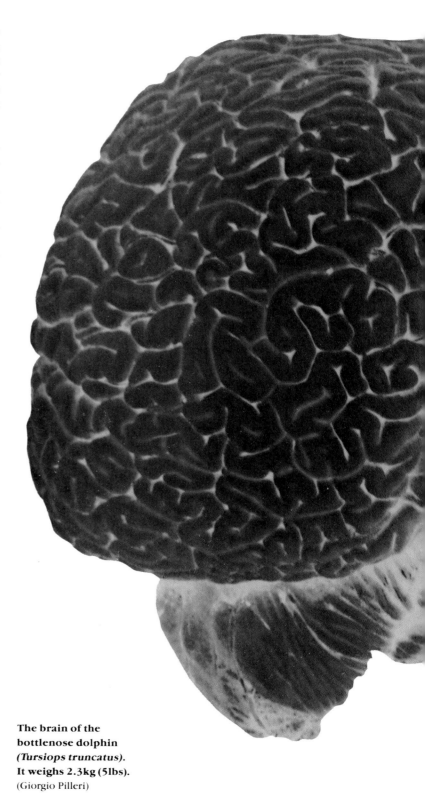

The brain of the bottlenose dolphin (*Tursiops truncatus*). It weighs 2.3kg (5lbs).
(Giorgio Pilleri)

Communication

The so-called 'varied' repertoire of sounds actually consists of a very limited number of vocalizations, namely whistles and clicks. The latter are used solely for echolocation, the former for identification and indications of mood.

According to David Gaskin, who has conducted a thorough review of the subject, dolphins do gather information about their environment and broadcast it but there is no 'intent', in human terms, involved. They use whistles and body language to identify themselves individually but there is no evidence of enough variety in the sounds to constitute anything approaching a language.

It would be specious to argue that dolphins are not communicative creatures. Not only is there abundant evidence that they exchange information acoustically but it is equally obvious that they communicate by body contact - through rubbing, stroking and biting.

Visual cues and chemical secretions - dolphins have a good sense of taste - may also communicate important basic information such as sex and age and possibly provide an impression of reproductive prowess or mood.

The issues of dolphin intelligence and communication have been inseparable in most people's minds, and the presumed existence of one has been taken as proof of the other, a classic tautology. Not surprisingly then, most experiments to evaluate dolphin intelligence have measured the animals' capacity for cognitive processing, as exhibited in their understanding of the rudiments of language.

From the early work of researchers like Dwight Batteau and Jarvis Bastian through the more recent work of Louis Herman and associates, dolphins have been asked to accept simple information, in the form of acoustic or visual symbols representing verbs and nouns, and then to act on the information following a set of commands from the experimenter.

The widely publicized results have been somewhat disappointing. Although they have demonstrated that dolphins do have the primary skills necessary to support understanding and use of a language, they have not distinguished the dolphins from other animals in this respect. For example, some seals, animals we do not normally cite as members of the intellectual or communicative elite, have been found to have the same basic capabilities.

What, then, do the results of experiments to date mean? Either we have not devised adequate tests to permit us to detect, measure and rank intelligence as a measure of a given species' ability to communicate, or we must acknowledge that the characteristics which we regard as rudimentary evidence of intelligence are held more commonly by many 'lower' animals than we previously thought.

The fact remains, however, that when one encounters dolphins one is struck by their sense of 'awareness'. The scientific evidence may be inconclusive and disappointing but we humans seem unwilling to let the question of their intelligence and communication rest.

Echolocation

Echolocation - the location of objects by their echoes - is a highly specialized faculty that enables dolphins to explore their environment and search out their prey in a watery world where sight is often of little use.

As sound travels four and a half times faster in water than in air, the dolphin's brain must be extremely well adapted in order to make a rapid analysis of the complicated information provided by the echoes.

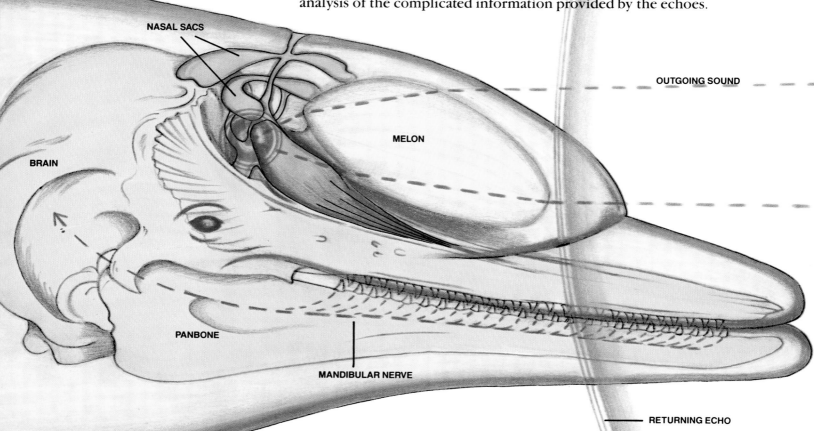

NASAL SACS

OUTGOING SOUND

MELON

BRAIN

PANBONE

MANDIBULAR NERVE

RETURNING ECHO

Although the ability to echolocate has only been proved experimentally for a few odontocete species, the anatomical evidence - the presence of the melon, nasal sacs and specialized skull structures - suggests that all dolphins have this ability.

The dolphin is able to generate sound in the form of clicks, within its nasal sacs, situated behind the melon. The frequency of this click is higher than that of the sounds used for communication and differs between species. The melon acts as a lens which focuses the sound into a narrow beam that is projected in front of the animal.

When the sound strikes an object, some of the energy of the soundwave is reflected back towards the dolphin. It would appear that the panbone in the dolphin's lower jaw receives the echo, and the fatty tissue behind it transmits the sound to the middle ear and thence to the brain. It has recently been suggested that the teeth of the dolphin, and the **mandibular nerve that runs through the jawbone, may transmit additional information to the dolphin's brain.**

As soon as an echo is received, the dolphin generates another click. The time lapse between click and echo enables the dolphin to evaluate the distance between it and the object; the varying strength of the signal as it is received on the two sides of

the dolphin's head enable it to evaluate direction. By continuously emitting clicks and receiving echoes in this way, the dolphin can track objects and home in on them.

The echolocation system of the dolphin is extremely sensitive and complex. Using only its acoustic senses, a **bottlenose dolphin can discriminate between practically identical objects which differ by ten per cent or less in** volume or surface area. It can do this in a noisy environment, can whistle and echolocate at the same time, and echolocate on near and distant targets simultaneously - feats which leave human sonar experts gasping.

THE BIG BANG THEORY

Dolphins may also be able to immobilize or even kill their prey using bursts of high-frequency sound. This idea was proposed in passing by a number of scientists but was first systematically investigated by the American and Danish marine mammal researchers Kenneth Norris and Bertel Mohl, in the first 'full-scale review' of the idea in 1983.

This 'big bang' theory suggests that, even if the dolphins cannot kill their prey outright with bursts of sound, they can impair their prey's equilibrium or sensory system, making them easier to capture.

The 'big bang' theory may explain: how dolphins catch prey that can easily out-distance and out-manoeuvre them; why dolphins have lost a large number of their functional teeth and their once-powerful jaws; and the high degree of co-operation between dolphins, necessary because they are carrying around the equivalent of a 'loaded gun'.

These so-called 'loud impulse sounds' have been recorded during predation in the wild by bottlenose dolphins and killer whales, made when the animals were hunting mullet and salmon respectively.

Norris and colleagues presented further evidence in 1989, based on experiments where they exposed anchovies to pneumatically-generated 'loud impulse sounds' similar to those recorded in the wild. They discovered that these sounds killed and injured the anchovies. More scientific evidence will be needed before conclusive proof of this theory can be obtained.

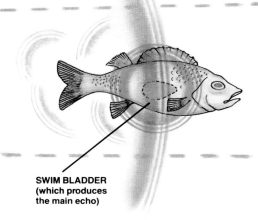

SWIM BLADDER
(which produces the main echo)

Illustration: Andy Gammon/ Margaret Klinowska

Right: **These two sonograms are visual representations of the 'ranging clicks' of a young bottlenose dolphin in a bay off the west coast of Wales, and were recorded using hydrophones suspended from a small boat. The top sonogram shows the increasing frequency of the dolphin's clicks as it approaches an underwater camera and then lies stationary in front of the camera emitting a continuous stream of high-frequency pulses.**
The bottom sonogram is a magnification of the last portion of the top one, and shows a second line of pulses (pink/blue) which are not being made by the dolphin. It has found the frequency at which the camera housing resonates, and is emitting clicks at that frequency.
(A.D. Goodson, M. Klinowska, R. Morris)

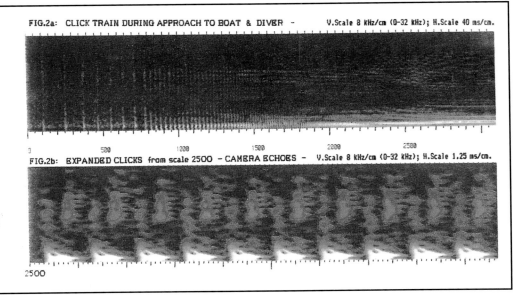

FIG.2a: CLICK TRAIN DURING APPROACH TO BOAT & DIVER - V.Scale 8 kHz/cm (0-32 kHz); H.Scale 40 ms/cm.

FIG.2b: EXPANDED CLICKS from scale 2500 - CAMERA ECHOES - V.Scale 8 kHz/cm (0-32 kHz); H.Scale 1.25 ms/cm.

2500

Stranding

Dead dolphins are frequently found stranded on shorelines around the world and the reasons for this are not hard to find. Some are debilitated by disease or old age; others have been injured by predators or have become accidentally entangled in fishing gear. Harder to comprehend are the single or mass strandings of apparently healthy live animals, recorded as far back as the days of ancient Greece, which almost invariably results in their death from such secondary effects as overheating, suffocation and pneumonia.

Below: **The head of a short-finned pilot whale, stranded on the East Coast of the USA.**
(Centre for Coastal Studies)

Many theories have been put forward to explain why live strandings occur. These have ranged from the unlikely suggestions that the animals are attempting mass suicide or following some atavistic urge to return to land, to the more plausible ideas that their echo-ranging systems are impaired, whether by parasitic infestation of the inner ear or by the confusing nature of the coastal topography. Another theory is that healthy individuals may be following a seriously ill or injured dominant member of the pod or herd.

In the early 1970s, the growing general interest in the biology and conservation of cetaceans led to the establishment of stranding programmes in many countries. Data from such programmes require care in interpretation, since the more people there are watching for and reporting strandings, the more strandings there appear to be.

However in the UK such records of both live and dead strandings have been kept by the British Natural History Museum, in co-operation with the Receiver of Wrecks and HM Coastguard Service, since 1913. It is on the basis of these that scientist Margaret Klinowska has developed a novel explanation as to why live strandings occur.

She argues that cetaceans travel by following geomagnetic contours. By comparing the distribution of live strandings in the UK with the magnetic characteristics in particular areas, she has found a high correlation between the incidence of strandings and the occurrence of sites where the magnetic contours are orientated perpendicular to the coast rather than parallel to it. In following the contours, the dolphins are led to their deaths on the shore.

She has also pointed out a pattern of daily variation in the total geomagnetic field which may function as a biological 'travel clock' for cetaceans. Solar activity can affect this pattern, causing irregular fluctuations which disturb the clock.

If the clock is out, they are not where they 'think' they are on their magnetic contour map and, as a result, can make turns too early or too late and get into unfamiliar areas, where simple contour following may lead them on to land. This can explain why they 'willingly' go on to the beach - they 'think' it is the right way. It also explains re-stranding, because again their basic strategy has let them down in an unfamiliar area.

Joseph Kirschvink and his scientific colleagues in the US have obtained similar results which also support this 'magnetic travel' hypothesis.

This new hypothesis has enriched the scientific debate about the causes of live strandings but a great deal more research in many other parts of the world will be needed if we are to reach a full and final explanation of this most intriguing and dramatic of natural phenomena.

Background: **A geomagnetic contour map of part of the north-west coast of the British Isles.**

Below: **A short-finned pilot whale stranded on the beach at Simonton Cove, San Miguel Island, in the California Channel islands, May 1982.**
(Brent Stewart)

THE WORLD OF
DOLPHINS

'They are the lads that always live before the wind. They are accounted a lucky omen. If you yourself can withstand three cheers at beholding these vivacious fish, then heaven help ye; the spirit of godly gamesomeness is not in ye.'

Moby Dick – Herman Melville

The streamlined body of a common dolphin leaping through waves in the Gulf of California, or the Sea of Cortés, between Mexico and Baja California *(Sylvan Wick – Marine Mammal Images)*

The Earth is 71 per cent ocean; this is the larger world the dolphins inhabit.

In order to set these creatures in context, we have chosen to present the many species in groups according to the environment they inhabit. We begin with the species that are found in all oceans and then move, from north to south, through the arctic, the northern oceans, the temperate and tropical oceans, and then to the more limited habitats of the coastal and river dolphins.

We have included all the toothed whales – 45 species – that are classified in the two Superfamilies, Platanistoidea and Delphinoidea. (The only other toothed whales – sperm, bottlenose and beaked whales – are classified in two other separate Superfamilies, Physeteroidea and Ziphioidea).

Knowledge about these intriguing sea mammals is hard to obtain and often slow to accumulate. Much of what we now know is the result of years of painstaking research, of thousands of hours of field observations, sifted and edited by scientists, experts and enthusiastic amateurs. Much of the information is contradictory. There are many schools of thought and theories abound.

The dolphins care little for our search for knowledge about them. Theirs is an ancient and boundless world in which they frolic. Their beauty and grace are reflected in these pages.

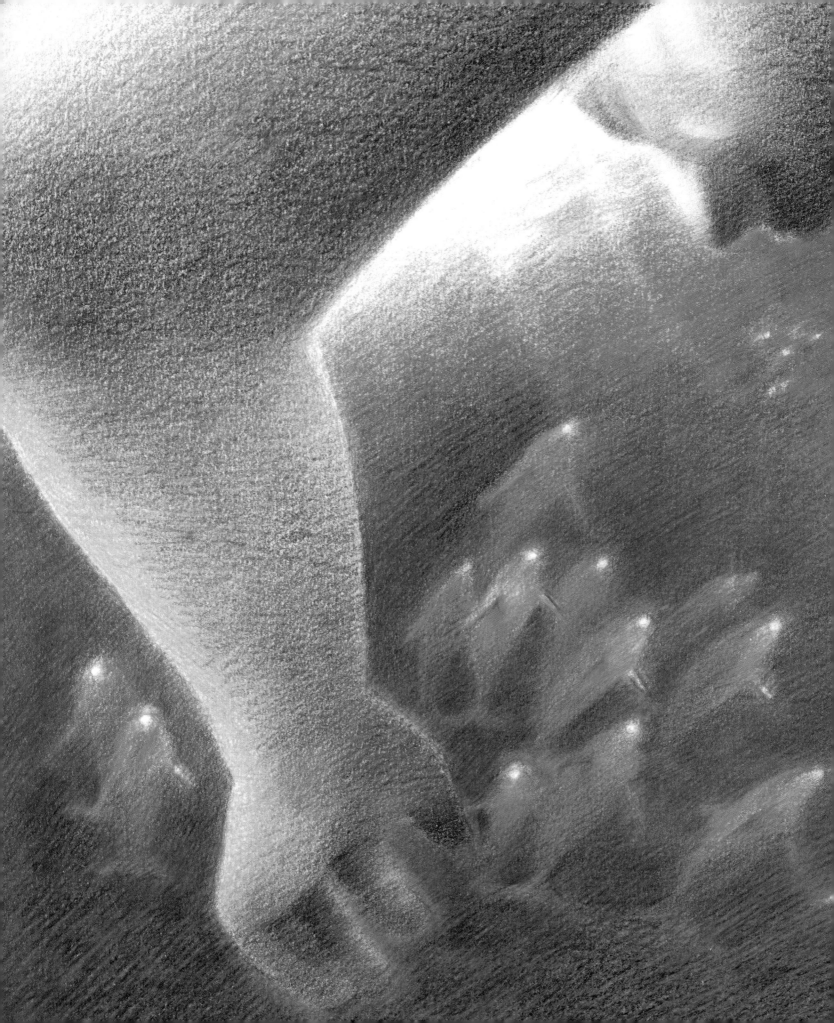

INTO THE BLUE

"Of the thirty-odd species of Oceanic Dolphins, none makes a more striking entrance than *Stenella attenuata*, the spotted dolphin. Under water spotted dolphins first appear as white dots against the blue. The beaks of the adults are white-tipped, and that distinctive blaze, viewed head-on, makes a perfect circle. When the vanguard of the school is "echolocating" on you – examining you sonically – the beaks all swing your way, and each circular blaze reflects light before any of the rest of the animal does. You see spots before your eyes.

Illustration: Ian Andrew

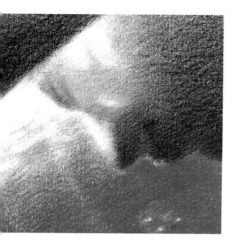

The habitat of the spotted dolphin is clear, deep, tropical ocean. Its home waters are warm, lovely to look at, sparse of life – a marine desert. Spotted dolphins roam that country like Bedouins. Their oases are the plumes of upwelling and nutrients in the lee of islands; their ululations are cries rising high above the hearing range of human beings; their dunes are the blue swells. They gather occasionally in herds of a thousand or more – several schools in a temporary federation – but more often they are seen in bands of a few hundred. Like many of the ocean's hosts, they are fewer than they once were.

Awaiting a tribe of spotters in their element is a peculiar experience. You hang from the surface by your snorkel, marking time with a slow churning of your fins. The swell lifts you by the hair, drops you, lifts you again. Beneath you lie two miles of ocean – a bottomlessness, for all practical purposes, an infinity of blue. When you are new to it, the blue void has a pull. It wants you, tries to call you down. A thousand coruscating shafts of sunlight probe it, illuminating nothing. Nothing is there to illuminate, nothing to establish scale or distance. A tiny gelatinous fragment of salpa, drifting up ten inches from your faceplate, startles you. For an instant it could be anything – a strange man, a whale, a shark.

From that lambent blue field, featureless yet somehow forever shifting, empty yet pulsing with all the imagined sharp-toothed things that might come out of it, come the spots indeed. You blink behind your faceplate, but the spots remain. They are real, not hallucinations. Around each white dot a gray dolphin materializes. Five or six quick strokes of the flukes and they are upon you, sleek, fast, graceful legions. They come a little larger than life, for water magnifies. They animate the void. With barrages of clicks and choruses of high-pitched whistling, with speed and hydrodynamic perfection, with curiosity, mission, agenda, and something like humor, they fill up the empty blue.

The first rank of dolphins race past. Behind them a second rank of dots appear, doubtful at first, like the first stars of twilight. The dots jiggle oddly as the beaks cast about for you, and then hold steady when they have fixed on you. Another rank of dots, and then another: the society of *Stenella attenuata* sprints by in waves, the squads of adult males, the gangs of juveniles, the nurseries of females and calves.

The squads of adult males execute close, synchronized flybys and pummel you with sound – loud bursts of echolocation that are both a threat and a piercing sonic look at you. The males acoustically "see" the air spaces of your lungs, watch your skeleton articulate. The clicks of their echo-sounding proceed from the amplifier in the "melon" – the dolphin's bulbous forehead – but the beak tip is so white and prominent that the sound seems to come from that. The beak is the Geiger counter; you are the uranium. As the white tip swings in line

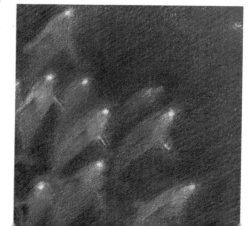

with you, the clicks come louder and faster, reach crescendo as the beak draws its bead, and then recede as the beak swings away again.

Tick tick tick tick ticktickTICKTICKTICKTICKtick tick.

When a squad of males sounds you out in unison, the sensation is like equatorial rain on a tin roof: first a few scattered drops, then the downpour. You don't hear the echolocation so much as feel it. Your whole body becomes tympanic membrane. You really are, for once, all ears.

The gangs of juveniles are curious but don't come so close. They fake boldness. The nurseries keep their distance, small calves nursing on the move or swimming at their mothers' backs, stroke for stroke in perfect synchrony, holding position just above and behind the maternal dorsal fin. Occasionally a larger calf strays off to swim with a rhythm of its own. Now and again a whistling dolphin emits a long, thin stream of bubbles from its blow-hole. This seems to signify mild distress, or a low-grade warning. Now and again a dolphin defecates, a slightly grayer stream of bubbles. From a distance the two sorts of contrail are hard to tell apart. If the dolphin is gliding at the moment of emission, the bubbles run out straight behind. If the dolphin is swimming, the action of the flukes beats the contrail into a wavy line.

Dolphins have no shame. They have no private moments. In courtship, foreplay, and sex they are public, and as they pass you see snatches of dolphin intimacy, if that's the word. One dolphin in a pair will yaw sideways, its pectoral fin pointing to the surface, and then, slowing to let its partner pass above, will allow the tip of its pectoral to trace delicately the length of the partner's belly, past the genital slit. Sometimes the romance is cruder. The amorous dolphin will jam its pectoral into the vicinity of the genital slit and impatiently, with stiff-shouldered jerks, work that area over hard. Mock fights occur, irritations, moments of play. You see only fragments, bits of behavior, for the school never lingers. To the sirens of their whistling (inaudible in the higher ranges even to dogs), to the klaxons of their clicks, they race for that distant fire that oceanic dolphins are forever chasing.

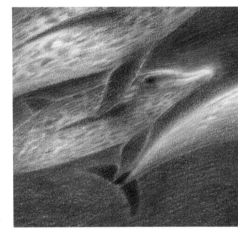

The last dolphin of the last wave pumps by, glances at you in passing, hurries to catch up. Its flukes dematerialize in the blue. The bubbles hang for a while, like vapor trails after the jets are gone. Often a faint whistling is audible, diminuendo. Sometimes, when the dolphins have been feeding, a few silvery flurries of fish scales drift in their wake. The scales catch the sunlight and go incandescent. They are subject to sudden, fitful dances and accelerations, caught up in vortices of turbulence that the dolphins have left behind. They are evidence that a tribe of dolphins really did pass this way. Then, settling away from the surface brightness, the scales go into eclipse. The sunlight ceases to glint from them. The whistling lingers on in the imagination. It haunts, briefly, the higher wavelengths of memory, and then goes silent even there. The contrails fizz out and dissipate. The ocean is empty blue again. **Kenneth Brower**

ALL OCEAN SPECIES

Killer Whale or Orca
Orcinus orca

Originally called *Delphinus orca* by Linnaeus in 1758, it was placed in a new genus, *Orcinus*, in 1860. The Latin word *orca* means 'a type of whale' and the Latin suffix *-inus* means 'like or pertaining to'. (It is interesting to note that the words *orc*, meaning horrible sea monster, and *Orcus*, the god of the infernal regions, are both derived from this same Latin root.)

The largest of the so-called dolphins, male orcas sometimes grow up to 9.5m (30ft) in length and weigh up to 8,000kg (17,600lb). The females measure 5.5-7m (18-23ft) in length and weigh 2,500-4,000kg (5,500-8,800lb).

The colouring of the killer whale is distinctive. The back and sides are black except for large white patches above and behind the eyes and a grey 'saddle' behind and below the dorsal fin. The exact size and shape of this saddle varies between individuals and between regional populations. (Antarctic orca populations also have a grey 'cape'.) The chin and belly are white and this colouring extends asymmetrically up the animal's flanks.

The flippers are large and paddle-shaped. In males, the dorsal fin, which is the shape of a tall isosceles triangle, can reach heights of 1.8m (6ft) and in large, old males it sometimes cants forward slightly. In adult females the dorsal fin is less pronounced and more curved, the two sexes diverging before they attain sexual maturity. Both sexes have between 10 and 12 pairs of conical teeth in each jaw.

Killer whales are top-level marine carnivores and opportunistic feeders with diets that differ seasonally and regionally. No marine organism of any size seems safe from attack. Virtually all marine cetaceans and pinnipeds, penguins and other seabirds, sea turtles, many types of fish (especially herring and salmon), and even their own kind, are eaten at times. Although there are no authenticated cases of killer whales eating humans, a few attacks have been reported.

The killer whale is one of the most widely distributed marine mammals in the world, but is not especially numerous. It is found in almost all the world's seas and in every ocean, from tropical waters to the polar regions.

The exuberance and power of a breaching orca, one of the largest predators on earth.
(Eric Martin)

The killer whale is one of the largest predators on Earth measuring up to 9.5m (30ft) long, and 8 tonnes. Its only enemies are human beings.

As whale conservationist Paul Spong speculated: '. . . I am particularly fond of . . . the thought that *Orcinus orca* is probably a creature which has little or no experiential reason to feel fear; it may literally be fearless.'

Revered by a number of native cultures on the north-west coast of North America and Canada, the orca has been viewed more commonly over the centuries as a ruthless killer. In the first century AD, Pliny the Elder wrote in his *Natural History* that, 'A killer whale cannot be properly depicted or described except as an enormous mass of flesh armed with savage teeth.'

The species' common name is derived from the term 'whale killer', coined by eighteenth century whalers who witnessed killer whales tearing lips and tongues from great whales several times their size.

No aspect of the killer whale's natural history has received more attention than its habit of preying on other marine mammals. When hunting they display a great deal of co-operation and cunning. A 1979 article in *National Geographic* described an attack on a blue whale by killer whales:

'The predators exhibited marked division of labor. Some flanked the blue on either side, as if herding it. Two others went ahead and two stayed behind to foil any escape attempts. One group seemed intent on keeping the blue underwater to hinder its breathing. Another phalanx swam beneath its belly to make sure it didn't dive out of reach.'

On another occasion, killer whales were seen circling a rocky outcrop on which a group of Steller sea lions was resting. The whales circled them patiently as the tide came in, as if aware that the rising sea would eventually force the sea lions off the rocks. Their patience was rewarded as, one by one, the Stellers dived into the sea to their deaths. One big killer whale breached with a massive sea lion in its jaws and, with one bite, severed it in half.

Long-term studies of killer whale communities in the wild, which began in the early 1970s around Vancouver Island in British Columbia and Puget Sound in Washington State, have revealed a surprisingly organized and cohesive society. Today they are probably the most comprehensively studied and best-known of all small cetaceans.

Two factors have made such detailed studies possible, the first being the concentration of one population of so-

called 'resident' coastal killer whales in Puget Sound and the waters off British Columbia, allowing relatively easy access for researchers. The second was the discovery by Canadian scientist Michael Bigg, and his colleagues, that it is possible to identify each individual killer whale by means of differences in the size, shape and scarring of the whales' dorsal fins.

The orcas of Puget Sound and the waters off the British Columbian coast appear to consist of two separate ecotypes – dubbed 'residents' and 'transients' by Bigg and his colleagues – which live side-by-side but can be distinguished in appearance and behaviour. DNA analysis has confirmed that the two populations are genetically distinct.

The residents form two separate communities (northern and southern) composed of extremely stable matrilineal groups or 'pods' containing between 5 and 50 individuals, which subsist almost entirely on fish, especially salmon. There is much inbreeding within individual pods, and perhaps between pods of the same community, but exchange between the two separate communities is limited. The

residents range about 800km (500mls) along the coast and are frequently sighted in the summer and autumn.

The transients, on the other hand, form pods containing between 1 and 7 individuals which prey largely on marine mammals. They roam over a larger range, up to 1,450km (900mls) along the coast and are seen less often by human observers.

The travelling and diving patterns of these two ecotypes are also different. Residents tend to keep to established routes from headland to headland, do not change direction suddenly and have a fairly regular pattern of dives, rarely staying underwater for more than four minutes.

Transients, however, tend to swim into the numerous small bays dotted along the coastline, frequently make abrupt changes of direction and often stay underwater for more than five minutes, occasionally for as long as 25 minutes.

In this exciting sequence, the photographer has captured the highlights of a dramatic chase, as a killer whale leaps in pursuit of its prey, a Dall's porpoise. *(Pieter Arend Folkens)*

ALL OCEAN Orca

Like many dolphin species, killer whales are capable of emitting a wide range of vocalizations which fall into three distinct categories: whistles, variable calls and discrete calls. The first two, which take many forms, are used when the whales are socializing within a tightly knit group. The discrete calls – the most commonly produced sounds – are used when the pod is scattered or foraging and may be a means of maintaining contact between individual pod members.

Each pod produces a specific number and type of discrete calls which are shared by all members of the pod. The number of

An orca breaks the stillness of an icy sea, against a majestic backdrop of the mountains of the Pacific Northwest.
(Ken Balcomb)

different types of discrete call (there can be between 5 and 15 different calls) and the accent given to each call are specific to the pod and can therefore be said to constitute a 'dialect'. Pods whose dialects contain some of the same discrete calls constitute 'language groups'.

John Ford, the scientist who discovered the existence of these dialects, has written that 'dialects of any form are rare in mammals, and those of killer whales seem to be unlike those observed in any non-human species.'

Some mammals, such as prairie dogs, have minor geographic variations in their vocalizations, but only between isolated populations which never come into contact. Amongst cetaceans, humpback whales in the North Atlantic sing very different songs from those in the North Pacific but this is probably because the two populations have been isolated from each other for so long.

The presence of dialects among populations of orcas that are in contact with each other proves that their vocalizations are learnt rather than genetically programmed.

Left: **Blood tinges the spray in this rare photo, taken in Alaskan waters, of an orca flipping a Dall's porpoise into the air. The large interlocking teeth of the killer whale, seen in detail in the photograph of the skull** (above), **will make short work of this small prey.**
(Sharon Nogg/Gerhard Bakker/Marine Mammal Images)

Overleaf: **A more tranquil view of this mighty animal, its distinctive fin silhouetted in the sunlit seascape of Johnstone Strait, with the mountains of North Vancouver Island in the background.**
(Erich Hoyt)

45

ALL OCEAN

Pilot Whales

Second in size only to the orca, pilot whales are among the most distinctive and widely distributed of dolphin species.

The size of pilot whale pods varies widely from 10 to 50 animals, although aggregations of up to 250 individuals have been reported.

These pods can be broadly classified into three main types: travelling and hunting groups, sometimes known as 'chorus lines', in which the whales form a broad band, no more than a few individuals deep, but up to two miles across; feeding groups in which individual whales swim at random but always stay fairly close to other pod members; and loafing groups consisting of between 12 and 30 individuals in close proximity, floating (and probably sleeping) at the surface.

Bonding between pod members is strong. In addition a pod shows a tendency to follow a particular 'leader', normally a large, mature female. Even when the leader is injured or dying, or has beached itself, other pod members are extremely reluctant to desert it. This behaviour has made pilot whales relatively easy targets for coastal hunts and may also be one of the reasons why pilot whales become stranded in large numbers.

(The tendency to follow a leader, or 'pilot', may also account for the species' common English name; alternatively it has been suggested that since they follow squid and fish, they 'pilot' fishermen to a successful catch.)

Pods are largely matrilineal as females tend to stay in their mothers' pods, whereas males do not. Males, which are polygamous, reach maturity at a later age than females and die younger. Pilot whale populations therefore have an excess number of mature females.

Like many other dolphin species, pilot whales produce a wide range of sounds, including what have been described as 'shrill or plaintive cries' when in distress. In 1964, William Schevill reported that once, when hauling on board a dead short-finned pilot whale, he and his colleagues 'heard and recorded loud squeals from another that loitered near the boat until the victim was on board, whereupon the survivor stopped calling and rejoined the now distant herd.'

Above: **Sunlight streaks the solid bulk of a short-finned pilot whale as it swims near the surface of the Pacific.**
(Birgit Winning/EarthViews).
Overleaf: **The large and bulbous dark brown head of a captive pilot whale.**
(Eric Martin)

Long-Finned Pilot Whale
Globicephala melas

Short-Finned Pilot Whale
Globicephala macrorhynchus

In 1828, the genus *Globicephala* was created, from the Latin *globus*, meaning 'sphere', and the Greek *kephalos*, meaning 'head', to describe a number of large dolphins. Seventeen years earlier, the long-finned pilot whale had been described and named by naturalist Thomas Traill as *Delphinus melas*, the latter word meaning 'black' in Greek. The first specimen of the short-finned pilot whale was identified by J.E. Gray in 1846 and named after the Greek word *makros*, meaning 'long', and *rhynchos*, meaning a 'beak or snout'.

The maximum lengths and weights for the long-finned pilot whales are 6.2m (20ft) and 3,000kg (6,600lb) in males; 5.4m (17ft 7in) and 2,500kg (5,500lb) in females. The short-finned pilot whales are slightly smaller, reaching a maximum length of 5.4m (17ft 7in) in males and 4.25m (14ft) in females. Their weights are unknown.

Distinctive features of both these sturdily built species are the large melon, the almost imperceptible beak and the prominent dorsal fin, which has a long base and is set far forward on the back. As their names suggest, the two species have 'fins' (sickle-shaped flippers) of different lengths; in the long-finned pilot whale they are one-fifth as long as the body.

Both species have a dark brown to black colouration, and sometimes have a light grey saddle behind the dorsal fin. The long-finned pilot whale also has a more distinct white or grey anchor-shaped patch on its throat which sometimes extends on to its lower ventral flanks. It has between 8 and 12 pairs of peglike teeth in each jaw whilst the short-finned pilot whale has between 7 and 9 pairs of teeth in each jaw.

The migration patterns of both species are influenced by the movements of the squid which form the bulk of their diet, although they also eat cod and other fish. Both species are common and tend to inhabit different ocean areas, although there is some overlap. The long-finned pilot whale is found in temperate and sub-polar waters in all oceans except the North Pacific; the short-finned pilot whale inhabits tropical and sub-tropical regions of the Indian, Atlantic and Pacific oceans.

Above: **This dynamic and fast-moving group of common dolphins, photographed in the Pacific, is part of a much larger herd. Such herds are characteristic of this most abundant and gregarious of dolphin species.**
(Dotte Larsen)

Common Dolphin
Delphinus delphis

Linnaeus named this species in the tenth edition of his *Systema Naturae* in 1758 after the Latin *Delphinus* and Greek *delphis*, meaning 'the dolphin-like dolphin'.

This streamlined species reaches a maximum length of about 2.5m (8ft), the males being slightly larger than the females, and seldom weighs more than 75kg (165lb).

Its colouring is very distinctive. The back is black or brownish-black, the belly white. The flank markings are elaborate and attractive, yellow to buff at the front and streaked with light grey towards the tail, forming an hourglass-shaped pattern. The shading of these markings differs, however, according to which region the dolphin inhabits. The beak, which is long and well-defined, is generally black with a white tip. There are between 40 and 58 small conical teeth on each side of both jaws.

Common dolphins feed on many different species of fish and squid, depending on the seasonal availability. Generally they are unspecialized, opportunistic feeders.

The common dolphin is one of the most abundant of all dolphin species. It is found worldwide in tropical and warm temperate waters, both in pelagic areas and on the continental shelf, especially over steep-sided banks and sea-mounts, where upwelling currents carry food from below.

In the Eastern Tropical Pacific it is possible to encounter huge herds of common dolphins, comprising hundreds, or even thousands of animals, surging through the water, creating a noise that can be heard some distance away. By contrast, in the North Atlantic, two-thirds of schools contain less than 20 animals.

Common dolphins in the eastern North Pacific have been observed to follow a particular pattern of daily activity, which is related to the rise of a community of organisms known as the 'deep scattering layer' (because they 'scatter' the signal from ships' sonar).

This layer or organisms is primarily composed of zooplankton that remain in the dark depths of the ocean during the day to avoid the light but rise to the surface at night to graze on phytoplankton, bringing with them the fish and squid which feed upon them and who in turn form the dolphin's prey.

The dolphins rest in large herds throughout the middle of the day and, in the afternoon, move into the feeding areas where they disperse into small groups and begin to make exploratory dives. They remain feeding in these groups throughout the night and, in the morning, as the 'deep scattering layer' descends, they once more converge into large herds.

Occasionally common dolphins fall prey to sharks and orcas. David H. Brown and Kenneth Norris recorded an attack by a killer whale pod on a herd of common dolphins off Baja California. In a manoeuvre very similar to the technique they use to catch salmon, the killer whales circled the herd, drawing it tighter and tighter, until 'finally, one of the killers veered off, rushing the school, while the others continued circling. In this fashion the killers ripped at the school one at a time, killing many of the dolphins.'

Above: **A clear view of the hourglass-shaped markings that make the common dolphin so recognizable to ocean travellers.**
(Scott Sinclair)

ALL OCEAN

BOTTLENOSE DOLPHIN
Tursiops truncatus

In 1821, British naturalist George Montagu named this species *Delphinus truncatus*, from the Latin *truncare*, meaning 'to cut off', a reference to its short beak. In 1843, a new genus *Tursio*, meaning 'a fish resembling a dolphin' in Latin, was created for this species by J.E. Gray, another British naturalist; this name was later amended to *Tursiops* by the addition of *ops*, from the Greek word *opsis*, meaning 'appearance'.

Streamlined and robust, the bottlenose dolphin grows to a maximum length of 4.5m (14ft 9in), weighing at least 275kg (606lb). The males are larger than females.

There appear to be two main forms or 'ecotypes' of bottlenose dolphins – a smaller inshore (coastal) ecotype and a larger, more robust offshore (pelagic) ecotype.

In all populations, the belly is light grey to pink and the sides are lighter in colour than the back, but there is considerable variation in the degree of expression of the complex colour elements. The back and sides, for example, can vary through many shades of charcoal, lighter grey and brown shades. In some populations, the belly in particular is mottled. Adults are heavily scarred.

The length and thickness of the beak also vary among and within populations. There are between 18 and 26 relatively large teeth on each side of both the upper and lower jaws.

Both coastal and pelagic bottlenose dolphins eat fish and cephalopods and occasionally crustaceans. The relative quantities of each type of prey taken reflect their availability in each habitat, indicating that these dolphins are generalist rather than specialist feeders.

Like orcas, bottlenose dolphins have been regularly observed feeding co-operatively. For example, they sometimes encircle a shoal of fish and different members of the group will take turns to feed while others keep the fish in position. They have even been seen chasing fish on to the shore, beaching themselves, capturing the fish and then wriggling back into the water.

There are also many examples of commensal fishing in which dolphins co-operate with fishermen. In the early 1970s a team of French scientists led by René-Guy Busnel gave the following detailed account of such co-operation.

The Imragen, a fishing tribe living on the edge of the Sahara Desert between Cape Blanc and Cape Timiris in Muritania, rely on a large winter catch of mullet to see them through the year. From September to February, when the mullet swim along the West African coast on their southward migration, the Imragen wait and watch. When the sentries spot the slight colour change in the water which signals the presence of a fish school, several fishermen wade into the sea, knee-deep, and beat the surface rhythmically with sticks. Bottlenose dolphins (and possibly also Atlantic hump-backed dolphins) appear soon after and herd the fish towards the shore. As the nets fill with mullet, the dolphins swim among the fishermen and the nets, feasting on any escaping fish.

Busnel's description of Imragen-dolphin co-operative fishing is almost identical to accounts from Moreton Bay, Australia, in the 1840s and 1850s, when aborigines caught migrating mullet with the aid of dolphins.

A fully-grown bottlenose dolphin is a large and formidable adversary, its only predators being killer whales and sharks which are known to take small or sick individuals, and may occasionally take healthy adults.

Both coastal and pelagic ecotypes are very widespread in tropical and warm temperate waters, although the coastal bottlenose dolphins tend to have a more limited range than the pelagic populations.

Studies have shown that most coastal bottlenose dolphins live in small groups of about ten individuals and are restricted to a 'home range'; the size of this 'range', however, varies from population to population in different areas of the world, from more than 400km (250mls) off the South Africa coast to less than 16km (10mls) off the Florida coast.

Some bottlenose dolphins, often old males, appear to lead a largely solitary existence, adopting bays or inlets as their 'home range'. Sometimes, when these are close to areas of human habitation, the solitary dolphins frequently encounter divers, sailors and fishermen; after a while, they accustom themselves to the presence of humans, and can become very friendly and approachable. Examples of such behaviour have been recorded throughout history and in many parts of the world.

Right: **The familiar short beak and appealing 'smile' of the bottlenose dolphin – most people's idea of what a dolphin looks like.** *(Stephen J. Krasemann/Bruce Coleman)*

Above: **A pair of bottlenose dolphins feed at their leisure on a shoal of small fish.** *(Jeff Jacobsen/ EarthViews)*

A bottlenose dolphin and calf surface for air in a motionless ocean.
(Eric Martin)

The beluga and the narwhal are the two Arctic species of small cetacean. Both species are rarely found outside the polar and cold temperate waters of the northern hemisphere. Both the beluga and narwhal display a number of adaptations to life in cold Arctic waters. They are especially well endowed with a thick skin and a protective layer of blubber, which accounts for up to 40 per cent of their body weight. Whereas the cervical vertebrae of most dolphins are fused together, those of the narwhal and beluga are not. This gives them greater flexibility and enables them to move their heads more freely which aids navigation through the ice flows.

In the case of Arctic cetaceans like belugas and narwhals, ice dynamics place strict limits on their migratory behaviour. The movement of populations of both species is therefore quite predictable. They congregate along the retreating ice edges in spring, penetrating leads and fissures as the ice barrier melts. Belugas traditionally appear in specific estuaries or bays during the open-water season. Mothers and calves are especially conspicuous in these aggregations, although it is unclear whether birth actually occurs there or in more offshore waters. Calves generally stay with their mothers for two years.

Belugas and narwhals both eat large quantities of arctic cod as well as herring, smelt, flounders and halibut, but despite the similarity in their diets, the summer distributions of the two species differ noticeably. Narwhals congregate in deep, clear fjords whereas belugas gather in shallow, often turbid areas. What it is about their behaviour, physiology or ecology that causes belugas and narwhals to partition their arctic realm in this way remains unknown. Belugas and narwhals occasionally swim together and both frequently form extremely large aggregations of several hundred, or even thousands, of individuals.

ARCTIC SPECIES

THE BELUGA

The most common Arctic cetacean, the beluga or white whale, is widely, though not uniformly, distributed throughout seasonally ice-covered arctic and sub-arctic waters off the coasts of North America, Asia, Europe, Svalbard (Spitzbergen) and Greenland.

Belugas are usually found in water temperatures below 15°C (59°F) but stragglers may wander further afield. Southernmost sightings of the species have been in New Jersey and Puget Sound, on the east and west coasts respectively of the USA, and in the USSR's Sakhalin Island in the Sea of Okhotsk, and in the northernmost part of the Sea of Japan.

There have also been occasional sightings in the waters off the British Isles, the Netherlands, Denmark and West Germany. In December 1948, a solitary beluga was caught in a salmon net in the Loire, 18km (11mls) west of Nantes, in France. Between May and June 1966, a white whale travelled 400km (250mls) upstream through the interlinked Oude Maas, Waal and Rhine rivers. Belugas have also been seen 2,000km (1,250mls) inland in the Argun River, in the Khabarovsk region of the USSR.

Knowledge of the belugas' winter habits is poor. They favour areas of partial ice cover where wind and ocean currents keep cracks in the ice open. They may winter on the front of the seasonal ice pack or in 'polynyas' – shifting areas of open water within the ice.

In spring, as leads form in the pack ice and the ice retreats from the coast, some belugas migrate to relatively warm estuarine waters. Among the longest of these migrations is that undertaken by a population believed to winter in the Bering Sea and summer in the Mackenzie River north of the Canadian/US border. In spring, these whales pass through the Bering Strait and along the Chukchi and Beaufort sea coast of northern Alaska. They congregate in thousands in the Mackenzie River delta before the build-up of ice in September forces them westward and southward again.

There appears to be a high level of communication between pod members. Belugas are able to show a wide array of facial expressions with the aid of their flexible melon and mouth. In addition, many of the noises made by the beluga are audible to humans. Indeed, the beluga was nicknamed the 'sea canary' by the whalers of old, who could hear its squeaks, squeals and cries through the wooden hulls of their boats.

A rare photo of a population of belugas densely concentrated in an estuary of Somerset Island, located in Arctic waters between the Beaufort Sea and Baffin Bay.
(K.J. Finley)

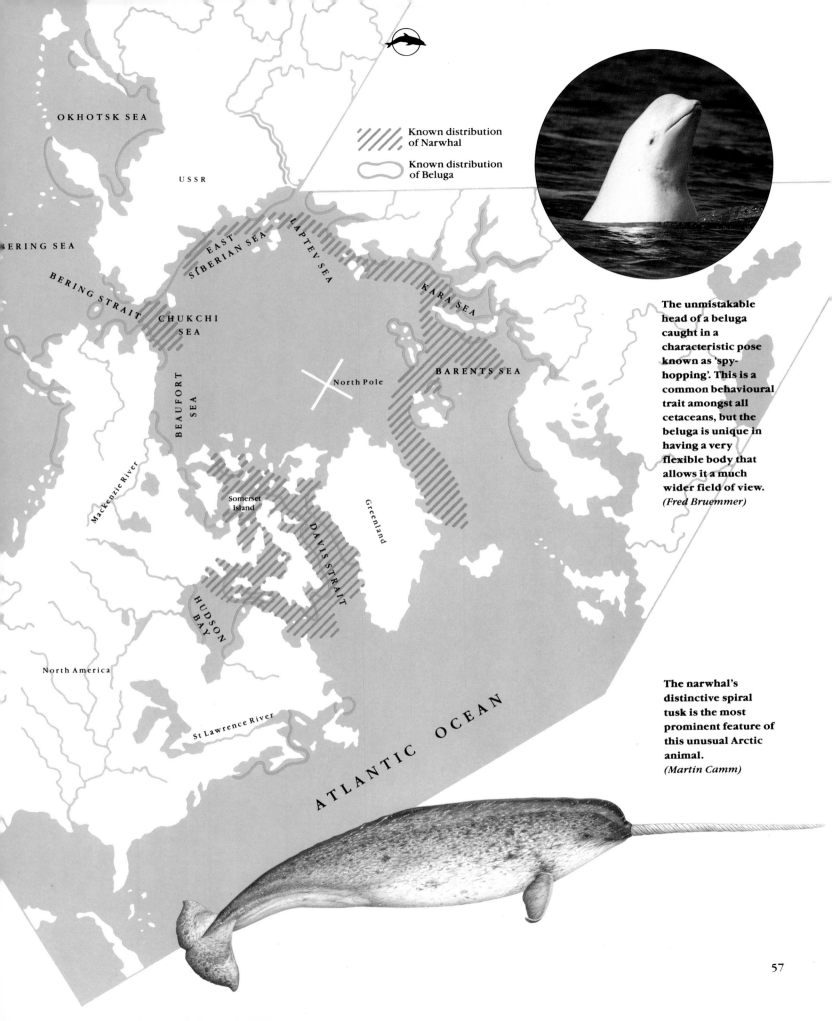

OKHOTSK SEA

USSR

BERING SEA

BERING STRAIT

EAST SIBERIAN SEA

LAPTEV SEA

CHUKCHI SEA

KARA SEA

BEAUFORT SEA

BARENTS SEA

North Pole

Mackenzie River

Somerset Island

Greenland

DAVIS STRAIT

HUDSON BAY

North America

St Lawrence River

ATLANTIC OCEAN

//// Known distribution of Narwhal

◯ Known distribution of Beluga

The unmistakable head of a beluga caught in a characteristic pose known as 'spy-hopping'. This is a common behavioural trait amongst all cetaceans, but the beluga is unique in having a very flexible body that allows it a much wider field of view.
(Fred Bruemmer)

The narwhal's distinctive spiral tusk is the most prominent feature of this unusual Arctic animal.
(Martin Camm)

M. CAMM

BELUGA or WHITE WHALE
Delphinapterus leucas

Between 1768 and 1774, Peter Simon Pallas, a German author and naturalist, made several expeditions to Siberia. On one of these trips he saw a pure white whale being harpooned in the Kara Sea. In 1776, he named the whale *Delphinus leucas* from the Greek *leukos*, meaning 'white'.

In 1804, the French naturalist Bernard Lacépède noted the absence of dorsal fins on subsequent beluga specimens and devized a new genus *Delphinapterus*, from the Greek *apterygos*, meaning 'without wings'. Its common name is from the Russian *belukha*, or 'white one'.

Female belugas are slightly smaller than males, which grow up to a maximum length of 5.7m (18ft 8in) and weigh up to 1,600kg (3,530lb), although there are many regional variations in their average lengths and weights.

The body is robust and the proportionately small head has a well-defined beak and a pronounced melon, whose shape is changeable. The flippers are convex at the tips in adults, like those of the narwhal. The trailing edge of the flukes becomes increasingly convex as the beluga matures. There is no dorsal fin but there is a serrated dorsal ridge which can be darkly pigmented. Adult belugas are creamy-white; calves and juveniles are brown, grey or blue and become completely white after reaching sexual maturity, which for females is at the age of five and for males is between the ages of 8 and 10. Belugas have between 8 and 11 teeth in each row of the upper jaw and between 8 and 9 in each row of the lower jaw.

Illustration: Martin Camm

ARCTIC

ICE

Left: Like some mythical beast, the narwhal cleaves the arctic waters with its long spiral tusk, the purpose of which is still not fully understood.
(K.J. Finley)

NARWHAL
Monodon monoceros

Linnaeus, who was familiar with this species' distinctive tusk and with the tales of Arctic explorers about sightings of unicorn-like whales, named the narwhal after the Greek words *monos*, meaning 'single', *odous* (genitive – *odontos*), meaning 'tooth', and *keras*, meaning 'horn' – literally, 'one-tooth, one-horn' – in his *Systema Naturae*. This is one of only two cetacean species of its size in the Arctic and is easily distinguished by its long tusk.

The narwhal's tusk is one of the most remarkable sights in the animal kingdom. Erupting through the upper jaw of male narwhals (and very occasionally females) these leftward-spiralling, modified teeth can exceed 2.6m (8ft 6in) in length.

The left tooth, which develops into the tusk, is almost always the narwhal's only externally visible tooth; a right tooth also exists, though this develops into a tusk only rarely, and there may be further vestigial teeth in the jaw tissue of juveniles. Double-tusked males are not unknown, but are extremely rare. Female narwhals do not generally develop external tusks but all have two embedded tusks in the upper jaw.

The function of this extraordinary appendage continues to elude scientists. The most often stated hypotheses include the following: that it is used to dig up the sea bottom in search of food; that it acts as a form of amplifier for the narwhal's echolocation clicks or communication signals; that it is indispensable as a means of breaking through thin ice to provide breathing holes; and that it is used in defence and/or to fight mating battles.

In recent years, researchers have seen narwhals using their tusks to spar and have discovered some scarred individuals. As erupted tusks are not normally found in females, the tusks may be used as a means of establishing dominance among males.

Excluding the tusk, males grow to about 4.7m (15ft 5in) and weigh up to 1,600kg (3,530lb); females are slightly smaller, being around 4.15m (13ft 7in) in length and weighing about 1,000kg (2,200lb). In adults the cylindrical body has a mottled brown/black colouring on the back; very old animals are almost completely white. There is no dorsal fin but there is a distinct dorsal ridge. The head is rounded with a slight beak. Their flippers are small and rounded: in adults, they curl upwards at the tip. The trailing edge of the tail flukes is markedly convex, a characteristic that increases with age.

Its main prey are arctic cod, Greenland halibut and other fish; squid and crustaceans.

The narwhal is widely distributed throughout the Arctic regions, predominantly north of 70° N. Large concentrations occur in the Davis Strait and in regions around Baffin Bay. Stragglers have been spotted as far south as the British Isles and the Netherlands.

Narwhals and belugas are not often reported stranded alive on beaches. However, they do get trapped by sea ice in shrinking pools of open water and the result can be the same as a mass stranding with large numbers of dead animals. The world was awakened to this problem when three gray whales were entrapped by ice near Barrow, Alaska, in October 1988. In spite of the great publicity surrounding this event, it was unrepresentative, as it is more often herds of belugas or narwhals, sometimes hundreds or even thousands of animals at once, which get into this kind of difficulty. When they do, they become vulnerable to capture by polar bears or if the entrapment occurs near a village, they are often shot and harpooned by local hunters who keep a special watch for a *savssat* – pronounced s'set – an Inuit term which means 'overcrowding' and is used to describe entrapments. In the past, local people have taken many hundreds of narwhals and belugas, during only a few days' or weeks' visit to a *savssat*.

The most spectacular recorded beluga entrapment occurred in December 1984 when an estimated 2,000-3,000 belugas became trapped in pack ice up to 3.6m (12ft) thick in Senyavin Strait, just south of the Bering Strait, in the Soviet Union.

The whales were first spotted by a native Chukchi hunter who alerted the authorities in the Soviet Far East. Helicopters and experts were dispatched to survey the nature of the problem and finally a decision was reached to summon the giant icebreaker, the *Moskva*, to help free the whales.

It took almost a month for the icebreaker to reach the whales through 19km (12mls) of thick ice. If getting to the site was difficult enough, persuading the belugas to follow the ship was even more problematic. As the government newspaper *Izvestia* reported, 'Nobody could tell the captain how, in effect, to perform the most responsible stage of the operation – in what language, so to speak, to talk to the Polar dolphins.'

After four days of frustrated effort, someone on board thought of using music to attract the whales. According to the Soviet press 'several melodies were tried out, and it turned out that classical music was to the taste of these Arctic belugas.'

ENTRAPMENT

With loudspeakers blaring, the ship was able finally, in late February, to lead the belugas to the open sea and freedom. In the event, an estimated 1,500-2,000 successfully escaped from the ice, some 500 died and 506 were 'taken' by local people.

Schools of free-swimming belugas, such as these (right) seen in Lancaster Sound, to the north of Baffin Island, are often trapped in large numbers in the ice as a result of rapidly changing weather conditions. In one of the largest of these incidents recorded to date, some 2-3,000 belugas were trapped for several weeks in thick ice (below) off the coast of the Soviet Union in December 1984.

(K.J. Finley: Popperfoto)

NORTHERN OCEAN SPECIES

Pacific white-sided dolphin
(Ken Balcomb/Bruce Coleman)

The four species featured in this section are never found south of the equator; all are restricted in distribution to one or both of the oceans in the northern hemisphere.

The Pacific white-sided dolphin is found in temperate North Pacific waters, well north of the Tropic of Cancer, except in the most easterly part of its range where it is sometimes seen as far south as the Gulf of California.

The northern right whale dolphin is also found throughout the temperate North Pacific. Once considered rare it is now known to be amongst the most abundant oceanic dolphin species in certain areas of the North Pacific.

Both the white-beaked and the Atlantic white-sided dolphins are found in the northerly and cool temperate waters of the North Atlantic, the range of the former extending slightly more to the north, and that of the latter slightly more to the south.

Both species are gregarious and abundant. White-beaked dolphins have been sighted most commonly in groups of between 2 and 5, and Atlantic white-sided dolphins in groups of between 6 and 8. However, they also assemble into aggregations of several hundred.

Pacific white-sided and northern right whale dolphins are more gregarious still. One observation of a school of white-sided dolphins in the Pacific recorded that 'thirty minutes were required for it to pass at a rate of two or three knots faster than the speed of the ship.' The two species inhabit almost identical ranges, frequently swim in company with each other, and occur in comparable herd sizes, sometimes forming aggregations of one or maybe two thousand individuals. The Pacific white-sided dolphin has also been seen in the company of other, larger cetacean species such as the Risso's dolphin, gray and humpback whales.

The white-sided and white-beaked dolphins belong to the genus *Lagenorhynchus* whose members are frequently referred to as 'Lags'. It has six members in all, including the dusky, hourglass and Peale's dolphins of the Southern hemisphere. They are all small to medium-sized, temperate water species of broadly similar body shape.

The name *Lagenorhynchus* is derived from the Greek words *lagenos* meaning 'bottle' or 'flask' and *rhunchos*, meaning 'beak', a reference to the shape of the species' foreheads and snouts.

The white-beaked dolphin is marginally the most northerly 'Lag' species and is at least seasonally abundant in the waters of Greenland, Newfoundland, Labrador and Davis Strait. An opportunistic feeder, its diet consists of squid, octopus, cod, herring, capelin, haddock and sometimes crustaceans.

The Atlantic and Pacific white-sided dolphins also feed on a variety of prey. Squid, herring, hake and smelt are the main components of the Atlantic white-sided dolphin's diet whilst its Pacific counterpart feeds primarily on squid, hake and anchovies and is a nocturnal feeder.

In the waters off California, where the Pacific white-sided dolphin has been most extensively studied, the dolphins follow the anchovies inshore during summer and autumn and into deeper water during the spring and winter. When actually feeding, they separate into groups of between 10 and 20 individuals, re-converging into huge herds for the seasonal migration.

The northern right whale dolphin is primarily a squid eater although analyses of the stomach contents of stranded specimens have revealed remains of at least 17 species of fish. It also undertakes seasonal migrations, probably following the squid, southward and inshore between October and May or June.

EAST CHINA SEA

SEA OF JAPAN

SEA OF OKHOTSK

USSR

BERING SEA

BERING STRAIT

Alaska

PACIFIC OCEAN

GULF OF CALIFORNIA

■ ATLANTIC WHITE-SIDED DOLPHIN
Lagenorhynchus acutus

■ PACIFIC WHITE-SIDED DOLPHIN
Lagenorhynchus obliquidens

■ WHITE-BEAKED DOLPHIN
Lagenorhynchus albirostris

The type specimen for the genus was beached in Great Yarmouth, England in 1846 and delivered to taxonomist John Gray who called it *Delphinus albirostris*, or white-beaked dolphin, from the Latin *albus* meaning 'white', and *rostrum*, meaning 'beak' or 'snout'. After collecting several more skulls with short beaks like the Great Yarmouth specimen, Gray created the genus *Lagenorhynchus*. He subsequently described the Atlantic white-sided dolphin, calling it *acutus* from the Latin word meaning 'pointed'.

The Pacific white-sided dolphin was classified in 1865 by Thomas Nicholas Gill, librarian to the Smithsonian Institution, on the basis of three skulls collected in San Francisco ten years earlier. The species name *obliquidens* is from the Latin *obliquus*, meaning 'slanting', and *dens* meaning 'a tooth'.

The largest of these three species is the white-beaked dolphin which reaches a maximum length of 3.1m (10ft 2in). Its colouring is normally dark on the back, sides and tail; white or light grey on the belly, throat and beak. There are also light patches on the side and behind the dorsal fin. Confusingly, the beak is not always white, and there are other regional variations in colour. It has between 22 and 28 small teeth on each side of both jaws.

The Atlantic white-sided dolphin is slightly smaller but equally robust, growing to a length of 2.7m (8ft 9in). The back, upper beak, tail and flippers are all black while the belly and throat are white. A band of grey runs along the sides for the full length of the body and there are distinctive patches of white and maize yellow or tan towards the rear. It has between 29 and 40 sharp, pointed teeth on each side of both jaws.

The Pacific white-sided dolphin reaches 2.3m (6ft 7in) and at least 150kg (330lb) in weight. The most distinctive feature is its hooked dorsal fin. The back, beak, flippers, flukes and front third of the dorsal fin are black, and the belly is white. Its flanks are a mixture of dark and light grey, separated from the white belly by a

long, black line. Viewed from above, the black colour of the back is interrupted by a pair of white stripes that run from the face, over the top of the head, past the dorsal fin and broaden out on the sides of the tail stock. It has between 21 and 28 teeth on each side of both jaws.

■ NORTHERN RIGHT WHALE DOLPHIN
Lissodelphis borealis

Lissodelphis is derived from the Greek word *lissos*, meaning 'smooth', a reference to the right whale dolphin's lack of a dorsal fin. *Borealis* is Latin for 'of the north', a name ascribed to it by Titian Peale in 1848 to distinguish it from the southern right whale dolphin which had been known for some years previously.

Males grow up to 3.1m (10ft) and females to 2.3m (7ft 6in). The body is usually slim with no dorsal fin or dorsal ridge. Its flippers are slim and sharply pointed at the tip. Largely black, it has white markings on its ventral surface which extend upwards beneath the flippers towards the throat and there is normally a small white mark at the tip of the lower jaw. It has between 39 and 49 teeth in each row of both jaws.

Above right: **White-beaked dolphin**
(Richard Sears/ EarthViews)

Right: **Northern right whale dolphin**
(Michael W. Newcomer)

Below: **Atlantic white-sided dolphin**
(Martin Camm)

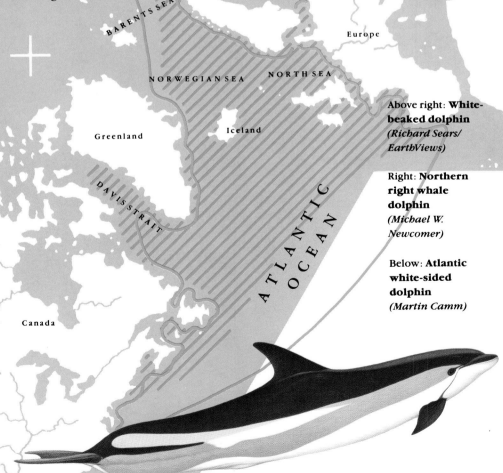

Europe

BARENTS SEA

NORWEGIAN SEA

NORTH SEA

Greenland

Iceland

DAVIS STRAIT

ATLANTIC OCEAN

Canada

USA

TEMPERATE + TROPICAL SPECIES

Of the thirteen species featured in this section, all but three are found in every one of the world's major oceans and ten are found on both sides of the equator. They all feed primarily on fish and squid; population estimates are generally non-existent, except for a few populations, and their precise distribution patterns are not known.

RISSO'S DOLPHIN
Grampus griseus

Grampus probably comes from the Spanish *grande pez*, meaning 'great fish'; *griseus* is the Latin for 'grey'. Risso was an Italian amateur naturalist who sent the first drawing and description of a specimen to Baron Cuvier, the famous French anatomist, in 1811.

Measuring up to 4m (13ft) in length, Risso's dolphin has a robust body from its head to its dorsal fin, tapering off thereafter. Its head has a prominent melon, with a deep furrow, and no beak. The flippers are long and pointed; the dorsal fin curved and very tall, up to 50cm (1ft 8in).

Newborn Risso's are grey, later becoming brown. By the time they reach maturity much of this pigment has been lost and their belly and most of the head have become white or very light grey. The rest of the body turns light grey except for the dorsal fin, flippers and flukes which remain dark. The whole body is covered by extensive white scarring. There are no teeth in the upper jaw in adults, and between 2 and 7 pairs of peglike teeth in the lower jaw. Older adults lose most, and sometimes all, of their teeth and those that remain are often extensively worn.

MELON-HEADED WHALE or ELECTRA DOLPHIN
Peponocephala electra

This species was first described by the British zoologist J.E. Gray in 1846, who called it *Lagenorhynchus electra*, *electra* coming from the name of a nymph in Greek mythology. Not until the early 1960s, after the first fresh specimens were examined independently by Masaharu Nishiwaki and Kenneth Norris, were doubts expressed about the generic classification; as a result, the two scientists created a new genus, which derives its name from the Greek *peponis*, meaning 'melon' or 'gourd', and *kephalos*, meaning 'head'.

The females grow up to 2.75m (9ft) in length and the males up to 2.73m (8ft 10in).

The body is slim with long pointed flippers and a fairly tall backward-curving dorsal fin. The head is triangular and slopes downwards to a point, and there may be little or no hint of a beak.

It is almost entirely black in colouring, although the belly is slightly lighter and there is often a subtle dark 'cape' on the back. The lips, anal and genital regions have little pigment, and sometimes appear pink or white. There is frequently a triangular mark of dark coloration on the side of the face. The upper jaw contains between 20 and 25 small·pointed teeth in each row, and the lower jaw between 22 and 24.

It can be aggressive and has been reported to attack *Stenella* dolphins as they escape from the purse seine nets set for tuna in the Eastern Tropical Pacific. Distribution is worldwide, in tropical and sub-tropical waters.

Left: **The scarred body of a leaping Risso's dolphin (Robert Pitman/ EarthViews)**
Right: **Melon-headed whales, their blowholes above the surface, float in aquamarine Pacific waters.** *(Howard Hall)*

SOUTHERN RIGHT WHALE DOLPHIN
Lissodelphis peronii

The word *peronii* comes from the name of the French naturalist, François Peron, who provided an early description of the species during a French expedition to Australia between 1800 and 1804.

On the basis of relatively few specimens, it appears to reach lengths of up to 2.35m (7ft 8in) in females and 2.3m (7ft 6in) in males. Sightings at sea suggest this may be an under-estimate and that they may in fact reach 3m (9ft 10in) in length.

Its body shape is similar to that of the northern right whale dolphin. Colouring is black and white in clearly defined zones – white on the ventral surface, extending over the beak and, to varying degrees, along the sides. The dorsal fin is mostly black whilst the upper flukes are dark grey at the back, graduating to a light grey at the front. There are between 43 and 49 pointed teeth in each row of both jaws.

Southern right whale dolphin
(Martin Camm)

FALSE KILLER WHALE
Pseudorca crassidens

This species was first described in 1846 by anatomist Sir Richard Owen, from a skull dug up in the Lincolnshire Fens in England. He called it *Phocoena crassidens*, from the Latin *crassus*, meaning 'thick', and *dens*, meaning 'tooth'. In 1860, when a hundred of these animals became stranded in the Bay of Kiel in Germany, Danish zoologist Johannes Reinhardt was able to examine several of them. He decided they looked like the killer whale *Orcinus orca* and so created the genus *Pseudorca* in 1862, from the Greek *pseudes*, meaning 'false'.

One of the largest dolphin species, the males may reach lengths of 6.1m (20ft) but more commonly they measure 5.5m (18ft) in length and weigh up to 1,400kg (3,100lb).

It has a long and slender body with a relatively small head. The forehead slopes downwards to a rounded snout, with the upper lip overhanging the lower jaw. The flippers are curved and pointed, with a hump or 'elbow' on the leading edge, and the dorsal fin curves backwards. They are black all over, except for some lighter shading on the chest and, occasionally near the eyes. There are between 8 and 11 large, pointed teeth in each row.

The false killer whale, as well as eating squid, feeds on large fish such as tuna and mahi-mahi. It has frequently been reported stealing the catch from fishermen's lines and has occasionally been reported as attacking other dolphins.

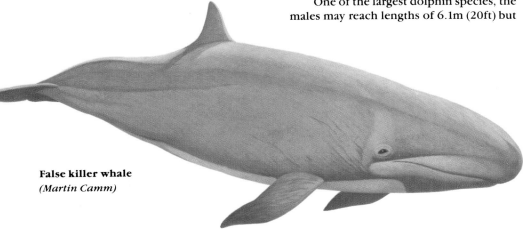

False killer whale
(Martin Camm)

A rough-toothed dolphin and calf
(James D. Watt/EarthViews)

ROUGH-TOOTHED DOLPHIN
Steno bredanensis

The word *bredanensis* comes from the name of the artist, Van Breda, who drew a portrait of the type specimen, which was stranded at Brest, on the Brittany coast of France in 1823. The word *Steno* is in honour of the celebrated seventeenth-century Danish anatomist Dr Nikolaus Steno.

The maximum recorded length for this species is 2.65m (8ft 7in). The males are slightly larger than the females.

The melon and the sides of the head slope smoothly into a long, relatively narrow beak, giving the whole front part of the body a conical shape when seen from the side or above. The body is fairly slim, especially in the tail area, with a moderately large, slightly backward-curving dorsal fin which is centred on the back.

There are variations in colouring but the back is normally a dark blotchy grey/purplish black, with light grey speckles on the flanks. The belly, throat and lips are white, often with a pinkish hue, and there are between 20 and 27 teeth, which have wrinkles on their surface, on each side of both jaws.

Right: **A scattered group of pygmy killer whales.**
(James D. Watt/EarthViews)

PYGMY KILLER WHALE
Feresa attenuata

In 1827, J.E. Gray identified a dolphin skull of unknown origin as *Delphinus intermedius*. Over the years, as more specimens emerged, he renamed it *Grampus intermedius* and then *Orca intermedia* until finally, in 1875 he fixed upon the name *Feresa attenuata*. *Feres* is a vernacular French name for a dolphin and *attenuata* is from the Latin for 'reduced, tapered or thin'.

The maximum reported lengths for this species are 2.87m (9ft 5in) for males and 2.43m (7ft 10in) for females.

The body is slender, the head rounded and the upper jaw protrudes slightly beyond the lower. There is no beak. The flippers have slightly rounded tips and the backward-curving dorsal fin is a prominent feature measuring up to 38cm (1ft 3in) in height. Its colouring varies between a dark brown and a grey/black on its back with slightly lighter colouring on the flanks. There is a white or grey area on the belly and on the chin. The lips may also be white, and there is an indistinct dark 'cape' on the back. There are between 8 and 11 pairs of teeth in the upper jaw and between 11 and 13 pairs in the lower jaw.

FRASER'S DOLPHIN
Lagenodelphis hosei

British cetologist F.C Fraser of the Natural History Museum, London, named this dolphin from the Greek words *lagenos,* meaning 'a flagon', and *delphis*, meaning 'the dolphin', in 1956. The skeleton had been collected by Dr Charles Hose, a naturalist who lived in Sarawak and Malaysia from 1884 to 1907. Until the early 1970s this remained the only record, but

Eastern Tropical Pacific alone. There are no estimates for any other part of the range.

The longest specimens recorded were a male and female from the southern Indian Ocean, they measured 2.64m (8ft 7in) in length and the male weighed 209kg (461lb). There appears to be some regional variation in body size. The body is robust and the beak short. The dorsal fin and flippers are relatively small. The body is bluish grey on the back and white on the belly with a striped pattern along the sides.

Fraser's dolphin
(Martin Camm)

then, in a matter of weeks, it was sighted in several widely separated places in the tropical Pacific and Indian Ocean. Many observations have now been made and the dolphin is known to be oceanic, avoiding shallow inshore waters, and found in tropical waters around the world. Records of strandings in temperate waters in France and Australia may represent vagrants. The dolphin is no longer considered to be rare, with 136,000 estimated to inhabit the

There are complex markings on the head. A parallel black band begins around the eye and extends to the anus. There are white bands above and below the black band. The upper lip, flippers, fin and flukes are dark. There are between 34 and 44 pairs of slender pointed teeth in the upper and lower jaws.

Most schools contain between 100 and 1,000 animals, but smaller groups of as few as four individuals have been seen.

DUSKY DOLPHIN
Lagenorhynchus obscurus

HOURGLASS DOLPHIN
Lagenorhynchus cruciger

The dusky dolphin was first described by J.E. Gray in 1828 as *Delphinus obscurus* from the Latin meaning 'dark' or 'dusky'. The hourglass dolphin was first described in 1824 as *Delphinus cruciger*, by French zoologists Jean René Quoy and Jean-Paul Gaimard, who saw a number of dolphins which bore black and white cross-shaped markings in the waters between Australia and Cape Horn. The name is derived from the Latin *crux*, meaning 'cross' and *gero* meaning 'I bear' or 'I carry'.

The dusky dolphin reaches a maximum length of 2.1m (7ft); the largest specimens of the hourglass dolphin measured to date were a 1.63m (5ft 4in) male and a 1.83m (6ft) female, but so few specimens have been measured that it is impossible to gauge its true size.

The body shapes of these two dolphins are similar to each other and to others in this genus. All are robust with a short, thick beak. The backward-curving dorsal fin is prominent and the flippers moderately long and tapered. The dorsal fin of the hourglass dolphin is shorter and more hooked, its flippers longer and more pointed, and there is a thick keel on the tail stock.

The colouring of both species is complex. The dusky dolphin is black on the back, the leading edge of the dorsal fin, the snout, tail stock and flukes. This black sweeps down to the flanks, widening towards the rear where it is interrupted by a forked slash of grey. The rest of the flanks are light grey and the flippers dark grey; the throat, chest and belly are white.

The hourglass dolphin has uniformly black back, flukes, snout, flippers and underside of the tail stock. The flanks are white, except for a black band running back from the eye which widens to meet the black of the back and then slopes downwards again, thus creating the 'hourglass' effect on the flanks which gives this species its name. The belly and throat are also white.

The hourglass dolphin has about 28 teeth in each row of both jaws, the dusky has between 24 and 36.

Right: **Like speeding torpedos, a group of hourglass dolphins shoot clear of the cold grey waters of Drake Passage, which runs between Tierra del Fuego and the South Shetland Islands.**
(Paul Ensor/ Hedgehog House New Zealand)

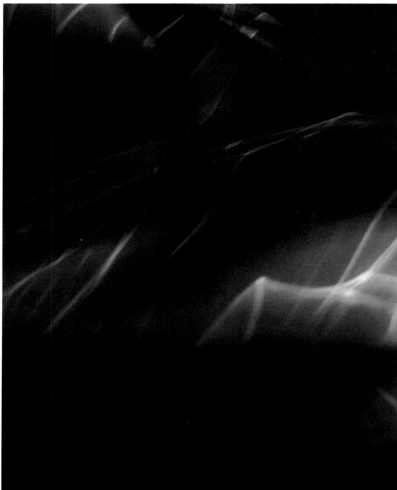

Right: **An intense and moody image of two dusky dolphins dappled by sunlight in the waters off Patagonia.**
(Jan and Des Bartlett/Bruce Coleman)

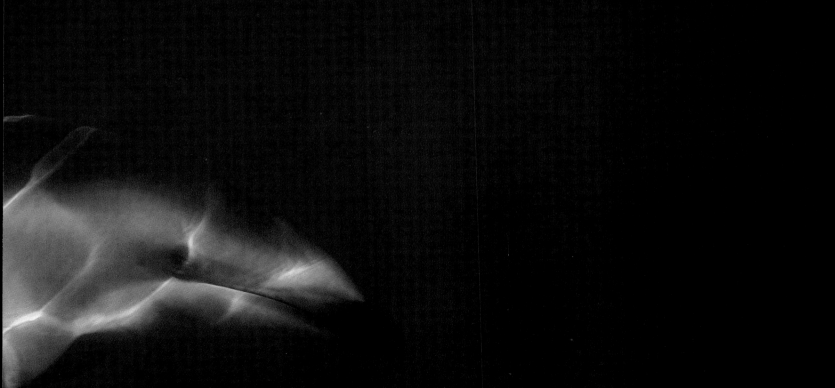

Above and right: **The dynamic and playful nature of the dusky dolphin is clearly revealed in these two images, themselves an interesting contrast in colours and shapes.** *(Barbara Todd/ Hedgehog House New Zealand)*

Natural acrobats

Several of the temperate and tropical dolphin species are highly accomplished acrobats. The spotted dolphins frequently leap high out of the water and appear to hang in the air before falling back. The false killer whale is also capable of high, twisting leaps and surprisingly deft turns of speed, considering its size.

But the acrobatic champions of the dolphin world are the spinner and dusky dolphins. As their name suggests, when swimming at speed, spinners often hurl themselves into the air, twisting and spinning as they do so. They may spin around four or more times during a single leap. This behaviour is most likely to be observed during the afternoon, after a period of morning rest, and at night during feeding time.

Dusky dolphins display a similar exuberance, at times leaping out of the water with such speed that they are able to somersault head over tail. Marine mammal scientists Bernd and Melany Würsig, who studied dusky dolphins for several years in the waters off Patagonia, identified at least three types of leaping behaviour, and suggested that each served a specific function.

The first is the 'head-first re-entry leap', in which the dolphin executes a leap and enters the water without making much of a splash. This, the Würsigs believe, could be a means of looking for feeding seabirds which might indicate the location of a nearby shoal of anchovies.

Secondly, there are the 'noisy leaps'. These are executed once a shoal of anchovies has been located and involve the dolphin landing on its back or side, apparently making as much noise as possible. This may serve either to signal the location of the fish to other dolphins, or to confuse and frighten the anchovies.

The third type of leap, for which there is no apparent explanation, is an exuberant display of twisting, turning and somersaulting, which is seen after feeding. The Würsigs comment: 'the dolphins seem to be performing, and it is difficult to imagine that they do so for any reason other than "pure joy".'

Above: **A Hawaiian spinner dolphin makes a headlong dive into the clear blue Pacific.**
(Steve Leatherwood)

73

TEMPERATE + TROPICAL

ATLANTIC SPOTTED DOLPHIN
Stenella frontalis

PANTROPICAL SPOTTED DOLPHIN
Stenella attenuata

*S*tenella was named by J.E. Gray in 1866. It is derived from the Greek *stenos*, meaning 'narrow', apparently in reference to the long, narrow beak characteristic of all members of this genus. The species name *attenuata* is from the Latin meaning 'reduced, tapered or thin' and *frontalis* from the Latin meaning 'pertaining to the forehead'.

The pantropical spotted dolphin can reach a length of 2.57m (8ft 5in) in the male and 2.4m (7ft 10in) in the female. In the case of the Atlantic spotted dolphin, males reach lengths of 2.26m (7ft 4in) and females 2.29m (7ft 6in). Maximum weights are around 119kg (262lb) for the pantropical and 143kg (315lb) and 127kg (280lb) respectively for the male and female Atlantic spotted dolphins. In both species there appear to be two ecotypes – coastal and pelagic – and the pelagic forms tend to be smaller and less robust.

The colouring of these animals is complex and difficult to describe because of the enormous variations, but adults of both species can usually be distinguished by their spotted appearance. The pantropical spotted dolphin generally has a mottled dark cape covering the dorsal region and the upper half of the flanks which narrows towards the head and the tail. This dark area is interrupted by a light diagonal patch behind the dorsal fin. The beak is also dark as are the mottled flippers. The ventral region is light cream in colour and often mottled.

The Atlantic spotted dolphin has a similar cape but it is darker and less distinct than that of the pantropical dolphin and therefore forms a less distinct contrast with the ventral colouring. The spots on the Atlantic species can be darker in the ventral area than on the back and upper flanks. The calves of both species are born without spots and the degree of spotting increases with age.

Exhaling a fine spray from its blowhole, a coastal spotted dolphin speeds across the ocean surface.
(K.D. Sexton. Courtesy of NMFS)

Both species have long, thin flippers and curved dorsal fins. The Atlantic spotted dolphin has between 32 and 42 teeth in each row of the upper jaw and between 30 and 40 teeth in each row of the lower jaw; the pantropical spotted dolphin has between 35 and 48 teeth in each row of the upper jaw and between 34 and 37 in each row of the lower jaw.

SPINNER DOLPHIN
Stenella longirostris

CLYMENE DOLPHIN
Stenella clymene

J. E. Gray described *Stenella longirostris* (originally *Delphinus longirostris*) in 1828 on the basis of a skull of unknown origin. The name derives from the Latin *longus*, meaning 'long' and *rostrum*, meaning 'beak'. In 1846, he determined that a skull in the Natural History Museum in London, which was very similar but had fewer teeth, was from another species. This he called *Delphinus metis*, but he had already used *metis* to describe what turned out to be the skull of a bottlenose dolphin, so in 1850 he changed the name to *clymene* (in Greek myth, the daughter of Tethys and Oceanus). This classification was widely regarded as suspect, however, and *Stenella clymene* was long considered nothing more than a regional variant of *Stenella longirostris*, until 1975 when the scientist William Perrin noticed a resemblance between two skulls from the Texas Gulf coast and that of *Stenella clymene*. His findings were published in 1981 and it is now accepted that *Stenella clymene* is indeed a separate species from *Stenella longirostris*.

Several physically different regional stocks of spinner dolphins have been described. The largest male yet recorded came from the Eastern Tropical Pacific and measured 2.35m (7ft 9in) in length and weighed 75kg (165lb). The largest female was from the tropical Atlantic and was 2.04m (6ft 7in) long. The smallest adult animals, a 1.36m (4ft 6in) male and a 1.29m (4ft 3in) female, were from a dwarf population in the Gulf of Thailand. The body shape of all spinner dolphins is much the same as that of other *Stenella* species, the body being slim and the beak long.

In the case of the clymene dolphin, the beak is shorter and the body more robust than those of the spinner dolphin. Males reach a maximum length of 1.96m (6ft 5in) and females a maximum of 1.88m (6ft 2in). The maximum weight is 86kg (190lb). The dorsal fin varies in shape between the different stocks but in general it is tall and erect in the spinner dolphin, canting forwards in adult males, and more hooked in the clymene dolphin. The flippers of both species are long and taper to a point and in the male spinner dolphin the underside of the tailstock has a pronounced bulge.

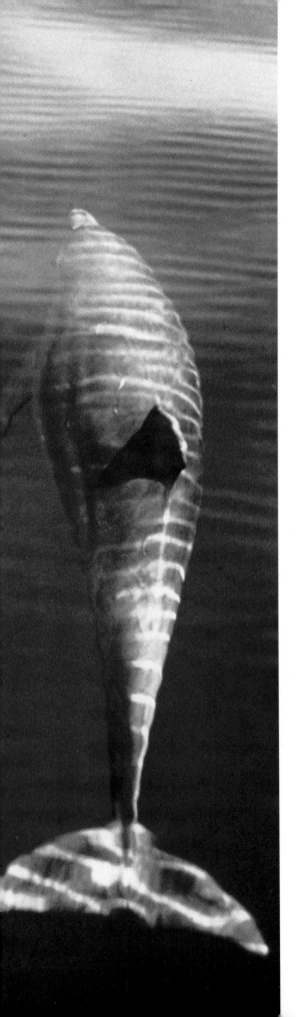

Colour too varies a great deal but in general there are three elements – a dark grey or brown dorsal area, light grey or tan flanks, and a much lighter grey, or white, underside. In some stocks, such as the eastern spinner, these differences in colouring are obscured and the body is an almost uniform grey. In all stocks, the lips and tip of the snout are dark in colour.

The spinner dolphin has between 48 and 64 sharply pointed teeth in each row of the upper jaw and between 47 and 62 teeth in each row of the lower jaw; the clymene dolphin has between 39 and 49 teeth in each upper row and between 38 and 47 in each lower row of teeth.

STRIPED DOLPHIN
Stenella coeruleoalba

The first specimen, which was caught off the east coast of South America near the Rio de la Plata, was described in 1833 by the German zoologist Franz Julius Meyen, who named it *Delphinus coeruleoalbus* from the Latin *caeruleus*, meaning 'sky blue' and *albus*, meaning 'white'.

The striped dolphin is the largest member of the genus with a maximum body length of 2.7m (9ft). The males are slightly larger than the females and their body shape is similar to that of other *Stenella* species. The beak is prominent and separated from the melon by a distinct crease. The dorsal fin, which has a slight backward curve, is positioned in the middle of the back.

In general, the dorsal area is dark to bluish grey in colour. The flanks, tail stock and flukes are light grey. The white of the belly is sharply separated from the grey of the flanks by a black line which runs from the eyes to the genital region, where it widens into a genital patch. There is often a secondary parallel black line. The beak and flippers are also black with a black line running from the eyes to the flippers. The light grey on the flanks extends upwards in a diagonal stripe just beneath the leading edge of the dorsal fin and the darker dorsal colouring reaches downwards in a V-shape just behind this stripe.

There are between 45 and 50 sharp, slightly inward curving teeth on each side of both jaws.

Left: **A spinner dolphin, striped by sunlight, glides just below the rippled surface of a calm sea.**
(V. Taylor/Panda Photo/Ardea)

Below: **The streaky markings on the head of a striped dolphin.**
(Dotte Larsen)

COASTAL SPECIES

All these species inhabit mainly shallow coastal waters in different parts of the world, apart from the Dall's porpoise which lives primarily in the open ocean but, in some areas, seasonally ventures on to the continental shelf. All feed principally on fish, cephalopods and crustaceans. There are two major groups: the true porpoises and the *Cephalorhynchus* dolphins.

All true porpoises are small (maximum length 2.2m (7ft 3in)). They have rounded heads with no beak (except for a faint hint in the Dall's porpoise) and the teeth are not conical and pointed, like those of most other dolphins, but shaped like little spades.

The *Cephalorhynchus* dolphins live in the Southern Hemisphere. They are small (less than 1.75m (5ft 9in) in length) robust animals, with a characteristic flattened and pointed head. Females are larger than males and the coloration around the genital area is sexually dimorphic (i.e. different for males and females). Little was known about the species until comparatively recently, but over the last ten years much has been learned – including the external appearance of two of the species.

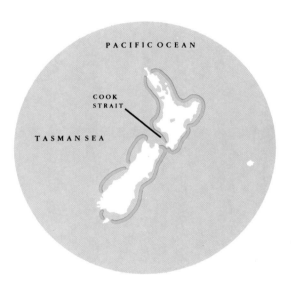

The incongruous and startling appearance of the Irrawaddy dolphin.
(Steve Leatherwood/EarthViews)

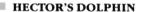

HECTOR'S DOLPHIN
Cephalorhynchus hectori

In the late nineteenth century, Sir James Hector, curator of the Wellington Colonial Museum in New Zealand, first described the species and sent the dolphin (which had been shot in the Cook Strait) to the Belgian palaeontologist, Van Beneden. Sir James Hector had assumed it to be a form of dusky dolphin but Van Beneden realized that it was a new species and in 1881 he named it after its discoverer.

Hector's dolphin lives in New Zealand waters, particularly around the South Island. Little was known about the species until two students, Stephen Dawson and Elisabeth Slooten, began a series of surveys and studies in the early 1980s. Working alone and from donated funds, they succeeded in obtaining population estimates, elucidating much of the biology of this species and in alerting the public and government to some serious gill net entanglement problems which were threatening local populations.

The maximum size and weight for females is 1.53m (5ft) and 57.27kg (126lb) and for males 1.38m (4ft 6in) and 52.72kg (116lb). Females are larger at all stages of maturity. The head has no beak and slopes smoothly from the blowhole as in all members of this genus. There is also the characteristic rounded dorsal fin with the convex trailing edge.

The flippers have rounded tips and are usually slightly serrated along the leading edge. The animals have a complex pattern of white, grey and black areas. The sides of the head, flippers, dorsal fin and tail are all black, as is the tip of the jaws. The throat, most of the lower jaw and belly are white. The area over the melon is grey, outlined with a thin black line running across the head behind the blowhole. Males and females have differently-shaped dark patches around the genital area. There are between 26 and 32 pairs of teeth in the upper and lower jaws.

These dolphins live in small groups which vary from one to seven animals. They feed throughout the water column on a variety of fish and squid.

A pair of rare Hector's dolphins.
(Steve Dawson/ Hedgehog House New Zealand)

IRRAWADDY DOLPHIN
Orcaella brevirostris

Named by J.E. Gray from a skull collected by Sir Walter Elliot in the harbour of Vizagapatam in the Bay of Bengal, *Orcaella* is a diminutive of the Latin *orca*, meaning 'a type of whale' and *brevirostris* comes from the Latin *brevis*, meaning 'short', and *rostrum*, meaning 'beak'.

Females reach a maximum length of 2.32m (7ft 7in) and a weight of 190kg (416lb); males are slightly larger and heavier. It has a streamlined body and a blunt head with a prominent melon and no beak. The flippers are broad and paddle-like and the dorsal fin, located just aft of the mid-point, is very small with a rounded peak. The colouring varies but is generally grey to dark slate blue with a paler belly. There are between 17 and 20 teeth in each row of the upper jaw and between 15 and 18 in each row of the lower. There are usually slightly more teeth in the upper jaw than the lower.

They are found in tropical and sub-tropical coastal waters and some major river systems throughout the Indo-west Pacific region, from the Bay of Bengal to the east Australian coast. Their diet varies with habitat but generally consists of various fish species and some shrimps. They usually live in small groups of less than six animals. In some areas these dolphins are reported to assist fishermen by driving fish into their nets, in others they are feared and blamed for stealing fish and damaging nets. Khmer and Vietnamese fishermen revere them as sacred animals, but Khmer-Islam fishermen kill them for food.

There is considerable concern for the riverine populations because of habitat destruction through deforestation and the environmental disruption brought about by the wars in south-east Asia. The coastal populations are also under increasing threat from habitat destruction. Very little is known of this dolphin and further studies are urgently needed if whole populations are not to disappear before there is even a general awareness of their existence.

Close-up of the head of a tucuxi, primarily a coastal species that also ventures into the river systems and floodplain lakes of the Amazon and Orinoco.
(Maurico Prieto/Marine Mammal Images)

TUCUXI
Sotalia fluviatilis

In 1853, the French zoologist and physician Paul Gervais named a specimen from the upper Amazon *Delphinus fluviatalis*, from the Latin meaning 'belonging to a river'. In 1866, J.E. Gray created the genus *Sotalia*, and in 1884, the tucuxi was recognized as being a member of that genus. This species is found in marine and fresh waters. *Tucuxi* is the Portuguese name.

The dolphin is very small, about 1.8m (5ft 11in) in length. The tucuxi looks much like a small bottlenose dolphin, except that the beak is less clearly demarcated from the head, the body is stubbier, and the dorsal fin is less prominent and more triangular.

Its colour varies throughout the range, but in general the back is dark to light grey and the belly is white to pink, with this light colouring extending onto the ventral flanks.

There are between 29 and 34 teeth on each side of both jaws. The tucuxi feeds on a wide variety of fish species but, unlike the boto which regularly enters the flooded forests, the tucuxi stays mostly in river channels and floodplain lakes.

It is found in the Amazon and Orinoco river systems, including the upper reaches, and the coastal waters and other rivers of northern Latin America, the east coast of Central America and around some Caribbean Islands.

COASTAL

DALL'S PORPOISE
Phocoenoides dalli

In 1885, Frederick True of the American Museum of Natural History named this species *Phocaena dalli* after William Healey Dall, who had collected the first specimen while on an expedition aboard the *Humboldt* in Alaska. In 1909, US naturalist Roy Chapman Andrews collected a specimen of what he believed to be a new species of porpoise in Japan. He decided that it was closely related to Dall's porpoise and created a new genus *Phocoenoides* for both species. These two are now considered one species.

This stocky and powerfully built species grows to a length of 2.2m (7ft 3in) and a weight of 220kg (485lb). Its overall shape is highly unusual with a very small head and a pronounced ridge or 'keel' above and below the tail stock. The dorsal fin, which is in the middle of the back, is small, erect and almost triangular with a slight curve at the tip. The flippers are small.

The colour is striking, being predominantly black with a large white patch on the belly and flanks. The trailing edges of the dorsal fin and the flukes are also white. There are between 19 and 28 very small, slightly spade-shaped teeth in each row of both jaws.

Dall's porpoises are found right across the northern North Pacific Ocean. Recent population estimates indicate at least a million animals in the offshore North Pacific.

The clear white markings of a Dall's porpoise, photographed off Point Sur, California, in August 1979. (James Harvey)

HARBOR PORPOISE
Phocoena phocoena

Linnaeus included this species in his *Systema Naturae* as *Delphinus phocoena*, the latter name being derived from the Greek *phokaina* or the Latin *phocaena*, both of which mean 'porpoise'. The genus *Phocoena* was subsequently established by Baron Cuvier in 1817.

This small porpoise reaches no more than 2m (6ft 7in) in length and weighs a maximum of 90kg (200lb). Short and robust, it has no discernible beak. The triangular dorsal fin is set slightly behind the mid-point of the back. Colouring is indistinct, normally dark brown on the back, fading to light grey on the flanks and white on the belly. A thin dark line often runs from the mouth to the flippers, which are short and rounded, above which a whitish zone may extend up the sides of the body. There are between 19 and 28 small, spade-shaped teeth in each row of both jaws.

The harbor porpoise is found in the coastal waters of the temperate and sub-arctic Northern Hemisphere. There is also a population in the Black Sea. They are most often seen in groups of less than five animals, although larger aggregations have been reported. They are difficult to spot in the field, being of generally quiet and shy habits. They do not appear to undertake long migrations but move inshore in summer and offshore in winter.

Harbor porpoise
(Martin Camm)

North Africa

BLACK SEA   Europe

BALTIC SEA   NORTH SEA

BERING STRAIT

SEA OF OKHOTSK   BERING SEA   GULF OF CALIFORNIA

China   Japan   NORTH PACIFIC OCEAN

VAQUITA or GULF OF CALIFORNIA HARBOR PORPOISE
Phocoena sinus

In 1950, Kenneth Norris found a single bleached porpoise skull on a beach in the Gulf of California. In 1958, after collecting several similar skulls, he and William McFarland published the first full description of this new species, calling it *Phocoena sinus*, from the Latin *sinus* for 'bay, recess, or gulf'. Its common name comes from the local Mexican fishermen who know it as *vaquita* or 'little cow'.

The largest specimen of this species so far identified was a mature female 1.5m (5ft) in length; the heaviest of these animals weighed so far was a 46.7kg (103lb) male. Its dorsal fin is proportionately taller than that of other porpoises and is roughly triangular in shape. The sides are light grey, the belly white and it has a dark dorsal cape and tail stock with dark patches around the eyes and lips. There are between 17 and 21 teeth in each row of the upper jaw and between 17 and 20 in each row of the lower.

These animals are elusive and avoid sea vessels of any kind; when seen, they are usually in groups of up to four animals. Their external appearance and pigmentation were described, for the first time, by Robert Brownell and his colleagues in 1987; they obtained 13 fresh specimens from gill net fishermen. Nothing is known of this species' feeding habits or life history.

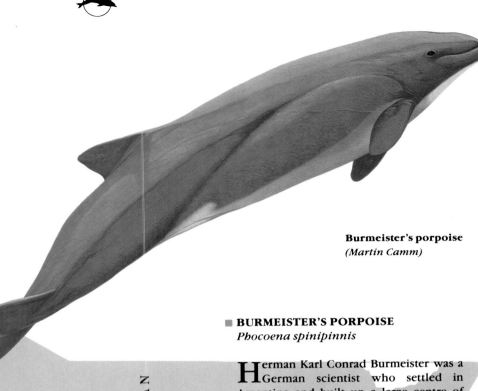

Burmeister's porpoise
(Martin Camm)

BURMEISTER'S PORPOISE
Phocoena spinipinnis

Herman Karl Conrad Burmeister was a German scientist who settled in Argentina and built up a large centre of cetology at the *Museo Argentino de Ciencias Naturales* in Buenos Aires. In 1865, he was the first to describe this new species of porpoise, which was captured alive by fishermen at the mouth of the Rio de la Plata. He named it *spinipinnis*, from the Latin *spinna*, meaning 'a thorn', and *pinna*, meaning 'wing' or 'fin', after the spiny bumps he noticed on the leading edge of the dorsal fin.

Similar in size and shape to the harbor porpoise, its maximum length is 1.8m (5ft 11in). It is distinguished by the shape of its dorsal fin, which is set well back on the body and has a short convex trailing edge and a long, low leading edge bearing spiny bumps. The flippers are large and broad at the base with a blunt tip. Its colouring is predominantly black with some light grey counter-shading on the belly and throat. There are between 14 and 16 spade-shaped teeth in each row of the upper jaw, and between 17 and 19 in each row of the lower.

Burmeister's porpoise lives in the coastal waters on both sides of southern South America. There was some debate as to whether the two populations were separate, but specimens have now been found around Tierra del Fuego, indicating that distribution may be continuous around the tip of South America. Very little is known about the species. The group size appears to be small, usually about three animals.

SOUTH ATLANTIC OCEAN

S. America

Tierra del Fuego

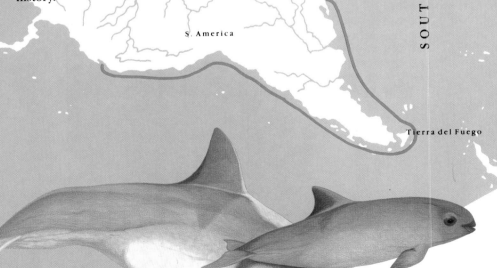

Vaquita and calf
(Martin Camm)

OUTH PACIFIC OCEAN

COASTAL

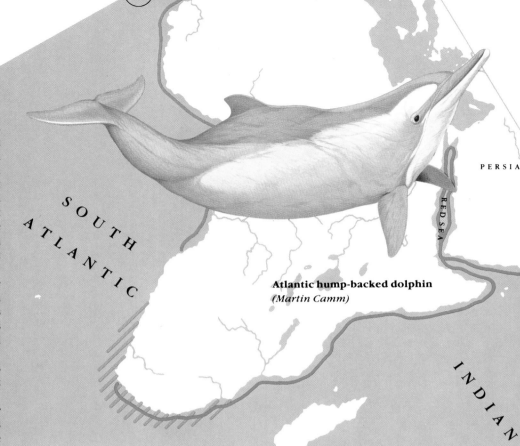

Atlantic hump-backed dolphin
(Martin Camm)

HEAVISIDE'S DOLPHIN
Cephalorhynchus heavisidii

The first specimen of Heaviside's dolphin was named and described in 1828 from the skin and skull of a specimen brought back to England by Captain Haviside, an employee of the British East India Company. The specimen was named incorrectly, however, in the belief that it was part of the anatomical collection of the prominent naval surgeon Captain Heaviside, which had been auctioned that same year.

Heaviside's dolphin lives in the Benguela current system off south-western Africa. Even the external appearance was not properly known until a description was published in 1988 by marine mammal scientist, Peter Best. The longest, physically mature, male recorded was 1.47m (5ft 8in) long and the heaviest animal weighed so far was 74.4kg (164lb).

The head is cone-shaped, like other *Cephalorhynchus* species, the flippers small and blunt. Many animals have irregular serrations on the leading edge of the flippers. The dorsal fin is roughly triangular, unlike the other species which have characteristically rounded and hook-shaped dorsal fins. The tail is crescent shaped with a small central notch. There are between 22 and 28 teeth in each side of the upper jaw and between 22 and 28 in the lower.

Heaviside's dolphin is a dark blue-black above with a grey cape over the head and thoracic region, a light grey flank blaze, and four well-defined unpigmented areas on the belly. Pigmentation around the genital area is different in males and females.

The average group size is about three animals. They eat a mixture of bottom dwelling, mid-water and surface living fish and cephalopods.

FINLESS PORPOISE
Neophocaena phocaenoides

Cuvier first described this species in 1829 and classified it as *Delphinus phocaenoides* ('the dolphin that is like a porpoise'). In 1846, Gray created the genus *Neomeris*, but this was later declared invalid as it had already been ascribed to a species of worm; as a result, the genus was renamed *Neophocaena* (*neo* being Greek for 'new') by the American naturalist Theodore Palmer in 1899.

Its maximum length is about 1.9m (6ft 3in). Its body appears more streamlined than that of other porpoises and its head is similar in appearance to that of the beluga

Heaviside's dolphin
(Martin Camm)

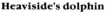

with a well-developed melon. There is no dorsal fin but it has a long dorsal ridge. The flippers are long and taper to a point whilst the trailing edge of the flukes is concave. It is almost uniformly grey in colour, although there is sometimes a bluish tinge on its back and sides. The ventral surface, upper lip, throat and anal region are often lighter in colour. There are between 13 and 22 teeth in each row of both jaws.

The known distribution is in warm rivers and coastal waters from the Persian Gulf to Indonesia, China, the Korean peninsula and Japan. They are found in all major rivers in this area, including the Yangtze, where they seem to be more successful than the baiji in coping with the difficult modern ecological conditions found there. They are certainly more abundant in the area and appear to be 'taking over' some of the baiji's former habitat. There is also some overlap with past distributions of the Ganges and Indus river dolphins. This has led to some neglect of the finless porpoise, because the other species are far more endangered. More information is urgently needed throughout the range before whole populations disappear as a result of habitat destruction.

■ INDO-PACIFIC HUMP-BACKED DOLPHIN
Sousa chinensis

■ ATLANTIC HUMP-BACKED DOLPHIN
Sousa teuszii

In 1757, the Swedish explorer Per Osbeck published a description of dolphins he had observed in the Canton river, which he named *Delphinus chinensis*.

The Atlantic hump-backed dolphin was first described in 1892 by Willy Kükenthal of the Jena Natural History museum in Germany, from a skull and descriptions sent to him by Edward Teusz from Cameroon in West Africa.

The genus name *Sousa* was given by J.E. Gray but its derivation is uncertain; it might be based on a vernacular Indian name for dolphin.

There are no major external bodily differences known between the two species, which are virtually identical but geographically isolated. They have a maximum recorded length of 2.8m (9ft 2in) and a weight of up to 285kg (628lb). The body is streamlined with a prominent beak. Flippers are broad at the base and taper to a point. The most distinctive feature is the dorsal region which consists of a small, slightly rounded fin atop a large hump. (The hump is smaller and the fin more pronounced in adults found east of Indonesia.)

Coloration varies greatly throughout the range but these dolphins are basically grey. Speckled and spotted individuals are not uncommon and all-white individuals have also been reported. The Indo-Pacific hump-backed dolphin has between 29 and 38 teeth in each row of both jaws, compared with between 26 and 31 in the Atlantic hump-backed dolphin.

The taxonomic status of *Sousa* species is not clear. There appears to be little difference between the population living off the West African coast (currently described as *Sousa teuszii*) and those from South Africa and the Indian Ocean (currently known as *Sousa chinensis*) although there are local variations. In particular those found to the east and south of Indonesia seem to be lighter in colour and to lack the characteristic 'hump' of those found elsewhere. A further study may show a total of four or more species exist – or that they are all just one species.

In all areas they may ascend rivers but it is not known whether they have true freshwater populations. The distribution coincides with the distribution of coastal mangrove areas and fears have been expressed that the wide destruction of these will have an adverse effect on the dolphins.

Sousas live in small groups in inshore waters and do not appear to range very far. Very little is known about the genus and, in view of habitat threats, more information is urgently required throughout the range.

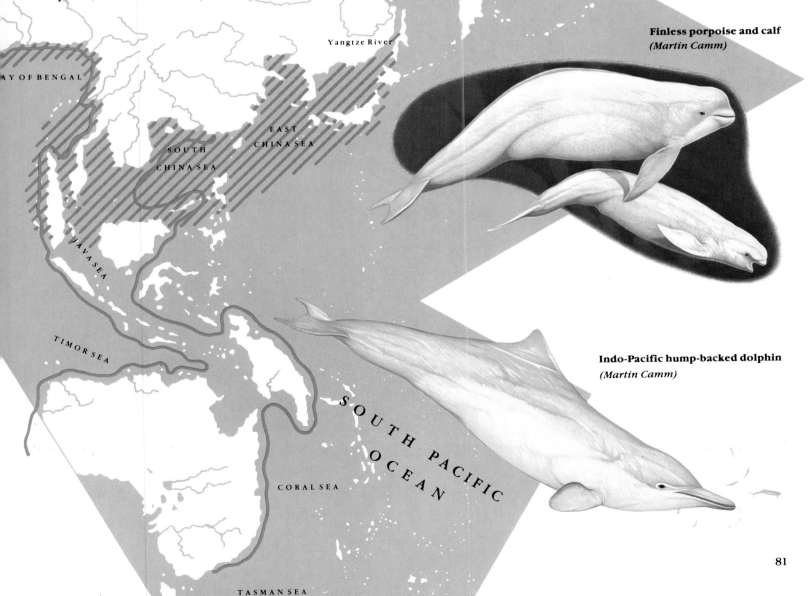

Finless porpoise and calf
(Martin Camm)

Indo-Pacific hump-backed dolphin
(Martin Camm)

COASTAL

■ SPECTACLED PORPOISE
Australophocaena dioptrica

The type specimen for this species was found stranded at Punta Colares on the Rio de la Plata in 1912. The whole animal was preserved in spirits and described by zoologist Fernando Lahille at the national museum in Buenos Aires. He named the species *Phocaena dioptrica* from the Spanish for 'two eyes' or 'spectacles' after the black ring around each eye. (*Dioptrica* derives from the Greek *dioptra*.) The genus *Australophocaena* was created in 1985 by Lawrence G. Barnes, from the Latin *australis*, meaning 'southern', and *phocaena*, meaning 'porpoise', to denote the limitation of the species' range to the southern oceans.

One of the largest members of the family *Phocoenidae*, it can reach 2.2m (7ft 3in) in length. Similar in shape to the harbor porpoise, its coloration consists of two distinct fields, a black back and white belly. There is a thin black line around the mouth which extends along the side of the head and the leading edge of the flippers. The dorsal fin is just beyond the mid-point of the back, towards the tail, and is rounded at the peak. There are between 18 and 23 small spade-shaped teeth in each row of the upper jaw and between 16 and 20 in each row of the lower jaw.

It has been discovered, in comparatively recent times, that the spectacled porpoise occurs in the Auckland Islands, Macquarie Island, South Georgia, Kerguelen Island and in the Falkland Islands, as well as off the eastern coast of South America, which was previously thought to be the only area in which it was found. It is not known whether the island populations are isolated or whether there is contact between them.

Until the mid-1970s only ten specimens had been examined, but the work of Natalie Goodall and her colleagues has added another 112 specimens to the records and details of a further 29 from Tierra del Fuego. This species is the most common inshore cetacean in that region but it is very rarely sighted at sea. It could be a victim of the illegal bait fisheries in the area, and there is an urgent need for more information so that its true status can be ascertained.

■ COMMERSON'S DOLPHIN
Cephalorhynchus commersonii

Commerson's dolphin was named in 1804 by the French research naturalist Lacépède, on the basis of descriptions sent to him by Philbert Commerson, the physician and botanist on the first French voyage around the world, who had seen these dolphins playing round the ship near Tierra del Fuego and the Straits of Magellan.

South American Commerson's dolphins reach a maximum length of 1.52m (4ft 11in) in males and 1.49m (4ft 10in) in females. The heaviest male recorded was 42kg (93lb) and the heaviest non-pregnant female 50kg (110lb) – a pregnant animal weighed 66kg (146lb). The larger and more robust form, living around the Kerguelen Islands, is an isolated population. Here females reach 1.67m (5ft 6in) and weigh up to 86kg (190lb), while males reach 1.65m (5ft 5in) and weigh up to 78kg (172lb).

Very little was known about Commerson's dolphins before Natalie Goodall and her colleagues started work in Tierra del Fuego in the early 1970s. The dolphins live off the east coast of southern South America as far out as the Falkland Islands.

Adults have striking black and white markings. The head and neck are white with a chevron of the same colour at the throat. The black extends over the flippers, and forms a continuous band underneath the belly. A wide area of white begins in front of the black dorsal fin and extends to the middle of the tail stock. The rest of the tail is black. Calves have elements of the adult's colour pattern, but in brown or grey on darker grey. The adult colour pattern is attained within the first year. The black genital patches are differently shaped in males and females. Tierra del Fuego specimens have between 25 and 33 teeth on each side of the upper jaw and between 24 and 32 in the lower.

They are usually seen in small groups, although aggregations of over 100 have been reported. They often feed in areas disturbed by tidal changes. Food items include schooling fishes and, unusually for cetaceans, bottom-dwelling invertebrates.

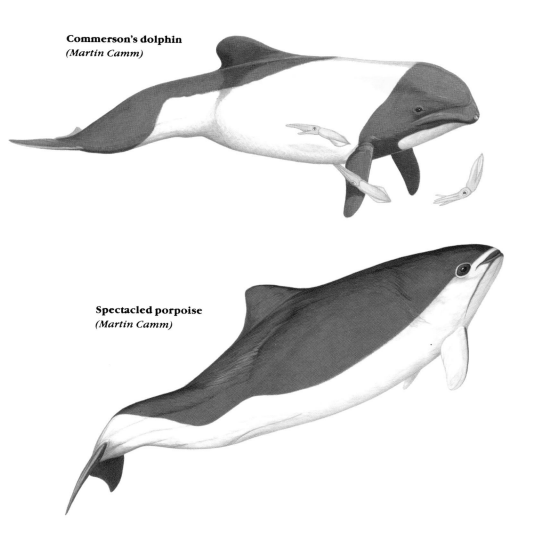

Commerson's dolphin
(Martin Camm)

Spectacled porpoise
(Martin Camm)

BLACK DOLPHIN or CHILEAN DOLPHIN
Cephalorhynchus eutropia

Eutropia is from the Greek *eu*, meaning 'good' or 'well', and *tropidos*, meaning a 'keel', referring to the shape of the skull.

The black dolphin is one of the least known cetacean species and its external appearance has only recently been described in detail by Natalie Goodall and colleagues. It lives in the coastal waters of Chile, on the west coast of southern South America. Females grow up to 1.65m (5ft 5in) in length and males up to 1.67m (5ft 6in). However, the females measured so far have not been physically mature and so it is not known whether there is real dimorphism in size. Substantial weights of up to 63kg (140lb) are reported. There are between 28 and 34 teeth in each side of the upper jaw and between 29 and 33 on each side in the lower jaw.

These animals typically have a flattened tapering head and rounded dorsal fin with a curved trailing edge. It has a grey back with a darker beak and distinctive asymmetrical lunate marks running from behind the blowhole to behind the eye. On the ventral surface there is a white patch on the chin and a dark grey area between the flippers. The area from the flippers to the tail stock is white with sexually distinctive grey genital patches.

This dolphin is usually seen in small groups of between two and five animals. They appear shy and often avoid vessels but will bow ride at times. Little is known about their diet but it seems to include a variety of fish, cephalopods and crustaceans. They are victims, to an unknown extent, of the illegal bait fisheries in the area.

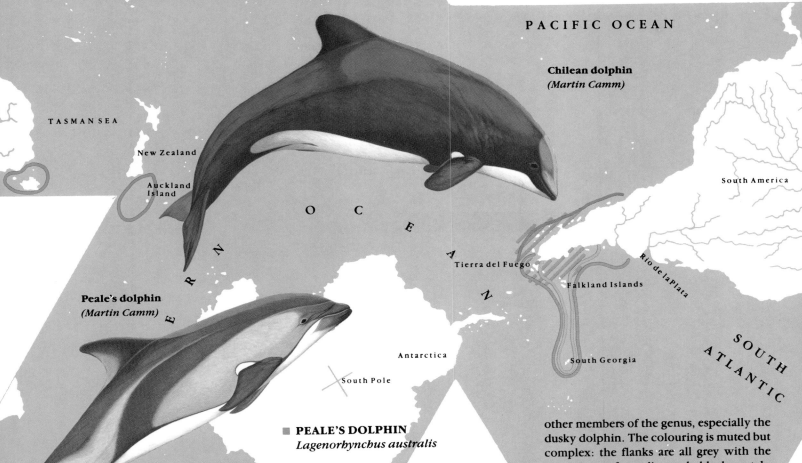

PACIFIC OCEAN

Chilean dolphin
(Martin Camm)

TASMAN SEA

New Zealand

Auckland Island

O C E

South America

A N

Tierra del Fuego

Río de la Plata

Falkland Islands

R N

Peale's dolphin
(Martin Camm)

E

Antarctica

South Pole

South Georgia

SOUTH ATLANTIC

O

S

Kerguelen Island

INDIAN OCEAN

PEALE'S DOLPHIN
Lagenorhynchus australis

This species was first identified by Titian Peale, painter and naturalist aboard the *USS Vincennes*, off the coast of Patagonia in 1839. He called it *Phocoena australis*, from the Latin for 'southern'. It was not seen again at sea until the 1930s and the first specimen to be collected was caught off Chile. In 1941 the US zoologist Remington Kellogg of the Smithsonian Institution placed it in the genus *Lagenorhynchus*.

Its maximum recorded length is 2.16m (7ft). The body shape is similar to that of other members of the genus, especially the dusky dolphin. The colouring is muted but complex: the flanks are all grey with the exception of a diagonal black patch, halfway along the body, which is joined to the dark dorsal region. The dorsal fin and flippers are also dark, as are the patches around the anus and the underside of the tail stock. The lower lip and chin are black. The belly and throat are white. There are about 30 teeth in each row of both jaws.

Peale's dolphin is little known. It lives in the coastal waters of southern South America and off the Falkland Islands. Nobody knows what it eats or how many there are.

ESTUARINE AND RIVER
S P E C I E S

The majority of dolphins and porpoises are found in the open ocean or in coastal marine environments. There are, however, four species which exist only in river and estuarine waters; another, the franciscana, is found in coastal marine waters and is included here because of its phylogenetic links with the four 'true' river dolphins.

The Ganges, Indus, Yangtze and Amazon river dolphins, together with the franciscana, compose the Superfamily Platanistoidea. All share similarities in appearance and, for a long time, they were all classed in one family. Over the years, however, scientists have come to consider that the five species' similarities are largely the result of 'parallel evolution', by which they adapted independently to suit their highly similar environments, rather than the result of any common ancestry. In consequence, the river dolphins are now classified in three different families: the Platanistidae (Ganges and Indus susu); the Pontoporiidae (baiji and franciscana) and Iniidae (boto).

Franciscana
(Martin Camm)

■ AMAZON RIVER DOLPHIN or BOTO
Inia geoffrensis

Inia is said to be a Bolivian Indian name for this dolphin. *Geoffrensis* derives from the name of the French naturalist Etienne Geoffroy Saint-Hilaire.

The largest of the river dolphins, the boto reaches a maximum length of 2.55m (8ft 4in) in males and a weight of up to 160kg (353lb); females grow up to 1.96m (6ft 3in) in length and weigh up to 96.5kg (213lb). It has a long dorsal keel and large flippers which curve to a point. The eye openings are larger than in other river dolphins and the eyes are functional. There are between 24 and 35 teeth in each row of both jaws.

Its coloration can be surprisingly vivid. Young botos are normally slate grey but, as they mature, the dark pigment fades to reveal the pink flush of the blood flow seen through their semi-translucent skin.

It feeds on a wide variety of fish species, including the large catfish which, because of its armour of heavy, bony fin spines, is shielded from all other potential predators.

The boto is widely distributed throughout the Amazon and Orinoco river systems in Brazil, Bolivia, Peru, Ecuador, Colombia, Venezuela and Guyana.

■ FRANCISCANA or LA PLATA DOLPHIN
Pontoporia blainvillei

This species was named in 1844 after Henri de Blainville of the *Museé National d'Histoire Naturelle* in Paris. The British naturalist J.E. Gray created a new genus, *Pontoporia*, for it in 1846, after the Greek *pontos*, meaning 'sea', because it was the first 'river' dolphin to have been found in the open sea.

Among the smallest of all cetaceans, adult males reach 1.58m (5ft 2in) in length and weigh 47.2kg (104lb); females reach 1.77m (5ft 10in) in length and weigh 52.1kg (115lb).

Its appearance is basically similar to that of the river dolphins. The beak is long and slender, the front of the melon is rounded and the blowhole crescent-shaped. The dorsal fin has a rounded peak and the flippers are splayed with serrated trailing edges. Brown-grey in colour, it is darker on the back than on the ventral regions. There are between 51 and 58 sharp teeth in each row of both jaws.

The franciscana is restricted to the coastal waters of Brazil, Uruguay, Argentina, and the La Plata estuary.

A boto swims through the flooded Amazon forest.
(Andrea Florence/ Ardea)

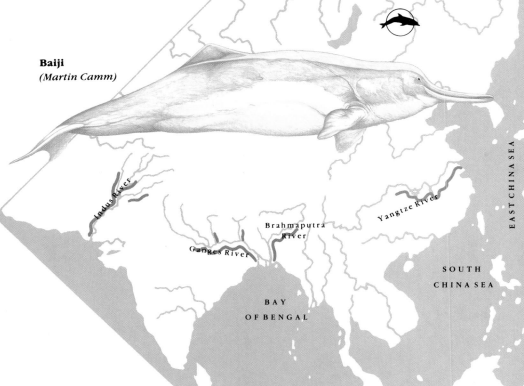

Baiji
(Martin Camm)

GANGES RIVER DOLPHIN or SUSU
Platinista gangetica

INDUS RIVER DOLPHIN or SUSU
Platinista minor

*P*latinista is the Latin word Pliny the Elder used to describe an animal living in the river Ganges with a beak like a dolphin and a long tail.

The Ganges susu was first scientific-ally described by the English physician and botanist William Roxburgh and the Dutch traveller Heinrich Julius Lebeck in 1801 (although independently of each other). They referred to the Ganges river dolphin as *Delphinus gangetica*. The genus *Platinista* was created in 1830 by the German zoologist Johann Wagler. The Indus susu was first described by Sir Richard Owen of the Royal College of Surgeons in 1853.

The two species are indistinguishable in appearance. Males can grow up to 2.12m (7ft) in length and weigh up to 84kg (185lb); females can reach lengths of 2.52m (8ft 2in) and weights of 83.5kg (184lb). Their most striking feature is the long, slender beak, which can account for as much as one-fifth of the total body length. The body is small and plump with large paddle-like flippers and wide, pointed flukes. There is a long dorsal keel but no true dorsal fin. The colour is a uniform grey. There are between 27 and 33 long, sharply-pointed teeth in each row of both jaws.

The Indus and Ganges susus are almost completely blind. The turbid waters of the rivers they inhabit are so full of sediment that visibility is severely reduced and good vision no longer a necessity. The eyes of the susus have become reduced to mere pinholes; they have no lenses or eye-muscle nerves, and only the thinnest of optic nerves. There is a retina but the eyes do no more than determine the direction and intensity of light. As a result they rely heavily on their well-developed echolocating abilities; both species swim on their sides and scan the water horizontally by moving their heads up and down while emitting a constant stream of clicks.

The Ganges river dolphin is found in the Ganges, Brahmaputra, Meghna and Karnaphuli rivers i.e. on the river systems of north-eastern India, Bangladesh, Bhutan and Nepal. The Indus susu is limited to five isolated populations, separated from each other as a result of dam construction, along the Indus river.

YANGTZE RIVER DOLPHIN or BAIJI
Lipotes vexillifer

*F*irst mentioned in Chinese records 2,000 years ago, its existence was not revealed to the West until 1914 when a visiting American, Charles M. Hoy, killed one and took its skull back to the Smithsonian Institution in the USA. Gerrit Smith Miller, the Institution's Curator of Mammals, published the first scientific description in 1918 naming it after the Greek *leipo*, meaning 'left behind', in reference to the species' restricted distribution, and the Latin *vexillum*, meaning 'flag' or 'banner'. Hoy mistook the Chinese ideogram for 'baiji' or 'white dolphin' for 'baiqui' meaning 'white flag' and this has caused confusion ever since.

The maximum length of this species is 2.53m (8ft 4in) for females and 2.16m (7ft) for males; they weigh 167kg (368lb) and 125kg (276lb) respectively. The dorsal fin is small and in the shape of a low isosceles triangle. The flippers are smaller than those of the susu and it is lighter in colour. The beak is slim and pointed. There are between 30 and 36 conical teeth, uniform in size, in each row of both jaws.

The head of a Ganges susu.
(Ted Stephenson/EarthViews)

Indus susu
(Martin Camm)

THE HUMAN THREAT

HUNTING AND FISHING

'While many in our culture tend toward a protectionist view of cetaceans, many people in the world continue to regard cetaceans simply as resources, no different from other resources available for human use.

Stephen Leatherwood – 'We're All in the Same Boat'
(*Windstar Journal*. Spring 1987)

The unsettling gaze of a trapped dolphin, staring helplessly through the strands of net that entangle it.
(Howard Hall)

Traditional hunts and fisheries for marine mammals have often developed in response to the absence of alternative protein sources on land. Some persist as anachronisms that have outlived their historical purpose.

Dolphins have long been the accidental victims of coastal fishing practices, but only on a limited scale. In recent years, not only have these fishing activities intensified but also new technologies have been introduced that allow 'industrial-scale' fishing on the high seas to be carried out with deadly efficiency.

Unregulated and indiscriminate, these methods make no distinctions between fish and marine mammals. In some cases, dolphins are deliberately targeted in order to catch fish more efficiently. As a result, literally hundreds of thousands of dolphins are now dying every year.

In addition, many fishermen are now turning to dolphins as a main catch because existing fish stocks have been depleted, either as a result of bad resource management or because of the effects of this intensification.

Ironically, small cetaceans are often blamed for depleting the fish stocks and are hunted as a result. Governments often encourage this view in order to avoid having to admit the failure of their fishery policies.

Many superficial solutions have been tried which seek to coerce nations or cultural groups into abandoning or modifying their fishing practices. But the problems the dolphins face are inextricably linked with the development and management of the resources of the world's oceans. Piecemeal solutions will not suffice.

COOK INLET

ARCTIC

BEAUFORT SEA

HIGH ARCTIC

BELUGA WHALE POPULATION ABUNDANCE AND CURRENT TAKE LEVELS

STOCK (based on summering locales)	Est. initial abundance	Current abundance	Approx. annual current take	Other impacts
CANADA				
St Lawrence River	at least 5,000	400 – 500	0	s,h,p
East Hudson Bay/James Bay	at least 6,600	2,900	50 – 90	h
Ungava Bay	at least 1,000	less than 100 (a)	15 – 25	unknown
West Hudson Bay	no estimate	14,000 – 27,000	200 – 300	s,c,h
Cumberland Sound	at least 5,000	400 – 500	25 – 45	unknown
High Arctic	10,000 +	6,000 – 19,000	550 – 1,150 (b)	unknown
Beaufort Sea	no estimate	11,500 – 17,000	135 – 385 (c)	o&g,s,h
UNITED STATES				
Cook Inlet	no estimate	400 – 500	less than 15	o&g
Eastern Chukchi	no estimate	2,500 – 3,000	31 – 187	o&g,s
Norton Sound/Yukon Delta	no estimate	1,000-2,000	50 – 119	o&g
NORWAY				
Spitzbergen	no estimate	unknown	0	unknown
GREENLAND				
High Arctic	no estimate	unknown	10 – 40	unknown
USSR	no estimate	unknown	unknown	unknown

(a) population may have already been extirpated and animals found here may be the result of a spill-over effect from other stocks

(b) estimated catch figure includes those killed by Greenland natives when this stock overwinters off the west coast of Greenland

(c) estimated catch figure includes those killed by Alaskan natives during this stock's migration to and from the Beaufort Sea in spring and autumn

o&g – oil and gas exploration/drilling
  h – habitat loss/modification
  s – shipping/boating disturbance
  c – capture for aquaria
  p – pollution

BAFFIN ISLAND

CUMB

FROBISH

WEST HUDSON BAY

LAKE HARBOUR ●

EAST HUDSON BAY

UNGAVA BAY

JAMES BAY

CANADA

ST LAWRENCE RIVER

SPITZBERGEN

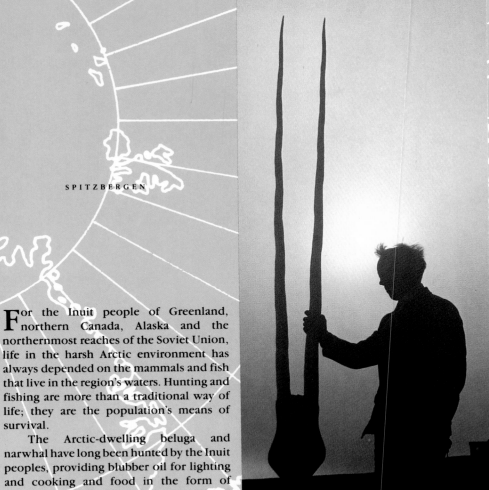

The striking
silhouette of a rare
double-tusked
narwhal's skull.
Although all males
have two teeth, it is
exceptional for both
to develop into tusks.
(Fred Breummer)

For the Inuit people of Greenland, northern Canada, Alaska and the northernmost reaches of the Soviet Union, life in the harsh Arctic environment has always depended on the mammals and fish that live in the region's waters. Hunting and fishing are more than a traditional way of life; they are the population's means of survival.

The Arctic-dwelling beluga and narwhal have long been hunted by the Inuit peoples, providing blubber oil for lighting and cooking and food in the form of *muktuk* – the name given to the whales' skin and adhering blubber – and meat, which is also fed to their sledge dogs.

NARWHAL

Demand for the male narwhal's long ivory tusk has provided an important incentive for Inuit hunters in some areas. Between 1965 and 1978, prices soared from Can.$1.25 per pound to Can.$50 per pound, before declining again during the 1980s, following EEC and US bans on the importation of narwhal ivory from Canada. Greenland Inuit were granted an exemption from the EEC ban and they still export to this market.

In the late 1960s and early 1970s, the combined 'takes' by Greenland and Canadian Inuit reached as much as 2,000 animals a year. Presently the number of narwhals killed and landed is between 700 and 1,100 animals annually; more are killed but sink before they can be retrieved.

The two discrete stocks of narwhals, to the west and east of Greenland, total between 24,000 and 30,000 animals. The western stock may presently be over-exploited.

BELUGA

In some areas of the USSR, belugas have been netted in communal fishing operations since the sixteenth century. At their peak in the mid-1960s, it is known that Soviet hunts took between 3,000 and 4,000 belugas a year and that, in recent years, this has declined considerably. It is not certain whether this is because the whales have been over-exploited and so are harder to find or whether there is less of a market for the belugas' meat and blubber, thus reducing the economic incentive for the hunt. Little new information exists either on the size of beluga populations in the Soviet Arctic or on the scale and impact of the remaining hunts, which are now conducted using rifles and nets.

In Greenland, the Inuit generally employ more efficient traditional hunting methods which involve spearing the belugas with harpoons attached to floats. These keep the whales at the surface until they can be retrieved by the hunters.

Where harpoons have been replaced by rifles, the hunts have become more wasteful as a large number of the belugas shot sink without a trace. Official records include only those belugas which are brought ashore and scientists and conservationists fear that, in some areas, the number of belugas actually killed may be twice as high as the number recorded.

The problem in Canada is even more complex because the Inuit there are continuing to hunt populations which have already been seriously depleted by large-scale commercial non-native hunts earlier this century. These hunters are understandably sensitive about attempts to limit their traditional practices due to this past over-exploitation by others. Yet many of these beluga stocks are now either in decline or facing extinction. In Ungava Bay, for example, a 1985 aerial survey spotted only two whales, the last remnants of a once thriving population.

In 1923 the stock of belugas in Cumberland Sound, on the south-east coast of Baffin Island, was conservatively estimated to contain at least 5,000 whales and now numbers no more than 500. A quota of 40 animals landed per year has been set by the Canadian government but this may well be too high because hunts further down the coast, at Frobisher Bay and Lake Harbour, may be taking animals from the same stock.

The development of oil and gas exploration in some Arctic regions, and the spread of other forms of pollution and habitat destruction, combined with possible over exploitation, makes the future of some beluga populations far from certain.

FAEROES

The Faeroes are a group of about 30 islands in the North Atlantic Ocean, located approximately halfway between Iceland and Scotland, which enjoy a semi-independent status under the jurisdiction of Denmark.

The population of 46,000, descendants of ninth-century Norwegian settlers, inhabit 18 of the islands and depend entirely on commercial fishing for their livelihood. The Faeroese rely on Denmark for their defense and for representation in most international fora, but have their own language, flag, bank notes, stamps and passport, political parties and parliament – called the *Lagting*. Unlike Denmark, they are not members of the European Community.

For at least four hundred years, the Faeroese have hunted the pods of pilot whales which swim close to their shores. This hunt, known as the *grindadrap*, takes place mainly in the summer months and has changed little in style or substance since it began, although the introduction of modern boats, radios and echo-sounders has made it easier to find and herd the whales.

A *grindadrap* begins whenever a pod of whales is spotted close to the coast. The boat which first sights the pod informs any others in the vicinity and together they form a semi-circle around the whales and begin gradually herding them towards bays.

Alerted to the whales' arrival by an announcement over local radio, islanders wade out from the beach into the water and attempt to bury hooks, or gaffs, attached to ropes into the whales' heads. The whales are then hauled ashore, where they are killed with a special knife, approximately 18cm (7in) long, called a *grindkniver*, which is used to sever the carotid artery and jugular vein.

The whales are cut up and the meat and blubber are distributed, free of charge, to the region's inhabitants with priority being given to those who actually participated in the hunt. The person who first spotted the whales is entitled to choose the largest whale or its equivalent in smaller whales; the whale foremen (*grindaforemenn*), who oversee the drive and killing of the whales, are each guaranteed one per cent of the meat.

A sharp 2.3kg (5lb) gaff is used to haul the dolphins into shallow water, where their throats are slit with a *grindkniver*.
(Athel von Koettlitz/ Environmental Investigation Agency)

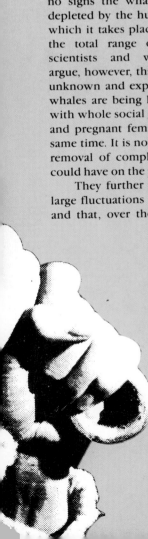

The bays of the Faeroe Islands *(background map)* **are the scene for the** *grindadrap,* **in which pilot whales are herded inshore and slaughtered** *(far left and right).*
(Dave Currey/Environmental Investigation Agency).

In recent years, Faeroese pilot whaling has received a great deal of international criticism. It is argued that the killing of the whales is cruel and inhumane; that the Faeroese no longer need the whalemeat to survive as they are now a modern society with a high standard of living; and that much of the meat is wasted.

Faeroese scientists argue that there are no signs the whale population is being depleted by the hunt and that the area in which it takes place is small compared to the total range of the species. Other scientists and whale conservationists argue, however, that the population size is unknown and express concern that these whales are being hunted indiscriminately with whole social groups, including calves and pregnant females, being taken at the same time. It is not known what effect the removal of complete groups in this way could have on the population's gene pool.

They further point out that there are large fluctuations in the size of the hunts, and that, over the last two decades, the

average number of whales killed annually has been the highest ever recorded. Between 1970 and 1979, an average of 960 pilot whales were killed each year. In 1981, 2,973 were killed, and thereafter, the average catch has remained high with the annual average for the 1980s standing at approximately 2,000 animals.

The Faeroese have now begun killing large numbers of other small cetacean species. In 1988, 544 Atlantic white-sided dolphins were killed in a single day.

This unstable pattern of increasingly heavy catches is very similar to that of a pilot whale hunt which used to occur off the Newfoundland coast in Canada but ended in the early 1970s after the stock was decimated by over-exploitation.

Of particular concern is the fact that the whales are taken from a population whose size has not been assessed. Scientists do not even know whether there are one, two, or more large pilot whale stocks in the North Atlantic. Nor is there any certainty about whether or not the whales are being affected by other human activities such as pollution, entanglement in nets or over-fishing.

Ironically, there is a great deal of evidence to suggest that pilot whale meat is hazardous to the islanders' health. Pilot whales in the North Atlantic, along with many other species of marine mammals, are heavily contaminated with mercury. This may be the result of pollution or chemical upwellings of naturally occurring mercury from the volcanic vents along the North Atlantic ridge.

In 1981 the Faeroes' own Department of Hygiene recommended that because of the levels of contamination, no islander should eat whale meat more than once a week and that the whales' liver shouldn't be eaten at all. It was recommended that the total per capita meat consumption should be limited to 14kg (31lb) a year. Although the annual per capita share of whale meat is actually nearer 30kg (66lb), the Faeroese insist that they have reduced the amount of meat they eat. However, they do still eat large quantities of blubber and more recent analyses have shown that it is here that most of the contaminants are likely to be concentrated.

In addition, at the time the Department of Hygiene made its recommendation, it had only been able to test for the presence of mercury in the whales' tissues. It has since been shown that the meat and blubber also contain very high levels of PCBs, DDT and dieldrin.

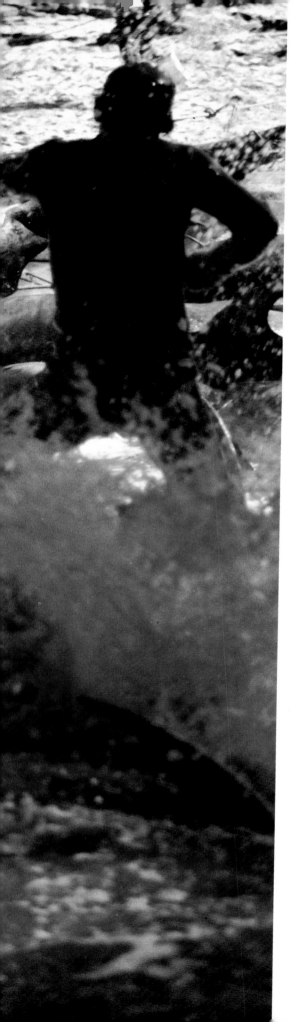

JAPAN

The Japanese diet has traditionally relied heavily on seafood for protein and, for centuries, the harvesting of these resources has involved the killing of marine mammals.

From around 1606, the catching of large whales was already common practice in the waters around the fishing town of Taiki. By the second half of the twentieth century, Japan had the largest commercial whaling fleet in the world.

Japan's role in the over-exploitation of several species of whales has made it the focus of intense international criticism. Much of this has proven bewildering to a society which, by and large, does not share the same degree of sensitivity as its critics towards marine mammals and which regards cetaceans as resources to be harvested in much the same way as fish.

The over-exploitation of larger whale species led to the imposition of a commercial whaling moratorium. As a result, Japan has been limited to hunting a relatively small number of minke whales for 'scientific' purposes. In recent years, an increasing number of dolphins and porpoises have been taken in Japanese coastal fisheries, generating a controversy which echoes the outcry over the dolphin kills at Iki Island in the 1970s.

IKI

The battle between dolphins and the fishermen of Katsumoto on Iki Island, in the south of Japan, dates back to the early part of the twentieth century. It was then that dolphins were first blamed for disturbing the breeding grounds of the yellowtail, the islanders' main fish catch. The killing of dolphins in the area remained sporadic, however, until 1976,

when yellowtail catches declined dramatically and the fishermen protested that it was because of an increased population of dolphins in the area.

This contention was widely disputed, not least because only one of the four species of dolphins the fishermen held responsible, the false killer whale, eats yellowtail and even then only as a relatively small component of its diet.

Many scientists argued that the decline was more likely to be the result of a combination of factors. The large net fisheries in the area, operated by Korea as well as Japan, probably over-exploited the local fish stocks. These may already have been affected by pollution off the coast and the sudden occurrence of a natural, though unusual, warm ocean current which began to flow through the area in the early 1970s, displacing the colder, more nutrient-rich, waters of the region.

Nonetheless, the fishermen remained convinced that the dolphins were responsible and, by way of a solution, began driving large numbers of the dolphins into bays and killing them.

Between 1976 and 1982, the Iki Islanders killed at least 4,147 bottlenose dolphins, 953 false killer whales, 525 Risso's dolphins and 466 Pacific white-sided dolphins.

The despair of the Katsumoto fishermen was understandable. Their own local laws prevented them from hunting yellowtail by any method other than hooks and lines, which meant that they were unable to compete with the large-scale commercial net fisheries.

In 1977, the fishermen even invited television cameras to film them killing the dolphins, believing that this coverage would generate sympathy for their plight. Instead, scenes of the carnage attracted attention and condemnation from all over the world. This came as a great shock to the Iki islanders, who genuinely couldn't understand why their actions should be considered so controversial.

Then suddenly in 1982, for reasons that are unknown, the dolphins stopped appearing in such large numbers around the yellowtail's breeding grounds. Today, some dolphins are almost certainly still taken in the waters around Iki, but the mass slaughter appears to be a thing of the past.

These dramatic images from Iki, of wet-suited fishermen spearing herds of panicking dolphins in shallow waters running with blood, were the kind of pictures that shocked Western observers and triggered off a widescale protest. (Howard Hall)

Such hunts were and are exceptional. However, the catching of dolphins for their meat is a routine matter in Japan and there are many quaysides and markets *(see overleaf)* that regularly sell their meat for resale in city supermarkets. (Steve Leatherwood)

JAPAN

COASTAL HUNTS

Elsewhere in Japan, dolphins and porpoises are hunted for meat all around the coast. Traditionally, this meat was sold for local consumption in the towns and villages where the dolphins were caught. Recently, however, dolphin meat has begun to appear more widely, in city supermarkets and restaurants.

Coastal dolphin hunts in Japan are conducted in two main ways. Most species, such as the striped, spotted and bottlenose dolphins and the short-finned pilot and false killer whales, are taken by driving the dolphins into bays, which are then barricaded with nets – the same method used at Iki.

The other type of hunt is conducted with hand-held harpoons from small boats. The Pacific white-sided dolphin is difficult to herd and so is frequently caught this way, as is the Dall's porpoise, which does not form large enough schools to be herded.

For many years, about 20,000 small cetaceans were recorded as being caught annually in Japanese coastal hunts. However, some scientists within Japan, such as Toshio Kasuya of the Far Seas Fisheries Research Institute, claimed that many of the catches went unreported and that the real total of small cetaceans killed annually was nearer to 40,000.

At the 1989 meeting of the Scientific Committee of the International Whaling Commission (IWC), Japan revealed that, according to its official statistics, 46,273 small cetaceans were reported as being intentionally killed in its coastal waters during 1988. (In addition, 3,318 were recorded as being caught incidentally in fishing nets).

This figure was the result of a massive increase in the number of Dall's porpoises killed, which rose from the previous average of about 10,000 a year to 39,737 in 1988. Alarmingly, all were taken from two stocks which together had been estimated to contain only 105,000 individuals.

The Japanese commissioner to the IWC argued in 1989 that this increase was prompted by the IWC's refusal to allow Japanese coastal communities to kill minke whales during the commercial whaling moratorium. Other delegates and scientists rejected this argument as simplistic, claiming the increase could just as easily be ascribed to fishermen seeking alternative prey as a result of dwindling fish stocks.

During the 1988 season there had been a large, orchestrated publicity campaign encouraging people to eat greater quantities of dolphin meat. Far from being used as a replacement for minke meat by small coastal communities, dolphin meat is now a valuable commodity which is being sold in many city supermarkets for extremely high prices; in 1990, 100g of frozen 'gondo', or pilot whale meat, was selling for 680 yen, the equivalent of £13.20 per pound.

Many scientists and conservationists believe the increasing number of dolphin kills is simply a sign that, after contributing to the over-exploitation of several species of large whales, the intransigent Japanese whaling industry is now turning to smaller whales, dolphins and porpoises as the next most available and exploitable species.

VAQUITA

MEXICO

The vaquita is one of the most endangered of the small cetaceans. Restricted in range to the upper part of the Gulf of California off Mexico's western coast, it has become seriously depleted as a result of widespread entanglement, mainly in gill nets used to catch a large fish called the totoaba.

Scientists working in the region first became concerned about its plight in the early 1970s at the same time that PESCA, the Mexican fisheries' authority, was worried about over-exploitation of the totoaba. The Mexican catch had plunged from a peak of 2,261 tonnes in 1942 to a mere 58 tonnes in 1975, the year in which PESCA imposed a ban on totoaba fishing. (The ban is still in force, although catches for research purposes have been allowed since 1985.)

It was thought that this ban would also benefit the vaquita but, unfortunately, it did the opposite. A black market for the fish was created and, as the ban was poorly enforced, nets continued to be set much as before. In addition, some local fishermen began setting gill nets to catch sharks and manta rays thus compounding the vaquitas' problems.

As far as we know, the fishermen do not eat the vaquita. They may use it for bait if it is caught accidentally but many may simply discard the bodies for fear of prosecution.

Scientists studying the vaquita in the wild are working in co-operation with Mexican conservationists to press the government of Mexico to devise a regional management programme for the upper Gulf that would address the effects of fisheries and environmental damage on the vaquita population. They are urging that a greater effort be made to determine the exact numbers of vaquitas remaining and to establish how many are still being caught in fishing nets.

Although there are no official estimates of its numbers, the best available information suggests there are probably no more than 200-400 vaquitas remaining. During an extensive survey of the upper Gulf in 1987, only 40 animals were sighted.

Just 30 years after it was first scientifically described in 1958, the vaquita has been pushed to the brink of extinction. According to Robert Brownell, a scientist with the U.S. Fish and Wildlife Service, who has studied the vaquita and followed its plight for more than two decades:

'It will be many years before scientists will be able to determine whether the population is increasing or decreasing. It is quite possible, therefore, that the vaquita could become extinct before scientists have clearly documented a decline in its population or learned much about its natural history.'

This rare picture of a rare species shows a female vaquita which drowned after being incidentally caught in a gill net, in waters near El Golfo de Santa Clara, in the north of the Gulf of California, on March 13, 1985. (Alejandro Robles/Marine Mammal Images)

TUNA-D

Most of the fisheries which kill dolphins do so accidentally. The tens of thousands of small cetaceans – and other marine mammals – which die annually as a result of commercial fishing operations are the unwanted, if inevitable, casualties of environmentally destructive fishing methods.

There is, however, one fishery which sets its nets around dolphins intentionally because it is the quickest and cheapest way to catch the most profitable fish. In the Eastern Tropical Pacific (ETP), an 18 million square kilometre (8 million square mls) area of water stretching from Mexico to Chile, between 80,000 and 130,000 dolphins are killed by the yellowfin tuna fishery every year.

For reasons that remain unexplained, schools of large yellowfin tuna which migrate through the ETP often swim just below herds of dolphins, a phenomenon believed to occur only in this part of the world. Fishermen, who have known of this association since the 1920s, used to take advantage of it without harming the dolphins.

The surface disturbances created by the dolphins were used to locate the schools of tuna. Operating from small coastal vessels, the fishermen would throw live bait overboard, sending the tuna into a feeding frenzy during which they would bite at anything, including the hooks lowered to catch them. The dolphins were able to detect the hooks with their sonar and were 'rewarded', as they too fed on the live bait.

The fishermen realized that the tuna swimming underneath the dolphins were almost exclusively yellowfin and were of a greater size than those yellowfin which swam alone. Thus they concentrated their efforts on looking for the tuna associated with dolphins because of the higher profits to be gained from landing the larger fish.

Then, in the late 1950s, the nature of the fishery changed from small-scale to highly commercial, with the development of the 'power block', a hydraulic pulley which permits the smooth and rapid retrieval of a large nylon purse-seine net, over a kilometre (3,300ft) in length. As a result, a mutually advantageous relationship was replaced by one that was to prove fatal for the dolphins.

Rather than hauling tuna aboard individually, it became possible to deploy a net around an entire herd of dolphins and draw, or 'purse', it closed at the bottom, thereby trapping both tuna and dolphins.

Purse-seining allowed far more tuna to be caught than was possible through bait-fishing, was less labour-intensive and thus more profitable. With the realization that bountiful and financially rewarding catches awaited those willing and able to take advantage of the tuna-dolphin bond, the fishery changed dramatically. The results were record catches of yellowfin and record numbers of dead dolphins.

Since 1959, it is estimated that over six million dolphins have died in the nets of the tuna fishery. Indeed, so efficient did it become that, by 1961, the Inter-American Tropical Tuna Commission (IATTC) – the regulatory body responsible for the management of tuna fisheries in the ETP – expressed concern about the status of yellowfin stocks.

The method used to capture the tuna has changed little during the past 30 years. Once a herd of dolphins is spotted from the purse-seiner or from a helicopter, speedboats are launched from the vessel. They give chase and drive in constant circles around the herd. Underwater explosives, thrown from the helicopter or speedboats, may also be used to herd and disorientate the dolphins. After a chase that may sometimes last for hours, the exhausted dolphins slow down and form a protective circle. The purse-seine net is then easily deployed around the entire herd and sealed at the bottom.

Many dolphins become entangled in the net and suffocate. Others may be crushed by the weight of the tuna in the crowded net, or by the power winch, as the net is hauled in. Flippers and beaks may be torn off as the dolphins struggle to free themselves. Those that escape one such encounter may soon find themselves netted again.

The huge mortality of dolphins caused by this fishery went largely unnoticed until brought to the public's attention by William Perrin, a young US fisheries scientist, who signed on with the US tuna fleet in 1966 and 1967 to study the behaviour of dolphins as the basis for his doctoral dissertation. In 1969, Perrin revealed that in the course of netting a single school of tuna, the fishermen would sometimes kill

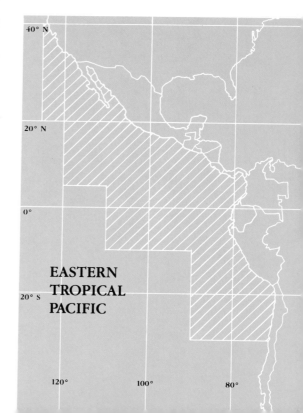

EASTERN TROPICAL PACIFIC

OLPHIN

as many as 1,000 dolphins. In all, he estimated that roughly 250,000 dolphins were dying in the nets of the US tuna fleet every year.

The ensuing public outrage over the number of dolphins killed was a major impetus for the development and passage of the US Marine Mammal Protection Act (MMPA) of 1972. Considered a landmark piece of legislation, it offered, on paper at least, strict protection for all marine mammals in US waters and placed a moratorium on their killing, capture and even harassment.

This powerful modern Mexican purse seiner, the *Arkos II* (above), is part of the largest national fleet in the ETP. Equipped with sophisticated navigational aids and fishing gear, it also carries a spotter helicopter to locate the herds of dolphins and the valuable tuna that swim beneath them.
(Pieter Folkens/EarthViews)

Looking like some Greek silver statue rescued from an underwater wreck, this dead spotted dolphin *(below)* is one of many thousands that fall victim to the nets of the tuna fishery every year in the ETP.
(H. Mushman/EarthViews)

One of the MMPA's 'immediate goals' was to reduce to 'insignificant levels approaching zero' the number of dolphins killed by the yellowfin tuna fishery. The act further prohibited the accidental or intentional taking of any 'depleted' stock of dolphins.

In reality the implementation of these measures has proved to be extremely difficult. Initially the tuna industry was given a two year exemption period, in order to allow the fishery time to develop techniques that would reduce dolphin mortality and thus solve the problem. During this time an estimated half a million more dolphins perished. A lawsuit initiated by conservationists forced the introduction of a system of rapidly decreasing annual quotas and an observer programme to ensure more accurate estimates of mortality and compliance with the law. At that time, more than 90 per cent of the fleet consisted of US vessels and thus these measures were expected drastically to reduce the total number of dolphins killed.

The first quota, in 1976, allowed the killing of 78,000 dolphins. This was steadily reduced over the next five years until it stood at 20,500 in 1981, which is where it remains today. Unfortunately, reductions in the US quota have not led to significant reductions in the total number of dolphins killed annually.

For one thing, while the US quota has remained steady, the size of the US tuna fleet in the ETP has declined dramatically, from 110 vessels in the early 1970s, each of which could hold from 600-1,000 tonnes of tuna, to 27 in 1990; as a result, each US seiner may and does kill more dolphins than before.

Even more importantly, the reduction of the US fleet has led to substantial changes in the composition of the international tuna fishing fleet. The US now accounts for less than a quarter of the 110 or so purse-seiners operating in the ETP. Many US vessels have simply re-registered under the flags of other nations, either to benefit from cheaper labour and fuel costs, or as some have suggested, to avoid US laws such as the MMPA. Between 1972 and 1980, 27 US vessels transferred to foreign registry; 10 vessels changed flags in 1984 alone.

The largest tuna-seining fleet in the ETP now carries the Mexican flag. The US fleet is now the second largest, followed by Venezuela, Ecuador, the South Pacific island state of Vanuatu, Panama, the Republic of Korea and Spain.

TUNA-DOLPHIN

Several of these countries have now constructed giant 'super seiners', each of which can hold almost 2,000 tonnes of yellowfin. The total capacity of the international fleet in the ETP is now more than 150,000 tonnes from a single voyage; the 1988 yellowfin catch in the region was a record 295,000 tonnes. According to the official figures of the IATTC, between 80,000 and 120,000 dolphins are killed every year by the international purse-seine fleet in the ETP. However, it is widely suspected that these figures under-estimate the true number of dolphins killed, for the following reasons.

Not all vessels carry official observers, and estimates of the total number of dolphins are extrapolated from the figures that these observers provide. Such a calculation is based on the assumption that unobserved vessels 'perform' in the same manner as observed vessels. However, when international observer coverage was expanded to include the boats of non-US fleets, and in particular Mexican boats, under a programme developed by the IATTC, the total recorded mortality estimates leapt from 57,000 in 1985 to 130,000 in 1986.

Furthermore official estimates do not account for, or record, mortally wounded animals. Dolphins which have lost their beak, flippers or tail, or whose nursing mothers have been killed, are not counted in the mortality figures if they are alive when released.

The industry *has* attempted to limit the number of dolphins killed in the ETP. The early 1960s saw the development of the 'backdown' procedure, in which the purse-seiner reverses direction when the net has been sealed shut at the bottom. This causes the open top of the net to elongate into a narrow channel. The flow of water causes the far edge of the net to sink, thus allowing the dolphins to escape over it . In 1971, vessels began replacing the upper-most part of the net with finer mesh in which dolphins were less likely to become entangled.

The great majority of 'sets' made by US vessels kill relatively few dolphins. The vast majority of the 20,500 dolphins killed annually by the US fleet result from a few 'disaster sets' in which these procedures fail because of unforeseen or unavoidable factors such as weather conditions or gear breakdowns. In such situations entire dolphin herds may be killed.

US law now requires that any nation wishing to export tuna to the US must demonstrate both that it has a regulatory programme and that kill rates are comparable to those of the US fleet. Nevertheless, even if all other nations could achieve the 99 per cent release rate claimed by the US fleet, the total mortality rate would still remain at a level of 80,000 dolphins a year.

The most commonly caught species in the ETP, and therefore the ones which warrant the most concern, are the spotted, spinner and common dolphins. Of greatest importance to the fishery is the 'northern offshore' spotted dolphin, as 90 per cent of all dolphin 'sets' involve pure or mixed herds of this stock. In 1979, fisheries scientists reported that this stock was 'depleted' or below its optimum sustainable population (OSP); it has since declined further but has not yet been afforded the protection it warrants. To do so would sharply curtail the practice of 'setting' on dolphins.

This underwater 'fish-eye' view is a study in contrasts between the sleek form of the eastern spinner dolphin and the jagged fins of the large yellowfin tuna. Science has yet to explain their mysterious bond. (NMFS/EarthViews)

Background: **The distinctive silhouette of a yellowfin tuna, characterized by its long fins. These tuna can grow up to 2m (6ft 6ins) in length.**
(Ian Andrew)

These are three frames from a real-life video, nasty, shot surreptitiously in 1988 by Sam La Budde, a biologist and environmental activist, while working on a tuna boat as a general deckhand and cook. His video, and the journal he kept, provided fresh first-hand evidence that dolphins were still being killed in huge numbers. In this set, an entire herd of legally protected and endangered spinner dolphins were killed for just one tuna.
(Sam La Budde/EarthViews)

Even more worrying is the status of the eastern spinner stock, which is estimated to have suffered a decline of 80 per cent since modern tuna-seining began. Although this stock has been formally designated as 'depleted', and thus has total legal protection, an estimated 20,000 are still being killed annually.

Regulation of the tuna-dolphin problem is extremely difficult. The IATTC runs a highly-regarded scientific pro-gramme designed to address the issue but its mandate is primarily to achieve the Maximum Sustainable Yield of tuna from the Eastern Pacific. Several participants in recent IATTC meetings have argued that to expend energy on protecting dolphin populations is in direct conflict with that mandate. Furthermore, several important

tuna fishing nations are not members of the Commission – including Mexico, the country with the largest fleet in the region.

There are other, more complex, issues involved. The large yellowfin tuna which swim beneath dolphin herds are an exceptionally valuable commodity and command a very high market price. They are easier to handle and process than the equivalent weight of small fish and, as a result, many fish processors are set up to deal only with large yellowfin.

These processors have encouraged the development of large-scale purse-seine operations in Latin America, furnishing loans for the purchase of vessels with a great enough capacity to exploit the deeper offshore waters where the largest tuna are to be found.

In order to repay these loans, the fishermen must make the maximum possible profit in the shortest possible time and they are therefore forced to catch large yellowfin, as opposed to smaller tuna.

That fishing for smaller tuna is not economically viable was demonstrated in 1986. The US had exceeded its dolphin kill quota by October that year and was thus prohibited from making further dolphin sets. Despite the ban, the fleet caught more tuna in the final quarter of that year than in

the equivalent periods of the two years before or after. Despite the increased tonnage, the industry claimed to have lost revenue since the catch was composed of skipjack and smaller yellowfin tuna, which have a lower market value.

As long as this situation continues the only solution to the tuna-dolphin problem is to devise new fishing methods which will enable large yellowfin to be caught in a way which does not harm, or possibly even involve dolphins. It is now known, for example, that tuna will congregate under virtually any floating object. Fish Aggregating Devices (FADs), large rafts beneath which fish gather, are already being used on a trial basis in some parts of the world.

However, because the yellowfin tuna fishery is so highly competitive, no single vessel or fleet is likely to experiment with new methods unless its competitors do so. In the absence of any international regulatory body with enough authority to impose such innovations, many con-servationists argue that the price differential between different sizes and species of tuna must be reduced or even reversed.

One important step towards this has been the introduction of a Bill in the US Congress proposing that all tuna produce sold in the US be labelled to state whether or not it was caught by methods which might have killed dolphins. It is hoped that this will encourage consumers to avoid buying certain tuna products and thus make it more profitable to catch tuna by other methods. Such a shift in the market may additionally provide the necessary economic incentives for the development of alternative fishing technologies.

With the depletion of fish stocks in inshore waters and the imposition of tighter national controls on increasingly valuable marine resources, fishing fleets are taking to the high seas, where they can catch previously unexploited fish populations which are beyond the control of any effective laws. Fish stocks in these deeper waters are less concentrated and more disparate and so the fishing fleets employ vast drift nets that enable them to sweep huge areas of the ocean in search of their catch.

DRIFT NETS

High seas drift nets, made of non-biodegradable plastic or nylon, can be up to 60km (37mls) in length. They are suspended vertically in the water with floats attached to the top and weights fixed to the bottom. Once set, the nets are then allowed to drift with the wind and currents, indiscriminately entangling any living creature that swims into them, including marine mammals.

Their use has been reported in virtually every ocean, especially the Pacific, Atlantic and Indian Oceans, and in many seas including the Mediterranean.

In the North Pacific alone, more than 32,000km (20,000mls) of net are set each night, which means that over the course of the year, a staggering one and a half million kilometres (1 million nautical mls) of net are deployed there in the course of a year.

Because high seas drift net fisheries are unregulated and conducted far out at sea, it is impossible to say how many marine mammals they kill annually. However, a few examples serve to demonstrate the destruction caused by this form of fishery.

In early 1989, a trial use of drift nets to catch skipjack tuna in South Pacific waters killed an average of four and a half marine mammals in each net 'set' – one marine mammal for every 10 tuna caught. The results of the trial prompted the State of Yap, which had initiated the experiment, to terminate the fishery permanently.

In 1986, one Japanese squid boat in the Pacific was observed to kill 59 small cetaceans in just 30 sets – a rate of almost two per set. Extrapolation from figures such as these is risky, but with 50,000-60,000 sets made by these fisheries annually, it is clear that the number of dolphins and porpoises dying each year in drift nets around the world could very well reach a six figure number.

It is believed that the small cetacean species most commonly caught are the Dall's porpoise, and the northern right whale, Pacific white-sided and common dolphins. Tens of thousands of Dall's porpoises are known to be killed by Japanese squid fisheries each year and in the Mediterranean at least 2,000 striped dolphins die annually in the Italian swordfish and bonito drift net fisheries.

Drift nets often break loose in the course of operations. They sail through the oceans, 'ghost fishing', until under the weight of the marine creatures they have ensnared, they sink to the bottom of the ocean. It is estimated that drift net fleets leave approximately 1,000km (600mls) of these 'ghost nets' floating in the North Pacific annually. At present rates of fishing, by the year 2000 there will be enough of this abandoned net to stretch one-third of the way around the world.

Many nations, such as New Zealand, Australia and a number of South Pacific states, are vigorously opposed to the use of such fishing technology by foreign fleets in their waters because of the disruption they cause to the marine ecosystem. In June 1989, the South Pacific Forum issued the Tarawa Declaration, which called for an

ALEUTIAN ISLANDS

HAWAIIAN ISLANDS

PACIFIC OCEAN

FIJI

SAMO

TASMAN SEA

NEW ZEALAND

CHATHAM ISLAND

Above: **Drift net
vessels in the Pacific,
such as this modern
Japanese ship,
deploy tens of
thousands of miles of
netting every night
during the fishing
season, primarily to
catch albacore,
salmon and squid. In
the process, they kill
untold numbers of
marine mammals,
turtles and birds.**
(Lorrette Dorreboom/
Greenpeace)

**The white rectangles
on this background
map of the North and
South Pacific
indicate the principal
areas where high-
seas drift netting
takes place.**

HITI

end to all drift net fishing in the Forum
areas and this was followed a few months
later by a resolution from the South Pacific
Commission calling for an immediate ban
on drift net fishing.

When it became known that drift net
fleets in the North Pacific were intercepting
large shoals of salmon bound for spawning
streams in the US, as well as huge numbers
of marine mammals and birds, the United
States reached agreements with Taiwan,
Japan and South Korea, requiring that they
allow US observers on their drift net vessels
or face an embargo of their products.
Unfortunately, these agreements are very
weak as there are, for example, only 14
American observers for a Japanese fleet of
over 500 vessels.

In December 1989, the United Nations
General Assembly passed a resolution
which prohibited further expansion of
drift net activities and called for their
provisional phase-out in the South Pacific
by 30 June, 1991 and throughout the rest of
the world by 1992. This 'provisional
moratorium' would still allow the use of
drift nets if research showed that their

impact could be limited through the
adoption of 'conservation and management programmes'. At present, this
research will be restricted to reports, from a
limited number of vessels, carried out by
observers appointed by the drift netting
nations themselves. Conservationists argue
that the indiscriminate nature of drift
netting is such that it can never be properly
managed, and should be banned.

Such is the determination of some
nations to act against the effects of drift net
fisheries that they have banned large-scale
drift nets completely from their waters.
New Zealand passed a law in 1989 making
it an offense for ships that use drift nets in
any sea or ocean, and any ships supplying
drift netters, to enter New Zealand waters.
Other countries are now instituting similar
measures.

Ironically, even Japan – which has
one of the largest drift net fishing
operations in the world – has banned
large-scale drift nets from its own waters
because of the impact they have had on the
ecosystem of its own Exclusive Economic
Zone (EEZ).

DRIFT NETS *ACTION*

These dramatic pictures were taken by Greenpeace photographers from the campaign ship *Rainbow Warrior* during an action against Japanese drift net vessels in the Tasman Sea in January 1990.

The common dolphin *(main picture)* was photographed, at great personal risk, by Dr Brian Coffey. The net was being plucked out of the water by the approaching drift net vessel when Coffey leapt into the water from a Greenpeace inflatable and took a series of shots. He only just managed to avoid the net and regain the safety of the inflatable before the vessel was upon them.

Four rare southern bottlenose whales were subsequently caught in the nets during the period the *Rainbow Warrior* was there; one was freed by Greenpeace divers.

The sunfish *(below)* was found alive by Dr Roger Grace, who managed to set it free by cutting through the net with a pair of household scissors.

The albacore and skipjack tuna *(far right)* and the short-billed spearfish *(bottom)* are just a few examples of the wide variety of fish and other species caught in such nets.

(Greenpeace)

LATIN AMERICA

Until a few decades ago, almost all the commercial fishing operations in the waters of Latin America were conducted on a small scale, along the coast, in estuaries or from the river banks. In some areas, such traditional fishing methods persist but in many others, the introduction of new technology and the injection of capital have resulted in a transition to less labour-intensive, larger-scale fisheries.

The mid-1970s saw the dramatic expansion of Latin America's fishing industry, particularly in the eastern Pacific, as several countries sought to integrate their economies into the international market to obtain foreign currency in order to pay off their debts and to find alternative food sources for their populations.

This expansion has inevitably given rise to concerns over the health of the marine ecosystem in this region. Some fish stocks have already been depleted and local populations of several species of small cetaceans have been effected, mainly by the increased use of monofilament gill nets.

Information on the exact numbers of dolphins killed is hard to come by but preliminary research has shown that bottlenose dolphins are caught in shrimp fishing nets in Colombia; several thousand bottlenose dolphins and tucuxi are caught off French Guiana in nets set for sharks, tarpon and mullet; and several hundred franciscana are entangled in shark nets off the coasts of Brazil, Argentina and Uruguay every year.

The effects of entanglement are not restricted to marine species. In the Amazon and Orinoco river systems, a huge increase in the size of commercial fisheries, and the introduction of nylon gill nets, is believed to have had a damaging effect on some populations of boto and tucuxi, although there are no reliable estimates of the numbers involved. Marine mammal scientists Vera da Silva and the late Robin Best, who examined 67 dead dolphins from these river systems between 1979 and 1984, found that all but seven had been killed in nets.

A further development in recent years has been the intentional killing of small cetaceans to provide bait for commercial fisheries.

The killing of dolphins and porpoises for bait has been recorded in Colombia and in Venezuela, where 7,000 dolphins of various species are caught every year as bait to catch sharks (although the government has now taken steps to outlaw this practice). The problem has been especially acute in southern Chile where, at one stage, between 4,000 and 5,000 small cetaceans were being killed annually to provide bait for the commercial crab fishery.

Previously, sea lions were caught for this purpose but, when their numbers declined in the late 1970s, the fishery began catching Commerson's dolphins. Over-exploitation of the crabs then led the fishery to move location and, as a result, Peale's and black dolphins became their main target.

Over the last ten years, new fishing technology, better boats and the introduction of a free-market economy have caused a seven-fold expansion in this fishery.

The flesh of marine mammals is preferred as bait because it can stay in the water for three days before it disintegrates, whereas fish bait deteriorates within 24 hours. It is also cheaper and more efficient to catch wild dolphins than it is to catch or buy fish; for example, one dolphin can provide bait for 350 crab traps.

In recent years, the number of small cetaceans taken for bait has decreased dramatically, probably due to the over-exploitation of local dolphin populations.

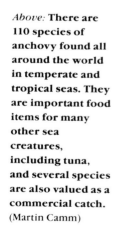

Above: **There are 110 species of anchovy found all around the world in temperate and tropical seas. They are important food items for many other sea creatures, including tuna, and several species are also valued as a commercial catch.**
(Martin Camm)

A delighted fisherman displays a dead tucuxi for the camera; unknown numbers are caught incidentally in gill nets, in the Orinoco and Amazon river systems.
(Steve Leatherwood photo-collection)

VENEZUELA

Orinoco River

COLOMBIA

PERU

Amazon River

PACIFIC OCEAN

CHILE

ARGENTINA

Bottlenose dolphins (left) and dusky dolphins (above left) are now a common sight in the markets and ports of the Peruvian coast. It is only through the efforts of conservationists like Julio Reyes and Koen van Waerebeek, who respectively shot these two rare pictures, that this new directed kill of dolphins has been revealed.

PERU – A CASE IN POINT

The largest take of small cetaceans in Latin America is in Peru, where as many as 10,000 porpoises and dolphins a year are believed to be killed in a directed hunt, the existence of which was first reported by scientist Julio Reyes. The development of this hunt demonstrates clearly the relationship between small cetacean problems in Latin America and the growth of the region's fisheries.

At the end of the 1960s, Peru was one of the most productive fishing nations in the world. The cold waters off its coast, fed by a north-flowing current rich in nutrients, brought an abundance of fish within the range of nearshore fisheries. This enabled fleets in Peruvian waters to make over a fifth of the world's commercial landings of fish. By far the most important catch was of anchovetas, which were netted in such huge quantities that the Peruvian economy effectively became dependent on them.

During the 1970s, a drastic change took place. In 1972, the combination of over-fishing and the arrival of an unusually severe El Niño, a recurring climatic phenomenon which severely reduced the productivity of near shore waters, brought about the collapse of the anchoveta fishery. In 1977, the catch was so poor that the fishery was closed down in the spring and banned for the rest of the year.

The collapse of the anchoveta stocks meant that many of those who had depended on the fishery were now forced to look for alternative ways of earning a living. Most moved to other forms of fishing, including longlining and gill netting, for a variety of small fish, crustaceans and molluscs. In the process, they would often accidentally catch dolphins and, rather than waste the bodies, would eat some of the meat. As the meat became popular, some entrepreneurs reasoned that there might be enough of a market to support a fishery directed specifically at the dolphins.

The most frequently caught species is the dusky dolphin, followed by Burmeister's porpoise and the bottlenose dolphin. Most of these are caught, deliberately or accidentally, in gill nets although, in recent years, there has been a sharp increase in the catch of common dolphins, most of which are killed by harpoons thrown from fast boats with powerful engines.

Situations similar to the one in Peru may well develop in other Latin American countries and in developing nations throughout the world. As coastal waters become over-fished, larger and more powerful boats are required to enable fishermen to move further out to sea and to catch previously unexploited stocks. However, as more boats appear in the area and competition increases so stocks decline and the fishermen have to move into still deeper water. This, in turn, gives rise to a further demand for new technology and even larger boats.

Thus begins an ongoing cycle of investment in technology, leading to increased catches, over-fishing and the need for yet more technology. Locked into this cycle, the fishermen, desperate to earn enough money in as short a time as possible to repay the loans on their boats and equipment, and to make some kind of profit, often find themselves forced to take every available resource from the ocean including marine mammals.

This spiralling demand for investment in new technology is further exacerbated by the need for the fisheries of developing nations to compete in a world market against countries with far greater resources. The fate of marine mammals can thus be seen as a small aspect of a large and complex economic, social and political situation.

SRI LANKA

For several decades, a great deal of government money and foreign aid has been directed towards expanding and modernizing Sri Lanka's fishing industry. The nation's citizens have been encouraged to eat more fish and Sri Lankan fishermen have been heavily subsidized in an effort to satisfy the consequent growth in demand for fish and fish products.

The direct result of the expansion of these fisheries has been the death of tens of thousands of small cetaceans in Sri Lankan waters. Many of these are entangled accidentally in coastal gill nets set to catch fish such as tuna and sharks, and others are taken by a large-scale commercial fishery which kills dolphins deliberately for use as bait.

In the past, dolphins were sometimes accidentally entangled in fishing nets in Sri Lanka's coastal waters. However, the nets were made of natural fibre such as jute and cotton and the dolphins could either detect them with their sonar or break free if they did become entangled.

Then, as part of an extensive programme funded by the UN Food and Agriculture Organization (FAO), designed to encourage the modernization of Sri Lanka's fisheries, nets were supplied that are made of stronger materials, which the dolphins can neither detect nor break. These gill nets are now also being used, in some areas, to catch dolphins deliberately and a market for cetacean meat, which did not exist prior to the FAO net programme, has now developed.

Conservationists are concerned that the total catch may be extremely high. Interviews with fishermen from Tangalle, in the south of the island, suggest that they generally take 10-25 dolphins a day in gill nets between March and July each year; if true, this would amount to an annual incidental kill of between 1,800 and 4,500 dolphins by fishermen from this one town alone.

A report written by marine mammal scientists Stephen Leatherwood and Randall R. Reeves (based on studies by Abigail Alling in conjunction with the Sri Lankan National Aquatic Research Agency [NARA]), was published in 1990 by the United Nations Environment Programme (UNEP). This estimated that between 25,000 and 45,000 small cetaceans may be brought ashore every year having been killed, deliberately or accidentally, in Sri Lankan waters. It isn't known how many dolphins are killed and used as bait at sea, although NARA had previously estimated that bait fisheries were responsible for 25 per cent of the total dolphin kill in the area.

Tragically, the size of this catch is likely to increase as the market for dolphin meat grows and the commercial fisheries in the region continue to expand, creating an increased demand for bait. At the same time, dolphins are being killed by harpoons fired from 3.5-tonne ships in some areas when catches of the usual target fish are poor. With the decline of fish stocks, particularly tuna, the number of dolphins being taken is likely to grow.

The Sri Lankan fishery is a case study in how well-intentioned aid programmes can have unforeseen and damaging effects. It is a difficult situation to tackle, given the enormous financial incentives for fishermen to modernize and expand their operations. Any efforts to conserve marine mammals, or for that matter fish stocks, in Sri Lankan waters will understandably meet with strong local opposition. Consideration has to be paid to the interests of those many Sri Lankans for whom the sea's resources provide their best, if not their only, means of securing a better standard of living. A programme, jointly sponsored by UNEP and NARA, is currently working to educate fishing communities about the problems of over-exploitation.

Effective regulations on fishing gear, seasons and areas could enable fisheries and dolphins to co-exist in Sri Lankan waters. However, fishermen, scientists and environmentalists must strengthen their co-operative efforts to ensure that these regulations are developed and implemented in the interests of all.

Right: **In Sri Lanka in recent years, butchering dolphins at the water's edge has become a more common sight, as the market for its meat has grown.**
(Amelia Pelligrini/WWF)

The rest of the world

Dolphins and porpoises are now killed, either deliberately or accidentally, in almost all the seas and oceans of the world but the true size, scale and effect of this take is unknown. Many small directed hunts are rarely observed and poorly recorded, and there may also be some hunts which are still unknown to researchers.

Small-scale hunts are known or believed to still exist in St Helena, the Indonesian islands of Lamalera and Lamakera and the Solomon Islands.

For more than 40 years, one of the largest directed kills of dolphins in the world took place in the Black Sea where Turkey, Romania, Bulgaria and the Soviet Union took tens of thousands of harbor porpoises, bottlenose and common dolphins annually. The USSR and Bulgaria imposed a ban on the killing of dolphins in their waters in 1966; Turkey, the last country to stop its Black Sea hunt, ceased operations in 1983 following international pressure.

Not all the small cetaceans which are killed deliberately are taken as part of an organized hunt. Killer whales are regularly shot on sight by coastal fishermen in Iceland, Norway and Canada because of fears that these predators might steal fish from nets and hooks, or deplete fish stocks.

Harbor porpoises, which mainly inhabit coastal waters, are especially vulnerable to the effects of inshore gill nets. In the Bay of Fundy and in the Gulf of Maine, situated on the eastern coast of Canada and the USA, at least 500-600 harbor porpoises are entangled every year in gill nets set to catch cod, pollock and other bottom-dwelling fish. This represents almost 7.5 per cent of this area's estimated total population – a cause for concern to many scientists and conservationists.

In the North Sea, it is estimated that some 3,000 harbor porpoises are caught annually in nets set by Danish cod fisheries. Some 1,500 are caught each year, directly as well as accidentally, in salmon gill nets off Greenland. Prior to 1976, when foreign fishing operations were phased out in Greenland waters, the total annual catch was around 2,500-3,000, out of an estimated total population of 15,000.

The effects of entanglement can be particularly acute on those species that have a limited distribution. Up to 100 of the scarce Heaviside's dolphins are drowned every year in fishing nets off the southern coast of Africa.

Hector's dolphin, which is perhaps the rarest of the marine dolphins and is found only in waters around New Zealand, is threatened in some areas by both commercial and amateur fishermen. Intensive scientific research combined with growing public concern has prompted the New Zealand government to designate Banks Peninsula, near the city of Christchurch on the South Island, a marine sanctuary. In this area, where most of the dolphins were being caught, nets are now prohibited during the summer months.

Commercial fisheries may also be inflicting longer-term damage on dolphin populations by over-exploiting the lower levels in the food chain. The collapse of the herring fishery in the North Sea, between the 1950s and the 1970s, was paralleled by a decline in the southern North Sea's populations of the bottlenose dolphin and harbor porpoise. There is also evidence that white-beaked dolphins have decreased off England's Cornish coast as the area's mackerel fishery has declined.

Large-scale fisheries which catch fish for meal and fertilizer may be threatening stocks of mackerel, sandeel and sprats in the North Sea, all of which form part of the diets of the small cetaceans found in this area. There are definite signs that harbor porpoises, in particular, are declining in

areas where sandeel stocks are decreasing.

The conclusions are stark. Dolphins are not only being hunted directly and caught incidentally but the very food they themselves need in order to survive is being over-fished. The increase in demand for the food resources of the ocean will surely intensify over the next decade. Much greater legal protection will be needed if many dolphin species are to survive.

The head and tail *(far left and above)* **of a common dolphin caught in a gill net – evidence of the damage such nets can cause to marine mammals.**

(Alisa Schulman/Marine Mammal Images)

THE
HUMAN
THREAT

ENVIRONMENTAL
DISRUPTION

This diseased bottlenose dolphin, its skin covered with sores and lesions, was one of many hundreds washed ashore on the east coast of the United States in 1987 and 1988.
(Michael Baytoff)

It is now widely recognized by governments, scientists and the general public that we are polluting the world on an unprecedented scale. The fragile net of interconnections that makes up the planet's living fabric is being disrupted by our actions: by patterns of exploitation and recreation, by flows of wastes and effluents, by thoughtlessness and greed.

Many dolphin populations are now subject to a cocktail of pollutants, a confluence of human pressures and a conflict of interests. The following case histories highlight both the urgency of the problem and the necessity of developing new solutions – legislative, technological, social and political.

The current plight of the dolphins and other marine mammals is the first indicator of wider problems in the marine environment. It may also be symptomatic of a deep-seated disharmony between human development and the natural world. The steps that we take to save them will have important implications for tackling other global problems, and for our own future.

RIVER DOLPHINS

Riverine habitats and the dolphins which live in them are highly vulnerable to the effects of a wide variety of human activities. The river dolphins are under increasing threat principally from entanglement in fishing nets, pollution through pesticides, heavy metals and effluent from industries, and the construction of dams for irrigation and hydroelectric power.

The latter are of particular concern. Dams may reduce the dolphins' food supply, by preventing migratory fish from reaching their spawning grounds, and restrict the flow of fresh water, thereby exhausting nutrients and oxygen supplies. More crucially, they restrict the dolphins' natural feeding range and separate dolphin populations into small, isolated groups that cannot interbreed and therefore do not have enough genetic variability to survive.

This striking image of an old fisherman in Pakistan cradling a dead Indus susu, was taken during an early expedition to capture some of these animals for further scientific study. It is symbolic of the concern that is now expressed for the fate of all the river dolphins, most of which are under threat from human activities.
(Giorgio Pilleri)

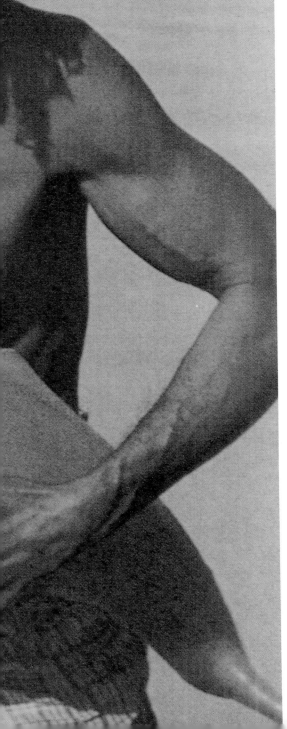

THE GANGES AND INDUS SUSUS

The Ganges susu, formerly quite abundant throughout its range, is now believed to number only 4,000-5,000 individuals; it is possible that there are as few as 40 remaining in Nepal. The construction of a large dam at Kaptai on the Karnaphuli River has prevented the migration of the dolphin to the adjacent river system of the Brahmaputra and Ganges. All the Ganges susus above the dam have disappeared, and those below it appear to be declining.

Every year 2,500 tonnes of pesticides and 1.2 million tonnes of fertilizers are used in the vicinity of the Ganges River. It receives the discharges from a wide variety of sources, including sugar mills, distilleries, pulp and paper mills, tanneries and chemical plants, as well as from about 700 towns and cities along its banks. The Ganges Basin is the home of more than 220 million people, 37 per cent of the total population of India.

In Nepal, the species' habitat is being degraded by logging, road building, irrigation and the mining of gravel and rock along the river banks and in the river beds themselves.

The species' close cousin, the Indus susu, has declined to a population of around 500. It is now extinct in parts of its former range. Like its close relative, the Indus susu has been divided into several populations by a series of irrigation dams. Three of the six populations may be on the verge of extinction: one may number only 2 or 3 individuals.

An Indus Dolphin Reserve was established in 1974 on the 170-km (105-mile) stretch of the Indus between the Guddu and Sukkur Barrages by the government of Sind Province.

THE BOTO

The size of the boto population is not known, but is generally thought to be stable and at less risk than the Ganges and Indus susus. Botos are nonetheless increasingly vulnerable as the aquatic ecosystems of the Amazon and Orinoco are disrupted.

Pollution is one of the major problems in parts of these river basins. On the Jari River, a single pulp mill discharged over 24,000 tonnes of contaminants containing chlorine, magnesium, potassium, aluminium and iron in one year, causing a major die-off of the fish on which the dolphin feeds in the river.

Another major problem is the 2,000 tonnes of mercury released into the forests and rivers of the Brazilian Amazon by gold miners, who use it as part of a primitive technique to purify the gold. Fish in the Maderia, an Amazon tributary, now contain five times the permitted methyl-mercury levels and these poisons are concentrated as they pass up the food chain to the dolphins and humans.

The Brazilian government has ambitious plans to build more than 60 dams for hydro-electric power in the Amazonian region by the year 2010, although only seven are currently completed and in operation. The damming of one river in the State of Pará in Brazil, led to the loss of 17 out of the 22 fish species found there; only two of the remaining five left are still abundant. The botos' general feeding pattern includes 50 species of fish; having their diet reduced to only two species might prove fatal.

THE FRANCISCANA

The franciscana appears to be less threatened by habitat degradation than the other river dolphins, although large numbers are taken in commercial fisheries. The areas of river and sea in which the franciscana lives also carry the heavy coastal traffic from ten major ports which between them handle most of the ship-borne trade to and from Uruguay, Argentina and Brazil.

High levels of man-made compounds such as DDT and the highly toxic PCBs were found in eight franciscana examined in Uruguayan waters in 1980.

CREATING A FUTURE

Concern for the fate of the river dolphins is such that, in October 1986, a major workshop sponsored by many governmental, scientific and conservation organizations was held in China on their biology and conservation. This workshop recommended a number of possible options for these species' conservation, management and future study; if applied successfully, these may hold out hope for the river dolphins' long-term survival.

It was agreed that, as an initial step, researchers in countries where river dolphins are found should ensure that they exchange information on their status and distribution as fully as possible. It was also urged that existing studies should be expanded and new ones implemented, as soon as possible, into the precise effects of environmental disturbance on river dolphin populations.

Dams, it was argued, should be sited near the headwaters of a river whenever feasible, leaving as much of the dolphin population as possible in a continuous habitat, and should not be placed on undisturbed tributaries. It would be less environmentally disruptive to place a series of dams on one river than single dams on several rivers.

The best and most immediate hope of preventing existing populations of river dolphins from becoming further depleted is to set up natural reserves where any large, relatively undisturbed, stretches of their range that remain can be set aside for the dolphins' protection and where discharges of contaminants, mining, fishing activities and boat traffic would be banned.

YANGTZE RIVER DOLPHIN

The baiji or Yangtze river dolphin is considered the most endangered of all cetacean species. The numerous threats it faces are representative of those confronting all river dolphin species. Zoologist *Mark Carwardine* visited the region in 1989 to report on the animal's plight.

The Yangtze is the third largest river in the world. Known locally as the Chang Jian, or Long River, it cuts right through the heart of the country, stretching 6,300km (3,900mls) from its source in western China to its mouth near Shanghai.

Certain parts of the river's natural landscape are overwhelmingly dramatic and relatively unspoilt, and tiny villages, terraced fields, spectacular canyons, striking limestone cliffs and beautiful countryside line its banks. But vast stretches are more typical of the ceaseless bustle of Chinese towns, lined with houses, docks, trading posts, enormous cranes and noisy factories.

Since there is no long-distance road transport in much of China, and only a thinly-spaced, overloaded railway system, the Yangtze forms a natural highway through the country. More than a sixth of all the country's exports travel along the river with the result that there is a constant stream of vessels plying up and down. There are rusty tramp steamers, container ships, giant ferries, passenger liners, sailing junks, barges and numerous tiny boats being rowed from bank to bank by oarsmen standing up in the traditional style.

This overcrowded river is the perilous home of what is probably the rarest cetacean in the world: the Yangtze river dolphin, or baiji as it is more commonly known in China.

This diminutive dolphin species was unknown to scientists in the rest of the world until a visiting American killed one

in 1914 and sold it to the Smithsonian Institution. Although it turned out to be a new species and genus of river dolphin it received surprisingly little scientific attention until the 1970s.

The Chinese people, of course, have been aware of the baiji's existence for centuries and fishermen living along the banks of the Yangtze have many strange and interesting stories to tell about it. Some say that the baiji makes peculiar roaring sounds at night; others claim it can start a severe storm and is the bearer of bad omens. It is thought by many to be the reincarnation of a drowned princess, while some fishermen believe that ill fortune descends upon anyone who dares to molest it. Overall, the local beliefs and customs concerning the baiji are generally harmless and may even have helped to protect it in the past. But with the increasing human pressures of modern-day China, superstitions will not be enough to ensure the baiji's future survival.

THREATS TO SURVIVAL
Baiji once occurred in the Qiantang River and far upstream in the Yangtze. Now, however, they are scattered in small groups along only 1,600km (1,000mls) of the middle and lower reaches of the Yangtze. They tend to congregate in certain areas of the river, such as the 135-km (80-mile) stretch from Luoshang to Xingtankao in Hubei Province, and the 120-km (70-mile) stretch from Anqing to Heishazhou in Anhui Province.

These dolphins have had legal protection in China since 1975 and it is unlikely that they are still being killed deliberately for meat or for their blubber, which was once considered to be of medicinal value.

The majority of deaths are caused inadvertently. Some dolphins die after becoming impaled on 'rolling hooks' – fishermen's lines with many large hooks attached to them that are strung along the river bed. Others become entangled and drown in some of the many gill nets which line the river's banks. In some areas, the number of dolphins caught in this way has been dramatically reduced, thanks to government intervention. Educational programmes for fishermen and local bans on these bottom longlines have certainly had an impact but fishing gear is still a major hazard.

Many baiji have been found with appalling injuries after collisions with boats and their propellers. The volume of boat traffic on the Yangtze is likely to continue to grow, especially with the recent trend of economic development in China, so the probability of such encounters is bound to increase.

The acoustic disturbance, caused by the heavy river traffic, may also interfere with the dolphin's sensitive sonar, which it relies on to locate food and navigate in the river's turbid waters.

Added to these problems are a suspected reduction in fish resources in the river in the past 40 years, the development

of irrigation facilities, proposed new major dam projects and the dumping by innumerable factories of uncontrolled waste into the river, where it is hidden but not lost in the Chang Jiang's natural turbidity.

ATTITUDES AND AWARENESS
The level of awareness of the baiji's plight in the country is extraordinary. It is now a Protected Animal of the First Order, along with the giant panda and other critically threatened species in China. The government has taken measures to educate local people through newspaper and magazine articles, a film, baiji postage stamps, and wide dissemination of the regulations for their protection.

More importantly, at various points along the Yangtze, there are Baiji Conservation Associations. These are run by local volunteers to promote baiji conservation, particularly among the fishermen, and to raise commercial sponsorship for baiji conservation projects.

The first of these Associations was set up at Tongling, a town with a population of 250,000 on the lower reaches of the Yangtze. Established in 1984, the TBCA began by persuading the local brewery to use the baiji as its trademark. This beer, which is now sold throughout China, has a picture of the dolphin on its label and its Latin name, *Lipotes vexillifer*, on the cap. Many other companies followed suit and Tongling now has a baiji hotel, a baiji department store, baiji shoes, baiji

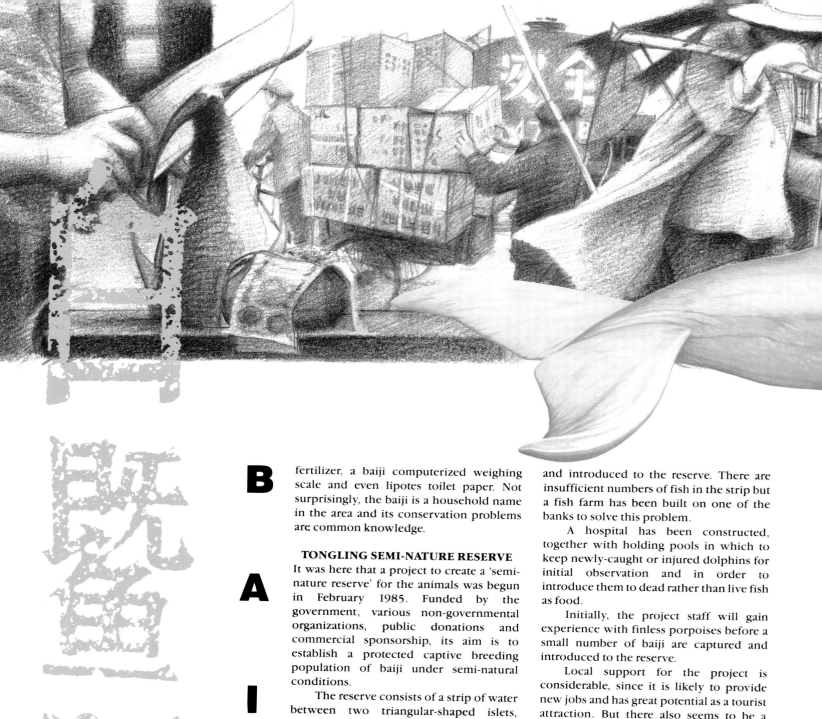

B

A

I

J

I

fertilizer, a baiji computerized weighing scale and even lipotes toilet paper. Not surprisingly, the baiji is a household name in the area and its conservation problems are common knowledge.

TONGLING SEMI-NATURE RESERVE
It was here that a project to create a 'semi-nature reserve' for the animals was begun in February 1985. Funded by the government, various non-governmental organizations, public donations and commercial sponsorship, its aim is to establish a protected captive breeding population of baiji under semi-natural conditions.

The reserve consists of a strip of water between two triangular-shaped islets, Heyuezhou and Tiebenzhou, in Anhui Province. Directly opposite the small town of Datong, and a little upstream of Tongling, it is in a stretch of the river already frequented by the dolphins. The strip is 1,550m (5,000ft) long and 40-220m (130-720ft) wide. Construction work has been necessary to ensure that the water level remains at or above five metres (16ft 5in) all year round, but water from the main river flows continuously through the channel.

There are metal and bamboo barriers at both ends to prevent the dolphins from escaping, once they have been captured

and introduced to the reserve. There are insufficient numbers of fish in the strip but a fish farm has been built on one of the banks to solve this problem.

A hospital has been constructed, together with holding pools in which to keep newly-caught or injured dolphins for initial observation and in order to introduce them to dead rather than live fish as food.

Initially, the project staff will gain experience with finless porpoises before a small number of baiji are captured and introduced to the reserve.

Local support for the project is considerable, since it is likely to provide new jobs and has great potential as a tourist attraction. But there also seems to be a general, and rather unique, feeling that saving the baiji from extinction is a natural duty of the people, whether anyone gains financially or not.

A second semi-nature reserve is now planned for Shishou, further upstream in a fairly remote area of Hubei Province.

THE FUTURE OF THE BAIJI
A major concern is that much of this conservation work is based on speculation.

Surprisingly little is known about the baiji in the wild. There was no effort to determine the number of surviving dolphins until 1979, when a three-year

Illustration: Ian Andrew

The Baiji, or Yangtze river dolphin – the most endangered of all cetaceans.
(Martin Camm)

survey estimated a maximum of 400 along the entire length of the Yangtze. There has been a rapid reduction in numbers in the years since. Today there could be as few as 200 baiji left and the numbers continue to decrease. Major research programmes are already underway, aimed at filling the gaps in our knowledge about the animal's seasonal movements and population structure.

As with many other rare species of animal, captive breeding may be the only chance to save the baiji. But some conservationists question whether breeding animals that will then have to be granted permanent sanctuary in a semi-natural environment can rightly be termed 'conservation'.

Unless captive breeding is accompanied by equally energetic efforts to address the interlinking problems affecting the animals' habitat, small numbers of the baiji will survive but the river in which they once lived and all life within it will die.

Belugas in the St. Lawrence

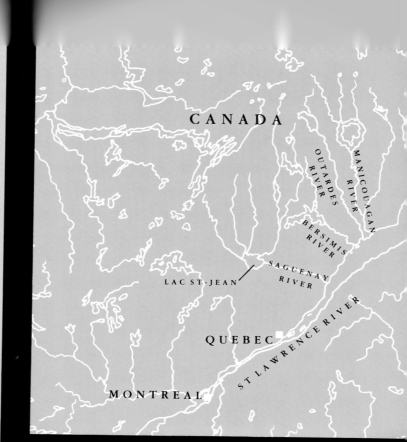

In 1885, there were at least 5,000 belugas in Canada's St Lawrence river. In 1990, only some 400-500 remain.

This decline probably began as long ago as 1700. Today the numbers continue to fall as a result of a combination of factors so varied that this single population of belugas can be said to have suffered from the effects of virtually every human activity that threatens other small cetaceans around the world.

Most of the initial damage was caused, over a period of 250 years, by a large commercial hunt, conducted first by Europeans and then by Canadians, who killed the whales for their blubber and oil. By the time this hunt ended in the 1950s, as a result of a decline in the market for whale oil, the beluga population had fallen to less than 2,500.

Belugas had meanwhile become scapegoats for periodic failures in the St Lawrence fisheries. In the late 1920s, the Quebec government argued that it was necessary to kill them in order to protect fish stocks and a cull was instituted with hunters being paid a bounty for each whale they killed.

During the 1950s, the St Lawrence River area underwent major industrial development with the increased growth of cities like Montreal and Quebec City, the establishment of international shipping ports and the construction of the St Lawrence Seaway, which opened up an unimpeded route for shipping from the Great Lakes to the Atlantic. This resulted in an increase in the amount of wastes and pollution reaching the river and a tremendous rise in the level of boat traffic in the region.

In addition, the construction of dams on rivers such as the Manicouagan, Outardes and Bersimis, all of which flow into the St Lawrence, may have critically altered important beluga habitats; the range of these animals is now believed to be about half the area it was 50 years ago.

GULF OF
ST LAWRENCE

Like a piece of white porcelain, the body of a dead beluga lies serenly on the shore of the St Lawrence. There are fears that this population of belugas may never recover from the devastating effects of pollution.
(Pierre Béland/INESL)

During the mid 1970s, independent studies by researcher Leone Pippard established the extent to which the St Lawrence beluga had been depleted. The population was granted protection from hunting in 1979 and as a result was declared endangered in 1983 by the Canadian government.

This first official sign of interest in the belugas' fate was followed by some startling discoveries in the early 1980s, by scientists Daniel Martineau and Pierre Béland. The beluga population was showing signs of being even more seriously affected by human activities than had previously been thought. In particular, the scientists found that the whales were suffering from a variety of unexpected diseases.

Autopsies conducted on whales washed ashore along the banks of the St Lawrence revealed an extraordinary array of disorders. One young beluga, aged two and a half years, had a perforated gastric ulcer with peritonitis, bronchopneumonia, dermatitis associated with a herpes-like virus, and chronic hepatitis.

Some of the reported disorders had never been recorded in toothed whales before, including bladder cancer, rupture of the pulmonary artery, and skin fibrosis.

Many of the whales were found to have been polluted by a mixture of some two dozen contaminants including polychlorinated biphenyls (PCBs) and the pesticides Mirex and DDT. PCBs in their blubber were recorded at levels as high as 576 parts per million (ppm). (Many countries consider fish too contaminated for human consumption if they contain levels of just 2 ppm.) The milk of some nursing females has been found to be contaminated with PCB levels up to 3,400 times higher than is considered safe in drinking water.

The instance of bladder cancer was considered particularly interesting because, in the late 1970s, it had been discovered that in the region directly adjacent to the territory in which the belugas lived, there were 60 per cent more cases of bladder cancer in human residents than was statistically likely.

A study of workers at the Alcan aluminium smelter (the region's largest employer) outside the town of Jonquière, situated between the Saguenay river and Lac St-Jean, revealed 73 cases of bladder cancer. The number of cases reported had risen to more than 130 by early 1990.

Most of these occurred in employees working on the 'potlines' where alumina powder is cooked into ingots. The study noted that such workers, who were exposed to extremely high levels of a group of chemicals known as polycyclic aromatic hydrocarbons (PAHs), were five times more likely to develop bladder cancer or tumours than other workers at the plant.

The high incidence of bladder cancer is not the only major health problem in the region. According to a federal government health study, the area also has the highest rate of birth defects in Canada. A study by the Quebec Department of Health found that the Saguenay/Lac St-Jean region had the province's highest rate of deaths as a result of malignant tumours, cardio-vascular and cerebrovascular diseases, and the second highest rate of stomach, lung and respiratory tumours.

In the search for a link between the presence of PAHs and the belugas' problems, brain tissue from three of the autopsied whales were sent to biochemist Lee R. Shugart at the Oak Ridge National Laboratory in Tennessee for analysis. The tissue was indeed found to have metabolized quantities of the carcinogenic PAH compound benzo-a-pyrene in concentrations that, according to Shugart, 'would produce cancer in other laboratory animals under similar conditions'.

The revelations about the health of the St Lawrence beluga population generated a great deal of media interest which significantly increased the public's awareness of the belugas' plight, but the action necessary to save these creatures and ensure their future survival has still not been forthcoming. Both national and provincial governments, while engaging in a great deal of rhetoric, and some research, have refused to take action until there is scientific proof of the specific cause of the belugas' decline.

In this respect, the story of the St Lawrence beluga is representative of the problems faced by all who are concerned about the future of small cetacean populations. By the time scientific proof is available, if indeed such proof is possible, it may be too late.

For the St Lawrence beluga, this may already be the case. Recent autopsies have continued to uncover new disorders: cancer of the liver, abdomen and mammary gland; a hermaphroditic beluga, (with both male and female genital organs); and a type of bronchial pneumonia associated with profound immunosuppression, similar to that found in human AIDS sufferers.

The latest evidence suggests that the birth rate of these belugas is not keeping pace with the mortality rate. Furthermore, as already noted, beluga calves are ingesting high doses of contaminants through their mother's milk. Even more disturbing is the discovery that carcinogenic PAHs have become attached to the belugas' DNA and have altered its genetic structure. The damage is thus passed on from generation to generation.

In the words of Dr Joseph Cummins, a geneticist at the University of Western Ontario, the St Lawrence belugas are, 'to all intents and purposes, absolutely doomed. I don't see how they can possibly survive, bearing the gene damage they do.'

Dolphin
DIE-OFF

In the summer of 1987, unprecedented numbers of dead and dying bottlenose dolphins were washed up along the coast of New Jersey, in the eastern United States. By early 1988, the total had reached 750, scattered along large stretches of the Atlantic coastline from New Jersey south to Florida. Including the many more that died unseen in the open ocean, it has been estimated that more than half the Atlantic coastal population of bottlenose dolphins died during this period.

Desktop set-up, featuring actual sites at which dead dolphins were recorded, based on data from the Marine Mammal Stranding Centre at Brigantine, New Jersey. (Andy Gammon/Leigh Simpson)

...side from the sheer number of ...dolphins involved, the condition of ...washed ashore was astonishing. ...ooked as though they had been ...n acid.

...vas like nothing in recorded ...id Brian Gorman, a government ... 'The dolphins were coming in, ...lling off, sores and lesions all ...dies . . .'

...ne time as the dead dolphins ...ppear, millions of dead fish ...ed up, on the beaches of ...nd in New York. Beaches ...coast were closed to the ...ere littered with raw ...and used syringes. ...stories of bathers ...wimming in polluted ...ing dolphins were a ...decaying coastal

Photo by Michael Baytoff

Dolphin
DIE-OFF

Within two weeks of first being notified of the phenomenon, the US Government's National Oceanic and Atmospheric Administration (NOAA) began organizing a major investigation, involving a wide variety of government agencies and scientists, into the cause of this massive and unprecedented die-off.

The team's initial findings suggested that the dolphins had succumbed to a wide variety of secondary infections and disorders. For reasons yet undetermined, the dolphins had been rendered unable to combat naturally occurring pathogens. So began the search for the factor, or factors, responsible for damaging the dolphins' immune system.

NOAA announced its findings 17 months later, on 1 February, 1989: the dolphins, they declared, had been poisoned by eating fish tainted with a naturally-occurring toxin produced by 'red tide' algae.

A 'red tide' is the result of an explosive growth of dinoflagellates (a class of one-celled, plant-like, organisms called phytoplankton) which occurs when certain environmental factors combine. High levels of organic or inorganic nutrients in the presence of adequate sunlight and the right water temperature and salinity levels provide the ideal conditions. Such blooms can cause a discoloration of the surface waters, thus justifying their name.

Among the plankton involved in 'red tides' is a species called *Ptychodiscus brevis*, which produces a poison known as 'brevetoxin', and it was this toxin, according to NOAA, that killed the dolphins.

The official theory was that part of a red tide bloom that occurred in 1987 in the Gulf of Mexico was swept into the Atlantic where it was ingested by fish such as manhaden. These and other fish migrated up the coast where they, in turn, were eaten by the dolphins. Those dolphins that were not fatally poisoned by the brevetoxin were sufficiently weakened to succumb to other infections.

DOUBTS REMAIN

However, the brevetoxin theory had its flaws. For example, red tides occur frequently in the Gulf of Mexico, yet no similar die-off of dolphins has ever been reported there. In addition, brevetoxin was found in only eight of the 17 animals tested and in widely varying levels. Clinical data on the specific effects of chronic exposure to brevetoxin does not exist.

Public scepticism led the US Congress to hold a hearing and convene a scientific panel on 7 and 8 May 1989, to review the investigation's conclusions. One panelist, Canadian marine mammal scientist Dr Pierre Béland, stated that although 'little hard evidence implicating brevetoxin exists . . . remarkably little effort was put into investigating other possibilities for the die-off.'

This sentiment was echoed by other members of the same scientific panel. Veterinarian pathologist Daniel Martineau presented a possible scenario in which organochlorine pollutants, particularly PCBs, may have played an important role in the die-off.

Indeed, PCB levels in the beached dolphins studied were among the highest ever recorded in cetaceans. Levels found in the dolphins' blubber ranged between 13 and 620 parts per million (ppm). There was one exception – a dolphin found to contain an incredible 6,800 ppm, the highest level ever recorded in a marine mammal. (Products in the US are required to be labelled as hazardous and handled in toxic waste containers if they contain 5 ppm of PCBs.)

That PCBs cause various lesions, including damage to the liver and to the nervous, reproductive and immune systems in a wide range of mammals and birds is well documented. Many of the dolphins found on the east coast had the same types of lesions as those recorded in

Dr Joseph Geraci, pictured here at a US Senate hearing, headed the government investigation into the dolphin die-off. (Jay Townsend/ Greenpeace)

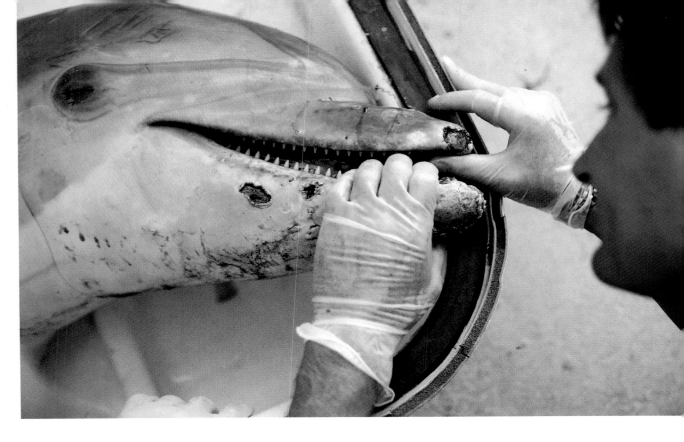

laboratory and domestic animals experimentally subjected to PCBs in their diet.

Alternative theories were presented during and after the investigation. For example, the US Department of Agriculture suggested that some event may have caused normally benign bacteria to increase in potency and wreak havoc on the dolphins.

Others posited a combination of events. Dr Gabe Vargo, another member of the scientific panel, questioned whether the mass mortality would have occurred if contaminants such as PCBs and DDT had not been present.

A number of ocean disposal sites used for dumping sewage sludge, acid waste and chemical warfare agents exist within the die-off area. There was no investigation of possible links between these sites and the die-off, nor into the possibility that there had been an accidental release from one of the military and civilian facilities in the area which manufacture chemical weapons and genetically engineered micro-organisms.

The US government certainly appeared anxious to avoid the implication of PCBs, or any other form of pollution, in the dolphins' deaths. In a leaked memo, read out at the Congressional hearing, one government scientist asked another for 'data generated on PCB/pesticides'. He added that no matter what was found in the dead dolphins, 'no special attention will be drawn to these data . . . [and] a blanket statement will be made that the levels were not out of the ordinary'.

PART OF A LARGER PICTURE

Set in a wider context, the dolphin mortalities may be just one sign of a slow collapse of coastal environments.

In some parts of the USA, lobsters and crabs are covered with mysterious 'burn holes'. Nearly a third of Louisiana's oyster beds are routinely closed because of pollution and half the shellfish beds in Galveston, Texas, are off limits to fishermen.

In 1988-89, some 18,000 harbour seals died in the North Sea, a death toll that accounted for approximately 60 per cent of each colony. The primary agent responsible is believed to be a new virus of the *morbillivirus* group which resembles the virus that causes canine distemper. Morbilliviruses suppress the body's immune system and allow secondary infections to proliferate but many scientists believe that pollution may have effected the extent and severity of the die-off.

Between 28 November, 1987, and 3 January, 1988, for example, 14 humpback whales were found dead on the beaches along Cape Cod and northern Nantucket Sound in Massachusetts. The whales were reported to have died after eating Atlantic mackerel which contained saxitoxin, another naturally occurring poison associated with red tides.

The countries which border the North Atlantic and other northern seas are some of the most heavily populated and highly industrialized in the world. The ocean is not only being depleted of its natural resources. It is also being used as a 'sink' for the waste products of millions of people and countless industries. Illustrating the magnitude of the problem, Dutch marine mammal scientist, Dr Peter Reijnders, recently reported that only one per cent of existing PCBs has so far reached the world's oceans, and that an additional 40-50 per cent is likely to make its way there in the future.

It is possible that red tides themselves are becoming more frequent, because of the increasing amounts of nutrients from fertilizer and sewage which are reaching the sea. These feed the micro-organisms responsible for red tides, causing them to multiply at explosive rates. Climatic change and atmospheric degradation may also play a role in this.

Dolphins are at the top of the marine food chain, and their health is an indicator of the condition of the entire aquatic environment. Perhaps the dolphin 'die-off' was a sign that, after decades of over-exploitation and abuse, the marine ecosystem simply cannot take any more.

CONTROVERSY

MILITARY USE OF DOLPHINS

Like the conning towers of surfacing submarines, the dorsal fins of two killer whales stand in stark relief above a grey seascape.
(Gerhard Bakker/Marine Mammal Images)

For the last 30 years, the US Navy has been involved in highly secret research programmes to study dolphins and to train them to detect enemy mines, attach tracking beacons and explosives to enemy ships and submarines, find and locate lost ordnance and to guard military bases. There are persistent rumours that they have also been trained to kill frogmen.

Details of these activities, highly classified on the grounds of 'national security', have come to light only because a number of people who were formerly involved with the programme have become disturbed by its aims and applications and have revealed some of what they know.

Information on the Soviet programme, begun in 1965, is even harder to find and the only source of such knowledge to date is from the CIA.

From 1960 to 1989, the US Navy is known to have trained and worked with 240 dolphins, of which 115 are currently enlisted in the programme along with some belugas and sea lions. A staff of 150 naval personnel and civilian trainers now manage the programme from clandestine bases in California, Florida and Hawaii. Leading civilian scientists from around the US, funded by the Navy, carry out additional research programmes into various aspects of dolphin behaviour and abilities.

Submarine-based missiles and naval warheads remain the front line of the superpowers' nuclear arsenal. The incredible speed, manoeuverability, sensitivity and sonar capabilities of dolphins are the very attributes that naval forces seek to emulate. Hidden from public view, these undersea research and development programmes are now established as an important component in naval strategic thinking.

This exclusive account, written by journalist *Dwight Holing*, and compiled on the basis of detailed research and original interviews, is one of the most definitive and up-to-date studies yet published of this dark area of military research.

MILITARY USE OF DOLPHINS

Dolphins were first drafted into the US Navy in 1960 when scientists at the Naval Ordnance Test Center at China Lake, California, acquired a Pacific white-sided dolphin from a now defunct marine park in Los Angeles, naming her Notty after the weapons laboratory's acronym. They hoped that their studies of the dolphin's streamlined shape and superb hydrodynamic efficiency would provide them with clues for improving the design of torpedoes.

Suspecting that the land-based laboratory tank in which she swam was affecting her performance, the Navy scientists began searching for a larger

One of the first dolphins to be trained successfully by the US Navy was this bottlenose dolphin named Tuffy.
(US Navy)

testing site. In 1963, under the direction of the Office of Naval Research (ONR), a small research facility was developed alongside a coastal lagoon at Point Mugu, California, home of the Pacific Missile Range and Naval Missile Center. Additional dolphins were subjected to a battery of tests in an attempt to learn more about their sensory systems, deep diving physiology and sonar.

Testing eventually moved from the confines of the lagoon to the open ocean. On 13 August, 1964, the Navy's first open-sea release took place when a young female Atlantic bottlenose dolphin, named Buzz-Buzz, was released near Point Mugu. She came back upon command. Ten days later, a Pacific bottlenose called Keiki was released in the open sea. He had been trained to keep up with a small boat, and in a series of speed tests he reached a top speed of 31.4 kilometres per hour (19.6 mph).

According to Blair Irvine, who trained dolphins for the US Navy from 1965 to 1969, a key goal of the work at Point Mugu was to get the animals to perform as retrievers. 'We wondered if you could teach a dolphin to go out and find a sound-emitting pinger,' he said. 'We were told to test this idea with practice ordnance, as a demonstration. Navy divers took a half hour to an hour to find one mine and put a line on it. We showed that a dolphin could potentially mark several mines much more quickly than that.'

Acoustic signals, usually a train of intense, broad-band clicks with maximum frequencies from two to four kilohertz were used as commands, and rewards of fish were given as positive reinforcement.

In August 1965, an irascible bottlenose dolphin, aptly named Tuf Guy or Tuffy for short, became the Navy's star pupil. Fresh from a successful series of tests aimed at determining deep-diving physiology, Tuffy was flown to La Jolla, California, where the ONR was operating Sealab II, an underwater base 60m (200ft) below the surface. Tuffy was soon carrying tools and messages between the surface and the lab, delighting the news media in the process.

The impact of the Sealab II demonstration was considerable. Tuffy proved that it was possible to train a dolphin to perform tasks that would be impossible for a human diver. No human could have made the number of repeated dives in rapid succession that Tuffy did without suffering the 'bends'.

The lesson was not lost on the Navy's weapons-testing officials, who quickly enlisted Tuffy's aid in recovering equipment routinely lost at sea. These included the re-usable cradles which separate from Regulus missiles after firing from submarines and fall into the water, or unarmed nuclear anti-submarine rockets (ASROCs) launched from surface ships during tests. Before launch, these devices were equipped with acoustic beacons; Tuffy was able to home in on the beacons'

signals and mark the location of the equipment which was then hauled to the surface by divers.

Tuffy's success inspired the Navy to try training two killer whales and a pilot whale to perform similar exercises but, despite some initial successes, they proved expensive to feed and difficult to transport. As a result, they were eventually dropped from the programme.

OPERATIONAL DEPLOYMENT

In 1967, the Point Mugu facility and its personnel were placed under a newly formed organization which was to become the Naval Undersea Center (NUC), with headquarters in San Diego, California. Following the formation of the centre, two more laboratories were established in Hawaii and Florida and, in a subsequent reorganization, the NUC became the Naval Ocean Systems Center (NOSC).

Interviews with many current and former trainers and scientists connected with the Navy's dolphin work have revealed that in the late 1960s, during the Vietnam War, the Navy stopped simply studying the dolphin's swimming and acoustic abilities and turned their attention to the development of the dolphin as a weapon – an animal programmed to detect, attack and help capture enemy divers.

At the time, the Pentagon was examining every possible weapons system. 'They began talking to us about possible deployment in Vietnam,' Irvine says. 'They had a problem. Higher-ups were getting worried about saboteurs floating down the river with mines into Cam Ranh Bay. They were saying we were really vulnerable there. They got us thinking about this seriously.'

Irvine had not opposed the idea of training dolphins to conduct surveillance patrols, but he was disturbed by hints that the Navy wanted dolphins to carry out attack missions.

Rumours have persisted ever since about dolphins being trained to kill underwater divers, attach limpet mines to ships and fix high technology listening devices to enemy submarines. The popular novel by Robert Merle, subsequently made into the film 'The Day of the Dolphin', starring George C. Scott, helped fuel these notions in the early 1970s.

James Fitzgerald, a former President of Kildare Corporation, a US manufacturer of sonar equipment, was one of the few people willing to shed light on these activities. He claimed to have run feasibility studies from 1964 onwards, into using dolphins as 'naval weapons systems'.

In Key West and nearby Grassy Key, he developed an 'antiswimmer system for ship protection' and a mine-hunting system. In October 1965, he conducted two weeks of field tests in the Bahamas, demonstrating that a trained dolphin could be deployed at a remote base. By 1967, he had trained five dolphins for particular tasks and two of these were deemed 'substantially ready for operational deployment in Vietnam'.

Fitzgerald promoted the idea of using the animals to the Navy's top officials, claiming that the dolphin was a natural 'marine operational system' that was just begging to be exploited. 'It's a self-propelled vehicle with an on-board computer with operational capability,' says Fitzgerald. 'All you have to do is program it.'

In tests, he claimed, the dolphins 'were 100 per cent effective. We trained them to either pull the mouthpiece of the regulator from the diver's mouth or push him to the surface. Then the dolphin would hit a response paddle hanging from a buoy that would trigger an alert signal. Between a man and a dolphin, there was no contest.'

In 1968, the US Navy expanded Fitzgerald's dolphin programme but then made the entire operation an internal project and cancelled his contract.

Fitzgerald said the Navy began using the system in Vietnam in 1971 when it sent a team of dolphins to Cam Ranh Bay for 15 months. The animals were also trained to work with underwater demolition teams (UDTs) in mine-sweeping operations, locating mines and other obstacles and either attaching acoustic beacons to them or informing divers of their location by striking a series of submerged paddles with

their snout. 'The frogmen,' says Fitzgerald, 'could then either blow the mines up or defuse them.'

Other reports suggest that dolphins were also used to plant mines. Ken Woodal, a former member of the Navy's elite 'special welfare group' or commandos, known as SEAL (Sea, Air and Land) unit, was quoted in a May 1985 news article as saying that he worked with three dolphins in Vietnam and that they were 'quite effective in attaching light mines to enemy wharves and piers'. They were trained to detach from a mine after planting it and then to swim to safety.

A long-term employee of the programme, who requests anonymity, confirms that the animals were actually given offensive tasks. The dolphins, he says, were used at night to intercept saboteurs who floated down the river and into the harbour where the US fleet was anchored. 'If someone was in the water at night,' the former employee says, 'you could be sure he wasn't friendly.' He says the dolphins clamped markers on the swimmers and alerted guards to their presence but claims rumours that they were used to kill frogmen are 'nonsense'.

Such a story became widespread in 1977 when Michael Greenwood, a former Navy psychophysiologist, reportedly told a secret US Senate committee hearing that

MILITARY USE OF DOLPHINS

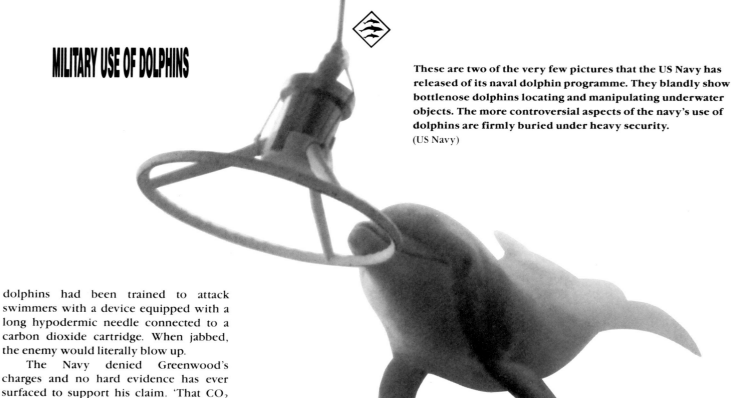

These are two of the very few pictures that the US Navy has released of its naval dolphin programme. They blandly show bottlenose dolphins locating and manipulating underwater objects. The more controversial aspects of the navy's use of dolphins are firmly buried under heavy security.
(US Navy)

dolphins had been trained to attack swimmers with a device equipped with a long hypodermic needle connected to a carbon dioxide cartridge. When jabbed, the enemy would literally blow up.

The Navy denied Greenwood's charges and no hard evidence has ever surfaced to support his claim. 'That CO_2 business all got started with a device that was invented to repel sharks,' explains the anonymous employee. 'It would certainly be a hell of an inefficient way to kill a lot of people. Why not just capture somebody unharmed and interrogate him?'

The next officially acknowledged combat duty for the Navy's marine mammals was on 14 October, 1987. A team of six Pacific bottlenose dolphins, along with a 25-man support staff, was airlifted to the Persian Gulf from the NOSC base in San Diego at the request of the US Commander of the Middle East Forces, Rear Admiral Harold J. Bernsen.

The Admiral was responsible for a fleet of US warships escorting tankers running the gauntlet through mine-strewn waters. Several bases onshore were used to support the fleet, including a barge stationed near Iran's Farsi Island from which mine-sweeping and other special operations were co-ordinated. It housed more than 200 American troops, including helicopter crews, SEAL commandos and UDTs.

During their seven and a half month tour of duty, the dolphins, according to a Pentagon statement, provided 'underwater surveillance and detection capability'. All further details about the project remain classified but it is known that it was not a great success.

None of the dolphins had had much training and the most experienced, a seven-year-old male, died shortly after arriving in the Gulf, from bronchial pneumonia precipitated by a bacterial infection.

STRATEGIC SONAR

The dolphin's exquisitely sensitive sonar has long captured the imagination of Navy scientists. Dolphins can pick out the most subtle features of submerged objects. In tests, blindfolded dolphins have been able to locate vitamin pills on the bottom of a tank, distinguish between identical sheets of aluminium and copper, and detect a stainless steel sphere only 7.5cm (3in) in diameter from a distance of 114m (370ft).

'The Navy would love to be able to do inside a destroyer what a dolphin can do in its head,' says former trainer Blair Irvine. 'A dolphin can probably tell if there's a submarine down there. The hard part is for humans to take that grey bulb with a fin on it and turn it into a black box.'

Lately Naval research into dolphin echolocation has escalated as current military strategy emphasizes the detection and destruction of long-range strategic nuclear missiles like Trident II, based on submarines. US Navy admirals believe that destruction of the Soviet fleet will be the crucial element in deciding the outcome of a global war and that dolphins can help solve their most critical problem of locating enemy submarines.

The Navy also wants to know which sounds interfere with the animal's echolocation ability, in order to develop a sonar jamming device to counter enemy-deployed dolphins.

In addition, the US Navy is studying the sonar capabilities of the beluga. These white-skinned whales are of particular interest because they inhabit the polar waters where many of the US and Soviet nuclear-capable submarine fleets patrol.

NATIONAL DEFENSE

Since the passage of the Marine Mammal Protection Act (MMPA) in 1972, the Navy has had to file a detailed application, subject to public scrutiny, every time it wants to capture a new group of animals. The MMPA placed the Navy's programme under the partial oversight of the Commerce Department's National Marine Fisheries Service (NMFS) and the Marine Mammal Commission, an independent US government body that monitors marine mammal research.

In 1987, the Navy succeeded in making military marine mammals 'blacker,' or more highly secret, than ever before. An obscure passage in the massive 1987 Defense Authorization Act made a distinction between those animals captured for 'national defense purposes' and those taken for Navy-funded scientific research, enabling the Navy to capture up to 25 marine mammals each year without regard for the provisions of the MMPA. The only restrictions are that the animals be treated 'humanely' and that no individuals from 'depleted' species be taken.

Conservationists are concerned because the Navy captures wild dolphins in the Gulf of Mexico. The status of the bottlenose dolphin here has not been determined but several local populations may already have been drastically reduced in size due to the large numbers of dolphins which have been caught there, mainly for use in commercial dolphinariums.

ALLEGATIONS OF ABUSE

There has also been a great deal of concern about the way dolphins have been treated by the Navy. In late 1988, marine mammal trainer Richard Trout went public with an account of how he had witnessed dolphins and sea lions being mistreated while he was working as a trainer at NOSC in San Diego. Among Trout's claims were that dolphins were habitually underfed and would, on occasion, have food withheld or be physically abused for not performing correctly.

The Navy denied Trout's claims but a three-month investigation by the Marine Mammal Commission, although concluding that Navy maltreatment of dolphins was not 'systematic', acknowledged some problems existed and urged the Navy to make several changes to its training procedures.

Concern for the welfare of the programme's dolphins has prompted some activists to take the Navy to court. In October 1989, a coalition of 15 animal welfare organizations filed a lawsuit in an effort to block the Navy's plan to construct a marine mammal facility with pens for 16 animals at the Trident nuclear submarine base at Bangor in Washington State. Here dolphins will be trained to provide perimeter defense for the eight Trident submarines at the base.

The $150-billion Trident II submarine-launched missile programme is intended to provide 50 per cent of US strategic or long-range nuclear forces over the next 50 years.

The 18-22 submarines which will carry these missiles are to be based at only two locations – Bangor and King's Bay, Georgia. A quarter to one-third of the fleet will be in port at any one time. The Navy plans to use dolphins to prevent Soviet Spetsnatz special forces from laying mines and thus blocking these submarines' route to the ocean. (The Navy has already conducted two tests using dolphins to clear mines from waters around a naval base for submarines carrying Poseidon strategic nuclear missiles at Charleston, South Carolina.)

The lawsuit charges that deploying dolphins at the Bangor base would be abusive treatment, and would violate several Federal statutes. There are also concerns that the use of dolphins for such activities would, in times of conflict, lead all dolphins to be looked upon as potential adversaries by divers, and accordingly injured or killed.

The plaintiffs further argue that bringing dolphins from the Gulf of Mexico to the icy waters of Puget Sound could prove fatal. The lawsuit cites as evidence the death of an Atlantic bottlenose dolphin in October 1988, 11 days after it had been transported to Washington State from the warmer waters of Hawaii.

Official records show that 13 of the dolphins enrolled in the US Navy's programme died between 1986 and 1988, at least five soon after being transported from one naval facility to another. Medical reports have revealed that nearly half of the dolphins stopped eating or suffered from stomach disorders.

Zico, the dolphin who died in the Persian Gulf, is a prime example. Dr Brad Fenwick, a pathologist at Kansas State University under contract to the Navy, believes stress may have contributed to Zico's eventual death from disease. 'Stress can lower an animal's resistance and make it more susceptible to infection,' he says. Dolphins may be stressed by such things as over-training, working with a new trainer or moving to a new environment.

EXPANDING ROLES

The Navy plans to increase the size of its marine mammal programme significantly in the years to come. ONR's chief, Rear Admiral Wilson, has asserted that military dolphins will be utilized in 'expanding roles', including protecting offshore oil wells from terrorists and combating underwater sabotage of their shipping. According to official documents, the Navy has enlarged its budget for the programme substantially in the past few years, appropriating $28.7 million between 1985 and 1989 for 'advanced marine biological research'.

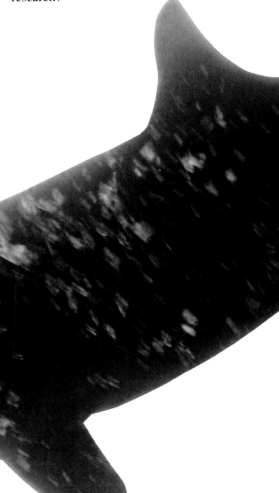

THE FLIPPER GAP

Evidence about Soviet marine mammal defense programmes is even harder to come by, the best source to date being a CIA report leaked to Jack Anderson of the *Washington Post* in May 1981.

This claimed that the Soviet programme closely resembles that of the US Navy, was begun in 1965 (the year of the Sealab experiments with Tuffy), and is carried out from five Black Sea facilities which include a small bio-acoustic laboratory and a dolphinarium.

The report states that 'the quality of Soviet research has improved steadily and in many areas is comparable' to that of the US Navy. As well as studying dolphins in order to try and improve missile and hull design, the Soviets are also 'training dolphins to perform various military and intelligence tasks . . . . which could include attaching intelligence collection packages and other devices to enemy submarines [a task the US Navy has never confirmed it is doing] and helping divers recover equipment from the ocean floor'.

The document also cites a successful Soviet experiment to investigate the detection of a sound-emitting object against adverse background noise, which 'could enable the Soviets to evaluate the potential benefits of developing acoustical jamming countermeasures to US navy dolphin programs'.

This prize-winning photo by British Royal Navy photographer Chris North, entitled 'Bow Chaser', shows a school of playful dolphins at dusk racing a Polaris nuclear submarine.

(Press Association)

The CIA's discussion of a 'flipper gap' and the potential for conflict in this area is a theme developed by Lieutenant Commander Douglas R. Burnett of the US Naval Reserve. In a September 1981 article he wrote:

'In a hostile confrontation, both sides will have to consider dolphins as potential enemy biosensors or weapons. In some situations, there may be no choice except to destroy dolphins or any marine mammal presenting a similar threat. Such a precedent could result in an unpredictable intrusion into the ocean environment. For example, it may be a sound tactical decision to protect shipping in a harbor by poisoning the surrounding waters to remove the threat of dolphin attacks which would, coincidentally, remove a sizeable portion of the area's ecology.'

He concludes that ' . . . the lead one country has in marine mammal technology will generate a countermeasure which will, in turn, create its own counter-countermeasure and so on in a ceaseless chain. A bilateral agreement between the United States and the Soviet Union might cap this chain before it reaches the level of a disastrous threat to the ocean environment and marine mammals. We have a unique opportunity to limit this threat without any loss to our national security. As the dolphin has traditionally been a friend to man, a bilateral agreement between the United States and the Soviet Union, regulating the naval use of marine mammals, would keep this tradition alive.'

Until such an agreement is reached, dolphins will continue to be exploited in the struggle for military supremacy.

CONTROVERSY
CAPTIVITY

Frozen in time, a bottlenose dolphin at the New England Aquarium is caught in mid-somersault by the late master of high-speed photography, Professor Harold E. Edgerton.

(Science Photo Library)

130

The dramatic growth in dolphinaria and zoos; the demand for dolphins in hotel pools; the 'New Age' desire to pet dolphins, swim with them and give birth in water in which they're swimming: these have all stimulated our demand for these charismatic, rubbery, wet, smiling creatures. The more we clamour for them, the more wild populations of dolphins become trapped by our desires.

About 4,600 dolphins, porpoises and small whales have been caught for display, research or military purposes in the last 30 years. As public tastes change, the industry moves from species to species, searching for new star attractions.

A deeply-felt and hard-fought argument over the whole question of keeping dolphins in captivity has been raging for the last 20 years or more. The arguments have been endlessly debated but positions remain polarized.

Some adopt an absolutist stance, abhorring the very notion of keeping any animal captive. Some argue a welfarist position, claiming the confinement of dolphins is cruel and inhumane. Others argue from an educational standpoint and stress the value of seeing dolphins at first hand, even though this experience is usually limited to watching them perform simple and repetitive tasks designed mainly for entertainment. Others dismiss such activities as nothing more than circus tricks and claim that real education now comes from global television, which brings us a constant diet of new footage fresh from the world's oceans.

In the absence of effective legislation, dolphins will continue to be held in captivity as long as they generate profits for the dolphinarium industry, which will go to great lengths to escape restrictive legislation and stay in operation.

In several parts of the world, the operations set up to supply live dolphins have exerted severe pressure on wild populations. This is perhaps best illustrated in the case of the bottlenose dolphins in the Gulf of Mexico which, since 1914, have suffered the longest and largest of these live capture operations.

Marine mammal researchers Wells, Scott and Irvine have demonstrated that, near the coast at least, bottlenose dolphins live in local 'resident' populations with limited ranges. Live capture operations have, in many cases, repeatedly taken animals from a select few of these populations, severely reducing their numbers.

Under the 1972 Marine Mammal Protection Act (MMPA), any depleted population, or any population whose status is unknown, should not be exploited at all. However, no quota system was established until 1977 and conservationists are concerned that the limits set – 2 per cent of a population in a given sub-area – are still too high.

These quotas take no account of other pressures on the dolphins, such as incidental catches by fisheries. Furthermore, 75 per cent of the dolphins captured are female and many are immature, resulting in long-term consequences for the future of the whole population.

In the case of orcas, their capture from the wild began with a series of fiascos but was to develop into a highly efficient international industry. The history of this industry, which was to make the killer whale into the biggest and most popular attraction of them all, has rarely been told in such detail. *Erich Hoyt*, author of the definitive book on these magnificent animals, has written the following disturbing account, illustrating many of the problems arising from the capture of marine mammals for captivity.

In November 1961 a collecting crew from one of the first dolphinaria in the US – Marineland of the Pacific – near Los Angeles in California, captured a female orca found swimming erratically in nearby Newport harbor. The 5.2m (17ft) killer whale was placed in a tank at Marineland where she repeatedly crashed into the walls. She died the following day.

In 1962 the same crew managed to lassoo a female whale with a hoop net in Puget Sound, off the north-west coast of the US, but the line tangled around the propellor shaft and immobilized the boat. When the whale and her male companion charged the boat, thumping it with their tail flukes, the frightened Marineland crew fired at the whales, killing the female and injuring the male, who swam off.

Two years later, the Vancouver Pacific Aquarium hired sculptor Samuel Burich to go out and kill an orca to use as a life-size model on which to base an exhibit. An orca pod was sighted close to the Gulf Islands, off the coast of British Columbia, and Burich fired a harpoon into a young whale's back but this failed to kill it. Before he could finish the job with a rifle, aquarium director, Murray Newman arrived by seaplane and suggested they try to bring the whale in alive. Using the line attached to the harpoon, they towed the orca through rough seas on a 16-hour journey to Vancouver harbour, where it was placed in a makeshift pen. Over the next few weeks, tens of thousands of people from around the world came to see 'Moby Doll', the first of these legendary killers to be placed in captivity, and to marvel at its docility. The

People watching orcas watching people at the Vancouver Aquarium.
(Thomas Jefferson/Marine Mammal Images)

harpoon wound healed but the whale wouldn't eat until, on the 55th day, it began to take food, devouring up to 90kg (200lbs) of fish a day. Within a month however, the whale was dead. The autopsy revealed that 'Moby Doll' was in fact 'Moby Dick', a male not a female.

The saga of 'Moby Whatever' convinced aquarium keepers that orcas would adapt to captivity, that they were not as dangerous as legend had portrayed them and that, like other zoo animals, they could be trained to perform stunts by using food as a reward. Moreover, their notoriety as killers combined with their panda-like attractiveness, had the potential to draw unprecedented crowds to aquaria. They were right on all counts.

In 1965, the Seattle Public Aquarium in Washington State paid $8,000 for Namu, a big male, that had been accidentally caught by Canadian gill net fishermen. Four months later, Ted Griffin, owner of the Aquarium, and his assistant Don Goldsberry, netted Shamu, a prospective mate for Namu, in Puget Sound. The two whales performed together in Seattle until the following year when Namu died. With the sale of Shamu to Sea World in San Diego, the trade in orcas began in earnest.

CAPTIVITY

The Griffin-Goldsberry team were the first to develop successful methods for the capture and transport of orcas, and their capture technique is still in use today off the coast of Iceland. Purse seine nets are used to surround a pod of orcas, sometimes in open water but more often in a shallow bay or inlet. Ironically, the whales could easily jump over the nets or break through them but few orcas have ever attempted to escape. Selected whales are then hoisted from the water in a sling and suspended in a box where they are cooled by water or shaved ice. They are then ready for transport by boat, truck or cargo plane to any location in the world.

By the end of 1968, Griffin and Goldsberry had carried out four such capture operations in the Pacific Northwest region and had taken 13 whales, three of which ended up at Sea World after spending some time in Seattle. The others were sold to aquaria in New York, Florida, Texas, Canada and England, and to the US Navy in Hawaii.

The growing market prompted a group of Canadian net fishermen across the border at Pender Harbour, British Columbia, to begin catching orcas. In 1968 and 1969 they made three trips and captured 12 orcas, which were sent to the Vancouver Aquarium, to Marineland of France and to Sea World's competitors in California – Marineland of the Pacific and Marine World near San Francisco. Several other fishermen in British Columbia caught orcas accidentally and these too were sold.

At this time, there were no regulations governing the catching of killer whales and, potentially, anyone who wished to try their luck at it could do so. In practice, however, a would-be captor had to know the sea and to have had some experience with marine animal collection and seine nets. That limited the field considerably. No one at that time knew much about orcas and early capture techniques evolved by trial and error. As a result, some orcas that were stunned by tranquilizer darts were lost in the ocean; several others became entangled in nets and drowned. That was the price of the learning curve.

When the whales arrived at their new homes, many died prematurely, some from injuries caused by their capture and transport, others from what aquarium directors today consider poor conditions: small tank size, inadequate water pumping facilities and excessive or inept handling in the tank. Before 1970, half of all aquarium orcas died during their first two years in captivity, most in the first year. There were a few exceptions. Ten orcas caught before 1970 survived ten years or more and two of these have now passed the 20-year mark – the record for longevity in captivity.

VALUE JUDGEMENTS

1970 was the peak year for orca captures in the Pacific Northwest, with 16 being taken from the wild, and stories about orcas received wide coverage in both local and national media.

In March of that year Sealand of the Pacific, based in Victoria, British Columbia, began their own whale-catching operation. Chimo, an orca captured on their first trip, was a striking all-white young female, whose albinism was caused by a rare genetic disorder called Chediak-Higashi Syndrome. By now orcas were selling for tens of thousands of US dollars but such was the attraction of this rare white orca that a US aquarium offered to buy it for half a million dollars. Sealand declined the offer and displayed Chimo until she died two years and eight months later.

While Chimo was attracting all the limelight, three members of her pod, captured at the same time, languished in nets at Pedder Bay, west of Victoria, refusing to eat. After 78 days, one of them died and the other two – a male and female that were scheduled to go to an aquarium in Texas – were freed one night by persons unknown. To this day, the pair can be seen swimming around Vancouver Island, and since 1979 they have been seen with a calf.

But the most extraordinary catch of the year came in August when Griffin and Goldsberry captured some 80 whales at Penn Cove, Washington. Never before or since have so many whales been captured at once. Although they were unaware of it at the time, Griffin and Goldsberry had captured three pods travelling together. Those 80 whales comprised almost the entire 'resident' orca population off southern Vancouver Island and in Puget Sound. For a day, until they released the majority of the whales, the fate of an entire 'community' or breeding stock of orcas was in the hands of two unregulated collectors.

As news of the capture spread, aquarium orders poured in. Seven whales were shipped to aquaria in Japan, England, France, Australia and the US.

A few months later, near the site of this capture, three young orcas, their bellies slit, their tails weighted with anchor chain, washed ashore, Griffin and Goldsberry denied knowledge of the corpses. Later, as evidence mounted, they admitted responsibility for four accidental deaths.

These events, and the continued capture of local orcas for world aquaria, led to a public outcry in the Northwest. As a result the Canadian authorities, and subsequently the state of Washington, imposed new regulations and permit requirements for capturing killer whales. Finally, in 1972, the US Marine Mammal Protection Act (MMPA) was passed by Congress and orcas were at last protected from being harrassed or killed, and would-be captors now had to apply for a special federal permit.

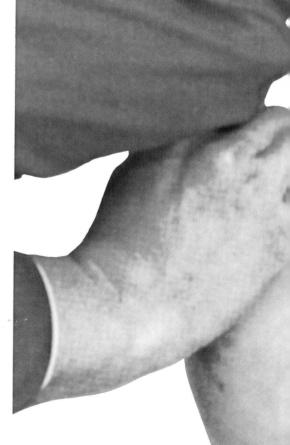

In a time-honoured routine, formerly used by lion tamers at the circus, a trainer puts his head in an orca's mouth, either to demonstrate the relative harmlessness of these giant creatures or to emphasize human dominion over this monster of the deep.
(Gerhard Bakker/Marine Mammal Images)

CAPTIVITY

Beginning in 1973, the Canadian federal government funded a field study to determine the orca population in the Northwest. The captors claimed they saw hundreds of orcas on their spotting trips, and estimated their total numbers in thousands. Using a detailed photo-identification study, Michael A. Bigg and his colleagues in Canada, and later Kenneth C. Balcomb in US waters, determined that about 300 killer whales frequented the waters of the British Columbia-Washington coast. In other words, the catchers had consistently been taking orcas from the same pods.

This evidence, combined with public opinion, has helped to limit the Northwest captures ever since and, in recent years, the 'cropped' pods have increased in numbers.

After the 1970 deaths of the 'Penn Cove Four', Griffin sold the Seattle Aquarium to Sea World and dropped out of the capture business. Until recently Goldsberry continued to participate in the capture of killer whales around the world as Sea World's Corporate Director of Collections.

Today, Sea World has four large marine parks, in California, Florida, Ohio and, most recently, in Texas. The company has built its marketing strategy on orcas, trademarking the name Shamu, as well as Kandu and Namu. Each park has at least two orcas; some, at times, have had up to six. The animals are moved around from park to park as needed. When one Shamu dies, a new one takes its place.

Sea World's need for new orcas has fuelled most of the controversy over captures since the early 1970s. In 1976, Goldsberry used aircraft and explosives to chase a pod of six orcas through Puget Sound, finally cornering them in Budd Inlet. The State of Washington filed a lawsuit against Sea World in federal court, charging that Goldsberry's inhumane treatment of the whales violated the terms of his collecting permit. The whales were held in nets for days as a result of a court injunction. The judge subsequently dismissed the case on condition that Sea World release the whales, relinquish its permit and agree never to collect orcas again in Washington State.

That's when Goldsberry went to Iceland. He did not want to be officially involved in the new capture operation but agreed to lend his expertise to W.H. Dudok van Heel, zoological director of the Dutch Dolfinarium Harderwijk, and Jón Kr. Gunnarsson, director of Sædýrasafnid, an aquarium near Reykjavik. Their first captures were two young whales, netted during the autumn of 1976, which were airlifted to the Netherlands; one remained there while the other was forwarded to San Diego's Sea World after six months.

The same team captured six orcas in October 1977, and a further five the following year. Sea World had now received nine new whales in two years, enough to satisfy their immediate requirements and they therefore dropped out of the project. Gunnarsson then took over the Icelandic captures using International Animal Exchange of Ferndale, Michigan, USA, to handle sales to the world market. The going rate for a healthy young orca in November 1979 was $150,000 excluding delivery costs from Reykjavik; in 1980, the prices ranged from $200,000 to $300,000.

By the early 1980s, Sea World wanted more Icelandic orcas. Their import application to the US National Marine Fisheries Service was refused, however, partly because the status of the species in the North Atlantic was unknown. Sea World considered capturing Antarctic orca, but the logistics were forbidding. Instead they prepared a permit application for Alaska.

In 1983, Sea World announced a grand scheme to expand their operations and mount a five-year capture plan in south-eastern Alaskan waters. They proposed capturing 100 orcas, 90 for research purposes and eventual release, ten to be kept for Sea World parks. Despite outcry from conservationists, the National Marine Fisheries Service issued the permit. Sea World agreed to mount a photographic identification study on Alaska's orcas in the summer of 1984. The Sea World Research Institute/Hubbs Marine Research Center assembled a competent research team and produced a solid scientific study but the state governor and many Alaskan residents and conservationists were strongly opposed to any captures. After months of protest, Sea World finally withdrew.

With the collapse of the Alaskan operation, Sea World tried several new strategies to obtain orcas. In late 1986, Sea World's parent company, Harcourt Brace Jovanovich, purchased Marineland of the Pacific for $23.4 million. Sea World officials promised to keep the park open but two months later moved Orky and Corky, the park's two star orcas, from Los Angeles to San Diego and closed down Marineland.

Sea World's most highly publicized route for obtaining new orcas has been through their breeding programme. On 26 September, 1985, the first 'Baby Shamu' was born at Sea World in Florida. Since then, five more Baby Shamus have been born, three in the autumn of 1988. Five of the six were still alive in February 1990. Prior to this, five orcas had been born alive in aquaria but none had lived for more than 46 days; a further five were stillborn.

On the basis of its breeding record, Sea World has been granted permits to import whales from aquaria in other countries on 'breeding loan' and has subsequently obtained whales from the Netherlands, England, and Canada.

Sea World has invested substantial research funds to determine the population of the North Atlantic killer whale and to review the history of their capture in Icelandic waters through the Sea World Research Institute/Hubbs Marine Research Center.

However, the results of these studies will not be known for some time. Researchers have so far identified only 143 individual orcas in the capture areas off Iceland, from photographs dating back to 1981. They feel this represents a conservative estimate of the Icelandic population; shipboard sightings may indicate as many as 4,000 orcas. The Icelandic Ministry of Fisheries has, in any case, been restricting capture permits to between four and ten per year. There are now two main permit holders, Jón Kr.Gunnarsson (Sædýrasafnid Aquarium) and Helgi Jónasson of the Fauna Co., both Icelanders.

Compared to many dolphinaria, the conditions at Sea World's parks are among the best. Orcas there receive good veterinary care and their survival rate has been above average for captive orcas. Yet Sea World's programme includes riding the animals, making them do numerous shows every day and exposing them to sustained close contact with large crowds, far larger than at other aquaria.

Former trainer Graeme Ellis, who worked with orcas at Sealand and at the Vancouver Aquarium, contends that this intensive programme may be all right initially for younger animals but that, after a time, the whales suffer stress and may become violent. There have been at least a dozen publicized cases of Sea World orcas turning on trainers. Several trainers have suffered broken bones and other internal injuries and some have sued for damages.

In August 1989, at Sea World in San Diego, Kandu charged another female orca, fatally injuring herself in what appeared to be a fight for dominance. Sea World said the death was an accident following routine aggressive play. Critics suggest it was 'artificial behaviour' brought on by stress after years in captivity; such violent displays have never been witnessed among orcas in the wild.

In 1989, Harcourt Brace Jovanovich sold Seaworld to Anheuser-Busch, the world's largest brewer, for $1,100 million.

COUNTING THE COST

Killer whales are the most popular of all marine attractions. Since the first capture, almost 30 years ago, 150 killer whales have been kept in 40 aquaria around the world. This includes 13 born in captivity, 56 from British Columbia and Washington State, one from California and 55 from Iceland. An additional 12 escaped or were released from captivity. Iceland is likely to remain the principal supplier of orcas to world aquaria for the forseeable future.

Also included are the 13 orcas which have been captured for Japanese aquaria in local offshore waters since 1972. Three that had survived being harpooned were sold to aquaria; the others were herded into shallow water by Japanese drive fisheries. Six of the orcas caught died within a year; one has so far survived for 10 years.

Several studies have looked at captive orca survival, reproduction rates and causes of death but only in selected animals kept under the best conditions. The cause of death in half of these cases was bacterial infection, with pneumonia topping the list.

A US study by marine mammal researchers Douglas DeMaster and Jeannie Drevenak determined that, on the basis of a limited sample mainly from US institutions where standards tend to be highest, orcas were living for an average of about 13 years from the date of their capture. Most of these were immature whales less than ten years old at the time of capture. In the wilds of British Columbia, long-term studies have revealed that male and female orcas live to about 60, females sometimes 20 years longer. Thus, to date, wild orcas are living two to three times longer than those in captivity.

Currently, 48 orcas are held captive in 18 aquaria around the world. The controversy continues.

A mighty orca leaps clear of the water to hit a ball at a dolphinarium in Mexico City.
(Sergio Nalasco/ Marine Mammal Images)

GREEN

PERSPE

PEACE

Centre: The head of a killer whale, poking out of the waters of Icy Straight, Alaska in July 1984, is framed by the Kwakiutl, a magic totem sign used by a seafaring tribe of North American Indians of the same name, who used it to symbolize their desire to live in harmony with the natural world. This crest, which represents two whales forming the infinite cycle of nature, was painted on many Greenpeace boats.
(Steve Leatherwood)

Far left: **An early Greenpeace crew member playing music to the whales in 1976;**
Above: **Campaigner Naoko Kakuta cradles a dead dolphin, caught in drift nets in the Tasman Sea, on board the new *Rainbow Warrior*.**
(Rex Weyler/Lorrette Dorreboom/Greenpeace)

CTIVES

OVER VIEW

Lesley Scheele spent five years as a biologist studying wild dolphins off Sarasota in Florida before joining Greenpeace in 1980, first as a canvasser, then as a campaigner on a variety of issues, from whaling to ocean dumping. In 1984, she became international co-ordinator of Greenpeace's small cetaceans campaign, and she is currently based in Fort Lauderdale, Florida.

' When I joined Greenpeace's international dolphin campaign, it was clear from the outset that the threats facing these small whales were many, varied and global in nature. However, unlike the whales, the dolphins had no international forum or framework working towards their protection. The actions necessary to protect these animals often had to be conducted in a vacuum rather than within a broader context.

We began to identify and catalogue the major threats facing small cetaceans throughout the world and quickly realized that dolphin populations were threatened by intentional exploitation, incidental kills and habitat degradation, or by a combination of these. We decided initially to target the most serious examples of each of these types of threats and focus on issues which not only posed immediate threats to dolphin populations, but would also serve as illustrations of the global problems.

For the most part, direct exploitation and incidental kills continue to occur as a result of poor fisheries management. The tuna/dolphin issue was considered the

most blatant form of direct exploitation and it remains a priority. Since the practice of deliberately capturing dolphins in order to catch tuna began, several dolphin populations have been seriously reduced. Conservation groups have struggled with the issue since the early 1970s – litigating, legislating and boycotting in an effort to end the killing. While reductions have been substantial, it is clear that as long as nets are deliberately set around dolphins, mortality will remain high, and no amount of fine-tuning what is an inherently flawed practice will change this. The practice, while entirely needless, continues because canneries pay a premium for tuna caught on dolphins. It is a prime example of the lengths humans will go to in order to exploit fish stocks as rapidly and efficiently as possible in order to realize maximum profits. The time for a worldwide end to this highly destructive fishing method is long overdue.

Above: **An atmospheric image of the new *Rainbow Warrior* in the Tasman Sea. Launched in 1989, the new boat is larger than its predecessor, which was sunk in Auckland in 1985 by French saboteurs.** *(Lorrette Dorreboom/Greenpeace)*

The use of high seas drift nets, with the consequent deaths of countless numbers of cetaceans, other marine mammals, sea birds and non-target fish, was an obvious priority for addressing the issue of incidental takes. These massive nets are so indiscriminate that even targeted fish populations are in danger. It is clear that a worldwide ban on drift net technology is needed.

Less commercial and more regional in nature, and therefore more difficult to address globally, is the extensive use of smaller, coastal gill nets. In some instances, however, there are potential regional solutions which can afford protection to the cetaceans, the fish and the fishery. Work undertaken on behalf of the Hector's dolphin in New Zealand positively demonstrated that such solutions can be implemented.

In the long term, I think that pollution, while the most insidious, may prove the most debilitating threat to small cetaceans. Because they are long-lived, reside at the top of the food chain and possess blubber, cetaceans accumulate and concentrate toxins in their bodies with a rapidity unique among mammals. Nursing mothers deliver these toxins in highly concentrated doses to their calves through their milk.

The case of the St Lawrence beluga clearly illustrates the role that pollution and habitat degradation can play in thwarting the recovery of cetacean populations. Because unequivocal proof of cause and effect is impossible to obtain, measures to reduce toxic discharges and protect their habitat have been slow. Despite the continuing efforts of conservationists and scientists, the belugas' future remains grim at best. For too long, the burden of proof has been on the conservationists, and this must be reversed to make the polluter accountable.

We know very little about dolphins, but time and again when we do begin to find out about them and discover the results of our actions, we find that we have failed to err on the side of caution. Taking the river dolphins as an example, some species have been so severely reduced that captive breeding programmes are now necessary to save them from extinction. The situation had to be this serious before these animals were formally declared "depleted", "threatened" or "endangered".

In their own right, dolphins deserve our protection. They have delighted and inspired humankind for centuries and they occupy a special place in our folklore, in our mythology and on the planet that we share. They are also in the unfortunate position of acting as living indicators of the effects of our unchecked exploitation and destruction of the oceans. The problems facing small cetaceans are clearly complex and must be addressed in a holistic manner. Several regional and national agreements which address not only the problems of the species, but also the health and stability of the environment are promising steps towards international solutions.

If the dolphins are to survive, then we as a species must recognize that the oceans they live in do not have unlimited resources and are not immune from our wastes.'

Left: **A pair of rare Hector's dolphins swimming off the east coast of New Zealand's South Island at Kaikoura.** *(Colin Monteath/ Hedgehog House New Zealand)*

Hector's Dolphin

*Greenpeace is one of the organizations that support the work of New Zealand biologists **Steve Dawson** and **Liz Slooten** who, since 1984, have been studying Hector's dolphins and campaigning for their protection. Both completed Ph.D theses on the species for the University of Canterbury in 1990.*

'When we started our studies of Hector's dolphin, 14 November 1984, the first task was a population survey. In the following six months we surveyed almost the entire South Island coastline twice, as well as the few areas around the North Island where Hector's dolphins have been recorded, and we arrived at a total population estimate of between 3,000 and 4,000 Hector's dolphins. This is an extremely low number for a marine mammal – several cetacean species, officially listed as endangered, number considerably more – and underscores the urgent need to discover more about the biology of this species.

Next we looked carefully at the reproductive rate, social behaviour and feeding ecology of these dolphins, so that we could determine if the species could recover from their reduced population.

Sadly, one of the findings we made was that the number of dolphins caught accidentally in gill nets was considerably higher than previously thought. Over four years, during which we studied the gill net fishery in the Pegasus Bay/Canterbury Bight region, 230 Hector's dolphins – that is about 30 per cent of the population in this important breeding area – were reported killed in the gill nets. Of those, 89 per cent were caught within four miles of the shore and 91 per cent were caught in the summer months of November to February.

In December 1988, the Department of Conservation (DOC) declared Banks Peninsula a marine mammal sanctuary, with a partial ban on net-setting in the summer months and restrictions on net-setting outside this period. Nonetheless, some dolphins continue to be killed in nets in the region. We need to make the sanctuary more secure in the face of opposition to it and to see if it should be extended to other areas of South Island.'

DRIFT NETS

Mike Hagler *spent thirteen years as a broadcaster and journalist in Los Angeles, Europe and Australia. He has lived in New Zealand since 1980 and has been Greenpeace Ocean Ecology campaigner there since 1989. He has been particularly involved in campaigning against drift nets in the South Pacific.*

'Drift net fleets first moved into the South Pacific in the mid 1980s when an organization called Japan Marine Research began some experimental drift net setting down there for albacore. By the 1988/89 season, 162 vessels were drift netting in the region – 130 from Taiwan, 30 from Japan and 2 from South Korea.

Most of these ships spend the rest of the year in the North Pacific or the Indian Ocean. They moved to the South Pacific because some of the stocks in the North were probably being over-exploited and there was obviously extra money to be made by fishing year-round in both hemispheres as, at that time, albacore prices were very attractive.

But it was clear from the outset that, by moving into this territory, the drift netters were potentially entering a diplomatic minefield. Their activities were bound to affect the poor, developing nations – to hit right at the heart of their resources – and would inevitably attract worldwide attention.

And so it proved. By the middle of 1989 things had started to heat up on the diplomatic level. New Zealand passed the Drift Nets [Prohibition] Act of 1989. This banned drift net ships from New Zealand waters and was based, to no small extent, on information supplied by Greenpeace.

We developed a working relationship with Geoffrey Palmer, the New Zealand Prime Minister, and suggested to him that a possible next step might be to propose a resolution against drift nets at the United Nations. This led to a meeting in his office with myself, Alan Reichman and Trevor Daly of Greenpeace, at which he said that he liked the idea very much and he would be using a scheduled speech at the UN to make a major statement on drift nets. In the

Above: **A Greenpeace campaigner holds the dead body of a young common dolphin, a victim of drift nets in the Tasman Sea, on board the *Rainbow Warrior* in January 1990.**
(Roger Grace/Greenpeace)

event, this led to a joint US – New Zealand resolution, seconded by a number of other countries, calling for an immediate ban on drift nets.

Not surprisingly, Japan fought hard in the UN and introduced an alternative resolution which basically just called for more research. A compromise emerged from this, calling for a provisional phased moratorium (rather than a ban) unless the

drift net fleets could prove that they could manage their fisheries effectively.

From our point of view, this outcome was far from satisfactory. The resolution states that the implementation of the provisional moratorium is essentially dependent on the results of the drift net fisheries' own research and contains a great many other loopholes. But at least it was a statement of some sort and it was buttressed by a whole host of political manouevres in the South Pacific itself, such as the Tarawa Declaration and the development of a drift nets convention in Wellington. So mounting pressure from all sides at all levels – regional, national and international – was beginning to make itself felt.

Then, in January 1990, we took the *Rainbow Warrior* out to confront the drift netters in the South Pacific and to document their activities, which had never been done before. This lack of documentation had allowed the Japanese to claim that there was no evidence that drift netting in the South Pacific was environmentally unsound.

We set out on 6 January, and found our first drift net vessel within a few days. Right from the start it was clear that species other than albacore were being caught but it took us some time before we found our first entangled dolphin. We soon found seven more in very quick succession. We didn't see any seabirds or turtles but a New Zealand Ministry of Agriculture observer on board a Japanese Marine Research vessel did record some. The dolphin catch rate recorded by observers was pretty much the same as ours: we came up with something like 2.1 dolphins per net set, theirs was in the region of 2.6.

We observed only 126km (80mls) of net while we were out there, a small percentage of the 6,000km (3,700mls) of net set in the area during that time. If you simply extrapolate from the figures that we had, it would mean that between 5,000 and 6,000 dolphins are dying each season in the Tasman Sea alone. The number of small cetaceans that must die each year in drift nets all over the world is frightening.

There's no doubt that the drift netters are worried by the political activity and public awareness that has developed since mid-1989 and they're fighting back hard. They're already claiming that it will be possible to use drift nets in an environmentally sound manner and that their use can be properly managed without the need for a ban.

I'm optimistic that we can win this issue within a short time with a concerted and concentrated effort on two levels; by lobbying governments and international forums and by raising public awareness and informing public opinion. People should be so concerned about this issue that they won't buy fish if they think it's been caught in a drift net. They should insist that the labels on fish and fish products state categorically that no dolphins were killed in the course of catching the fish.'

MEDIT

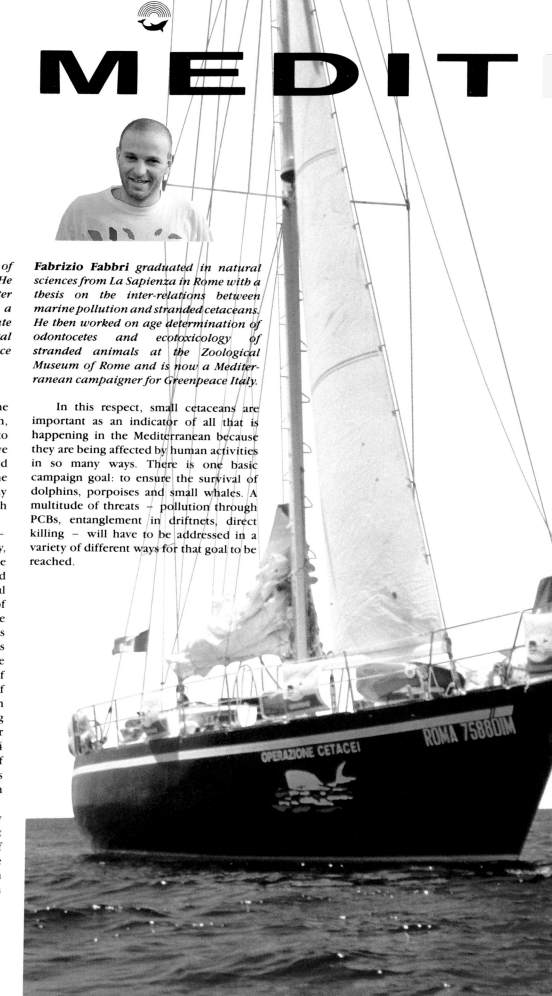

Xavier Pastor *is the co-ordinator of Greenpeace's Mediterranean Project. He joined Greenpeace in 1983, after spending more than ten years as a fisheries biologist for the Spanish Institute of Oceanography and was instrumental in the establishment of the Greenpeace office in Spain.*

Fabrizio Fabbri *graduated in natural sciences from La Sapienza in Rome with a thesis on the inter-relations between marine pollution and stranded cetaceans. He then worked on age determination of odontocetes and ecotoxicology of stranded animals at the Zoological Museum of Rome and is now a Mediterranean campaigner for Greenpeace Italy.*

'From the very earliest days of the Greenpeace Mediterranean campaign, it was clear that it wouldn't be possible to come up with a single goal for which we could aim, or just one strategy we could follow, as a way of saving the Mediterranean. There are just too many different problems that the sea faces, each of which requires a different approach.

There is, for example, over-fishing – by countries such as France, Spain and Italy, but also by fleets from nations outside the Mediterranean region, such as Japan and South Korea, who fish in international waters. There are direct discharges of organo-chlorines, heavy metals and the effluents from petrochemical companies and from pulp and paper mills. There is sewage, 80 per cent of which enters the Mediterranean without any form of treatment. There is an enormous level of tanker traffic: it has been calculated that in 1989 the amount of oil spilled during routine operations was equivalent to four *Exxon Valdez* disasters. There are about 34 nuclear plants around the coast and four of the five nuclear navies play war games here. So you can see that the Mediterranean faces many problems.

Nonetheless, although each may require a different approach, it is important not to lose sight of the fact that many of these problems are inter-related. The difficulties confronting the Mediterranean ecosystem are the result of a combination of all these human activities.

In this respect, small cetaceans are important as an indicator of all that is happening in the Mediterranean because they are being affected by human activities in so many ways. There is one basic campaign goal: to ensure the survival of dolphins, porpoises and small whales. A multitude of threats – pollution through PCBs, entanglement in driftnets, direct killing – will have to be addressed in a variety of different ways for that goal to be reached.

During the summer of 1989, Greenpeace Italy sponsored an ambitious project called *Operazione Cetacei*, which aimed to gather more information about cetaceans in Italian waters and to increase public concern for them. The project was conducted in co-operation with Dr Giuseppe Notarbartolo di Sciara, one of the most important marine mammal researchers in Italy, and it involved both the scientific community and a large number of volunteers from the Italian public.

The involvement of volunteers was perhaps the most exciting part of the project. On the fourth Saturday of July, 1989, hundreds of people in more than 250 boats took to the water to patrol tracts of sea assigned to them and to make notes of any cetaceans they saw. The operation also succeeded in motivating the scientific community in the region. We also organized a meeting on board the Greenpeace ship *Sirius* at which researchers from Italy, Spain, Tunisia, Algeria and Morocco discussed the first results from *Operazione Cetacei*.

When the project was completed, we were in possession for the first time of a general picture of the distribution of cetaceans in Italian waters. In particular, we were able to identify the areas where cetaceans are found in particularly large numbers.

Over 60 articles were published in national newspapers and magazines before, during and after *Operazione Cetacei* and one clear effect has been an enormous increase in the number of people in Italy who now know about, and support, our work on small cetaceans in the Mediterranean region.

In future years, we want *Operazione Cetacei* to expand so that we can involve environmentalist groups in Malta, as well as in countries such as Spain, Yugoslavia and Greece. Time is absolutely of the essence.'

Left: **The Greenpeace yacht *Highlander*, which bears the campaign symbol of 'Operazione Cetacei', was used to carry out scientific research in the Mediterranean.**
(Greenpeace Italy)

Moby Dick

In the summer of 1989, in response to concerns over the status of small cetaceans around the coasts of Britain and Ireland, the Greenpeace vessel *Moby Dick* visited Cardigan Bay in Wales and the Moray Firth in Scotland. Between them these two habitats are home to virtually the entire British semi-resident coastal population of bottlenose dolphins.

Greenpeace consultant Dr Peter Evans was able to photograph the dolphins in an attempt to identify individuals and to calculate the size of the groups, while other scientists took tissue samples in order to test for contaminants.

At the same time, the tour was used to make people aware, locally and nationally, that there were dolphins in these particular areas and that they were under threat. Greenpeace was able to arrange wide coverage of the visit in the national media and organized public meetings that have led to the setting up of local pressure groups.

Above: **A dolphin plays in front of the *Moby Dick* during the Greenpeace vessel's fact-finding mission to Cardigan Bay on the Welsh coast.**
(Frank Martin/The Guardian)

These groups are now pursuing successful independent campaigns in support of Greenpeace's goal of having these areas designated Marine Nature Reserves (MNRs). The 'Friends of Cardigan Bay', for example, have persuaded the Welsh Water Authority to host a major scientific meeting to discuss the problem of water pollution and the high levels of contaminants found in some stranded dolphins.

Isabel McCrea

FISHING

*Prior to joining Greenpeace International's staff – first as a fisheries researcher and later as International Fisheries Project Co-ordinator – **James Carr** had been employed as an environmental consultant and researcher. He also served as an adviser to a national delegation to the International Whaling Commission for two years. He studied an inter-disciplinary doctoral programme, at the University of California, Santa Cruz, focusing on comparative systems of fisheries management internationally.*

'Greenpeace is well known for the way in which it has campaigned, often successfully, against the direct exploitation of marine mammals. It is now arguable that the greatest threats these mammals face are not from intentional hunts but from the degradation of the marine environment, notably through pollution, and the enormous and continuing growth in commercial fisheries.

As demand increases and prices for fish products rise, there is a growing race to exploit known fish stocks. This has resulted in massive investments in bigger, more powerful and more efficient vessels and in technological innovations – fishing gear, factory processing, freezer capacity, transportation and marketing.

Technology is advancing more quickly than the ability to manage fisheries. Despite impressive progress in the past few years in marine biology and fisheries sciences, improvements in the efficiency and the catching capacity of the fleets are outstripping the ability of the fisheries management authorities to control the rates and types of exploitation. The sad results of this have been the many well-documented and spectacular collapses of fish stocks around the world and an increase in the death rate of marine mammals, birds, turtles and other wildlife.

There have been a number of attempts in recent times, most notably through the United Nations Law of the Sea, to improve the situation and develop a framework whereby fisheries could be managed more effectively but this legislation contains a number of fundamental flaws.

The Law of the Sea calls on interested parties to co-operate in the management and exploitation of the resources of the high seas. It was developed to give access to marine resources and to give control of that access to the coastal states. It was hoped that these states, by having a long-term interest in maintaining ecological stability in their own marine environment, would institute measures to ensure its conservation.

In developing countries, however, where there is a premium on hard currency and a relative lack of fishing technology, these resources have often been sold off to the highest bidders. One way to make this an attractive investment is to dispense with any conservation measures.

Such is the need amongst developing nations to acquire hard currency, often to service their foreign debts, that they will allow the large-scale exploitation of their marine resources even though they are invaluable sources of protein for their own populations.

In many coastal fishing communities, the fish stocks on which they have long depended are dwindling and they are unable to compete with the large-scale commercial fisheries which have been encouraged to enter their waters. As a result they have to turn to whatever resources remain, simply in order to survive, and the only available resources are often dolphins and porpoises. Few, if any, of the coastal fishing communities which have started killing dolphins for food in recent years have wanted to do so. Many have traditionally respected and admired them. They simply have no choice.

Another effect of the depletion of fish stocks is that the dolphins have also had to search for alternative food sources by moving inshore. Fishermen may perceive the dolphins as competing for the already reduced amount of fish and feel compelled to kill them to limit their numbers.

As long as the goal of the commercial fishing industry is maximum profit, there is no incentive to protect marine life. What is needed is the recognition, by fisheries managers and government agencies worldwide, that the effects of fishing (and particularly over-fishing) on marine wildlife must always be taken into consideration.

Runaway competition between nation states and corporate interests, or between various sectors within the fishing industry, needs to be replaced by greater co-ordination. This would ensure fair competition between all parties and allow the rational assessment of fish stocks in order to prevent a recurring cycle of over-exploitation, stock collapse, fishery decline and harm to wildlife.

This would in turn allow levels of catches worldwide to stabilize, ensuring the long-term viability of the fishing industry itself.'

'The drift nets campaign originated in 1983 with the *Rainbow Warrior*'s expedition to document and oppose the Japanese salmon drift net fishery that operated in the vicinity of the Aleutian Islands off Alaska (below). The carnage that we witnessed during that effort to save Dall's porpoises inspired us to launch a global political effort to have these 'death nets' banned. We delivered a paper on this to the Food and Agriculture Organization at the UN World Fisheries Conference in Rome in 1984. From there we went to the governments of Australia, Canada and the US, to try and get them to ban large-scale drift netting within their Exclusive Economic Zones, and then to various international commissions and conventions, and ultimately to the UN.'

Alan Reichman

(Photo: Richard Dawson/Greenpeace)

BELUGA

Bruce McKay *is an ecotoxicology campaigner for Greenpeace International in Montreal. A native of British Columbia, he has studied cartology and psychology. He moved to Quebec, where he became concerned over the plight of the St Lawrence River beluga, and persuaded Greenpeace to campaign on its behalf.*

'In 1984, an article appeared in the Montreal newspaper *La Presse*, with the headline 'Beluga Found With Cancer'. The article said this was the first case of cancer ever to be found in a cetacean and that the St Lawrence beluga was highly endangered and had a population of only about 500 animals. It referred to Daniel Martineau as the scientist who had discovered the cancer, so I phoned him, went to meet him and talked with him about the belugas, about pollution and about the burdens of contaminants they were carrying.

Up until then, the person who had done most to raise concern about the belugas was the naturalist Leone Pippard. In the mid 1970s, she and Heather Malcolm had studied them in the wild for four or five years and it was she who had first brought the attention of the Canadian government and public to the fact that this was a population that was clearly endangered. It was her work that resulted in the belugas being awarded 'endangered species' status in Canada.

There was virtually no work being conducted by government scientists, or indeed by anyone else at all, until Martineau and Pierre Béland began their autopsy programme in the early 1980s.

Following my meeting with Daniel Martineau, I sent a proposal to Lesley Scheele at Greenpeace in Florida asking for funding and within a month we had the money to work on behalf of the belugas. The first thing we did was to hold a press conference in Quebec City, which received nationwide coverage, to announce the start of the campaign.

The primary target was Alcan, the large aluminium multinational, to highlight the fact that industrial pollution was implicated in the problems faced by the belugas. We first conducted a direct action campaign, climbing up the smokestacks of one of the Alcan plants, but most of our work was centred on producing briefings and press releases. When we got hold of human health studies in the region, we sent out a press release summarizing the results. We did the same thing when the first analyses were conducted for the presence of PAHs in belugas.

All in all, the media response was phenomenal. Here was a marine mammal that almost nobody had heard about before. Within a short period, most of Canada knew not only that these animals existed in the St Lawrence and that they were on the brink of extinction but also that they were heavily contaminated with toxic chemicals.

The response of Alcan and the government was a little more muted. It's hard to say who echoed whom, but the general line from the company and the two governments – federal and provincial – was that there wasn't enough evidence to show firstly that the St Lawrence belugas were declining at all or secondly that, even if they were, contaminants were somehow implicated.

It was a typical response. In this kind of situation, faced with any environmental problem, governments won't act until either there's overwhelming evidence or public pressure compels them to do something. It's only in the last couple of years that the governments of Canada and Quebec have grudgingly begun to force the reduction of toxic emissions.

Alcan is still a disgrace but, in order to stay competitive and to fend off pressure from the government, it is slowly changing to a different kind of aluminium production process – one that will result in a gradual decrease in the emission of PAH pollution.

At government level, what is needed is a call for zero discharges of contaminants, as well as the protection of habitats against encroachment. There's an enormous number of things that need to be done. But governments will do nothing unless people act too.'

ACTION

Lisa Beale *was European co-ordinator of the Greenpeace small cetaceans campaign between 1988 and 1990. She is now based in Washington D.C., where she is director of the Ocean Ecology campaign for Greenpeace USA.*

'There is no doubt that people love dolphins and think they are fascinating, intelligent and beautiful. They certainly are amazing animals – mammals, like ourselves, that have become extremely well adapted to an environment completely different from our own. And because of the way we feel about dolphins, we get upset when we read about them becoming entangled in fishing nets or affected by pollution.

But in our concern for dolphins and their fate, we must not lose sight of why it is that they're under increasing threat in so many parts of the world. It's easy to express concern or outrage when we see thousands of dolphins being herded ashore and killed, or being caught in huge numbers in fishing nets, and it's easy to demand that something should be done – that there should be some kind of legal protection to stop such things happening in the future.

But such images do not tell the whole story. Deliberate and directed small cetacean hunts are not, in themselves, the main problem – although there are very serious and genuine concerns that such hunts may be endangering some populations. As we have seen, such hunts normally only escalate when fishermen can no longer make a living because their traditional fish resources have been over-exploited. In these cases, simply targeting the fishermen who are killing the dolphins, and campaigning for action to make such killing illegal, means treating the symptom rather than the malady and failing to understand the bigger picture.

A spectral beluga hangs motionless in icy green waters. *(Daniel Lefebvre/GREMM)*

Similarly, it is not enough to try and resolve the problem of entanglement through the use of acoustic 'pingers' – devices which reflect the dolphins' echolocation beams and make nets visible to them – which have been widely proposed as the obvious and best solution. Such devices could indeed halve the number of dolphins being caught in a particular fishery, but if that fishery then doubles its capacity and uses twice as many nets, then the same number of dolphins will be entangled. To be sure of solving the problem, you have to look at it in context, and the same is true of those situations where small cetaceans are being exploited for cultural or traditional reasons.

The dolphins' problems are symptomatic of the way in which humans view the marine ecosystem and, indeed, the rest of the planet. Too often, small cetaceans are looked upon as just another marine resource to be exploited or discarded in the name of profit.

Dolphins are dying in their hundreds of thousands because they're in the way. In the way of those who want to be able to discharge their industrial wastes straight into the sea because it's quick and easy. In the way of those who want to catch the largest amount of fish and make the maximum profit in the shortest amount of time. In the way of a species that believes it has the right to pollute and exploit the marine environment for its own short-term gain.

The campaign to save small cetaceans is not at all the same as the campaign to end whaling. It is not enough for governments to pass laws or draft conventions that stop people killing dolphins and porpoises if those same governments allow the unregulated discharge of contaminants into their coastal waters, or if their policies actively encourage the use of destructive fishing methods and technology.

Through our arrogance and ignorance we have already managed to wreak tremendous damage to extensive areas of our planet. By the time such damage shows up in animals such as dolphins, then you can be sure that there is devastation being wrought on a far larger scale further down the food chain. In that sense, dolphins are symbolic of what we have done, and what we are still doing, to the marine ecosystem.

We are destroying a vital part of our planet. I hope that by looking at what is happening to dolphins we can realize that, and do what needs to be done before it's too late!

Bends (embolism, caisson disease) Nitrogen poisoning triggered in divers by swift ascent from deep waters. Bubbles of the gas form in the bloodstream, causing body contortions and tissue damage that can be fatal.

Cephalopods Marine molluscs of the class Cephalopoda, including octopus, squid, cuttlefish and pearly nautilus, characterized by well developed head and eyes and a ring of suckered tentacles.

Commensal Adjective or noun applied to separate species that share identical resources tolerantly yet stop short of full interdependence or symbiosis.

Cerebral cortex Layer of grey matter on the surface of the brain, where functions such as vision, hearing and movement are integrated. In higher mammals, such as primates, the surface is convoluted, and the association areas are particularly well developed in humans.

Crustaceans Animals without backbones but plated with hard, calcium-rich crusts or carapaces, classified in the order Crustacea. Members include crabs, lobsters, woodlice, shrimps and barnacles.

DDT Dichloro-Diphenyl-Trichloroethane: An organochlorine insecticide, readily taken up by animals and retained in fatty tissues. DDT and the compounds derived from it are resistant to breakdown and accumulate in sediments and soils. The use of DDT is officially banned in most industrialized countries but not in the third world.

Delphinid General term applied to all dolphin-like odontocetes, specifically members of the superfamily Delphinoidea.

Dieldrin Insecticide related to DDT but of much higher toxicity and longer persistence. Its use is now regulated in many countries.

Directed hunt Hunt in which dolphins are the intended target (as opposed to incidental kill, e.g. in fishing nets).

Drive fishery Method of hunting dolphins (also some migratory fish) by driving and herding them into a bay where they are then killed.

Ecosystem Term used to describe the interdependence of species in the living world with one another and with their non-living (abiotic) environment.

Ecotypes Populations within species showing distinctive structural or physiological adaptation to local environmental conditions or pressures, e.g. the tendency towards melanism (black markings) in white butterflies in heavily polluted industrial areas.

EEZ (Exclusive Economic Zone) Protected offshore area 200 miles wide. Proposed in the second (1973) UN Conference of Law of the Sea (UNCLOS II) as the standard zone in which maritime countries should have wide jurisdiction over living and mineral resources of the seabed and water column.

El Niño Means 'the little one' or 'the Christ child' in Spanish but refers ironically to irregular (roughly every two to ten years) bouts of warming of unknown origin in Pacific surface waters, changing ocean current behaviour and prompting drought, floods and other natural disasters region-wide.

FAO (Food and Agriculture Organisation) United Nations body, founded in 1945 and based in Rome, seeks to increase productivity of the world's agricultural and fisheries operations.

Global warming Theory first proposed in the 19th century that surplus carbon vented into the atmosphere (mainly as carbon dioxide or methane gas) will trap solar energy that would normally rebound into space. Among predicted consequences are a mean rise in global temperatures leading to melting of the ice caps, releasing enough water to cause sea levels to rise,

warming of the oceans and disturbance of established climate patterns.

Greenhouse Effect The natural absorption of long-wave radiation by water vapour and carbon dioxide in the lower layers of the earth's atmosphere, which serves to increase the mean temperature of the earth's surface and provides comfortable living conditions for living things. (It is calculated that without this the mean temperature of the surface would be $-87°C$.)

Handlining Fishing by hand with rod and line or line alone for individual fish of high value such as bonito, tuna or swordfish.

Immuno-suppression Suppression of an immune response by chemical, physical or biological means.

IWC (International Whaling Commission) Intergovernmental body set up in 1946 to monitor and regulate whaling practices. In 1982, adopted an indefinite moratorium on commercial whaling, which came into effect in 1986.

Longlining Use of a winched line (often several miles long) to which shorter lengths of line carrying baited hooks are attached, to fish for large inshore or open sea food fish such as cod, halibut, tuna and swordfish.

Marine Mammal Commission A US body responsible for developing, reviewing and making recommendations on actions and policies for all US Federal agencies with respect to marine mammal protection and conservation and for carrying out a research programme.

Matrilineal groups Ones which consist of females and their accumulated offspring. Examples are killer whales, feeding groups of long-finned pilot whales, and probably other species in which the males mate with any female and form no permanent social bonds with any particular mate. So far, no cetacean species is known to form permanent bonds between mating males and females.

Maximum Sustainable Yield The theoretical point at which the size of a population is such as to produce a maximum rate of increase, which can then be harvested without further depleting the population.

Mirex An organochlorine insecticide developed to combat the introduced fire ant in the south of the USA, which has proved to be perhaps the most persistent pesticide ever produced. Its use is now officially banned in most countries.

Mysticete (baleen whale) Belonging to the suborder Mysticeti of whales possessing bristly plates (baleen) in the upper jaw, which is used for sieving small planktonic organisms (such as krill) from the ocean. Examples are right whales, blue whales, gray whales and rorquals (including humpback whales).

NOAA (National Oceanic and Atmospheric Administration) Organized in 1970, establishes US policies and manages US oceanic, coastal and atmospheric resources.

NMFS (National Marine Fisheries Service) US government body responsible for administration of issues directly relating to fisheries and marine mammals. A division of NOAA.

Odontocete Member of the sub-order Odontoceti, toothed whales, including sperm whales, narwhals and all dolphins and porpoises. Odontocetes are hunters of individual prey, such as fish and squid.

Organochlorines Rings of carbon atoms with associated chlorine atoms. Manufactured in great variety for industrial and domestic uses, and as pesticides. They are persistent in the environment once released, apparently because the chlorine atoms prevent or retard breakdown. They are highly soluble in

fat. This property makes it easier for an insecticide to penetrate the lipid (fat) -covered outer body of the insect, but also causes the compound to accumulate in the fat of animals, rather than being dispersed uniformly.

Osmotic membrane A semi-permeable membrane which allows solvent molecules (but not the solute) to pass through. It appears that cetacean skin acts in this way, allowing pure water to pass into the animal to make up any deficit when water from food digestion is not available. This happens when the concentration of salts inside the animal is greater than that in the sea water outside.

Ozone A form of oxygen with three molecules (as opposed to two in the form most abundant in the atmosphere). Ozone is toxic to living organisms, but there is a natural layer of ozone in the upper atmosphere which is essential for screening out much of the harmful ultra-violet radiation from the sun.

PAHs (Polycyclic aromatic hydrocarbons) A group of chemicals which are persistent and ubiquitous environmental contaminants (e.g. benzo-a-pyrene). All the compounds contain rings of six carbon atoms (a 'benzene ring') and the term 'aromatic' refers to their early discovery when some were found to be fragrant. They are known to induce cancers in laboratory animals.

Pathogen Substance or organism harmful to living tissues and creatures.

PCBs (polychlorinated biphenyls) A group of some 209 chlorinated compounds which have caused environmental problems very similar to those created by the organochlorine pesticides such as DDT. Used in a wide range of products (papers, paints, plastics, electrical components, mining equipment etc), their chemical stability makes them resistant to breakdown in the environment.

Pelagic Living or occurring in the upper waters of the open sea, as distinct from coastal or demersal (deep-sea) habitats.

Pinnipeds The collective name for the order of mammals which includes all seals, sea-lions and walruses.

Plankton Microscopic plants (phytoplankton) and animals (zooplankton) which form the base of the marine food chain.

Purse-seining Commercial fishing method where a long net is set round a school of fish to form a circular wall, then gathered at the bottom and drawn in to form an ever-smaller pouch till the fish are gathered alongside the vessel and taken aboard.

Range Natural extremes of possible distribution in a given species, including migratory pathways and seasonal haunts.

Resident Group or population which generally stays near a particular locale, or within a comparatively limited range (see also *transient*).

Seine nets Commercial bottom fishing method where a net is dragged between two long warps or cables with which it forms a kind of huge noose.

Set In industrial fishing, a single pass or use of the fishing gear.

South Pacific Commission Established in 1947. Aims to provide a common forum within which Pacific island peoples and their governments can express themselves on issues, problems, needs and ideas common to the region. Its 27 members include France, Britain, Australia, New Zealand, the USA and a number of South Pacific island states.

Stock As used in relation to cetaceans, the term 'stock' is a fisheries management unit, chosen for convenience. A stock may or may not consist of a single isolated interbreeding population.

Tarawa Declaration Resolution passed at the South Pacific Forum meeting on 10-11 July 1989, calling for the banning of drift net fishing in the Forum's region, and for the establishment of a proper management regime for albacore fishing.

Telemetry Radio or satellite measurement of remote phenomena, including tracking of movements of migratory animals equipped with tracer devices.

Transient Group or population of cetaceans 'passing through' an area, as opposed to spending most of their time there as 'residents'.

Trawl Large bag-shaped net or array of nets towed or dragged by a trawler vessel, or between a pair of vessels.

Type specimen Definitive specimen on which the scientific description of a species is based.

Ultra-violet radiation (UV) Energy radiating mainly from the sun at wavelengths intermediate between X-rays and visible light.

UNEP (United Nations Environment Programme) Established by a resolution of the UN General Assembly in 1972. Seeks to promote international cooperation in the field of the environment. It is divided into a number of smaller programmes (e.g. Oceans and Coastal Areas/Regional Seas programme) which in turn co-ordinate different action plans (e.g. on marine mammals, and on the Mediterranean).

Vestigial Of an anatomical feature, serving little or no structural or functional purpose so tending to become reduced in size over evolutionary time (e.g. tail-bones and appendix in humans).

There is no international body which specifically seeks to protect small cetaceans. However, there are a number of national, regional and international laws, conventions and agreements which can be, or are being, used to protect porpoises and dolphins or to reduce small cetacean mortality. It is in the nature of international agreements that they are often largely disregarded and poorly enforced by national governments and many are regarded by conservationists as requiring a great deal of effort for little reward. Others, however, point out that conventions can eventually be made to work, and that decisions by international bodies can often bring much-needed external pressures to bear on offending countries.

The following are considered to be among the most useful, or potentially useful, forms of legislation or convention.

Convention on the Conservation of European Wildlife and Habitat (Berne Convention)

Brought into force in 1982, under the aegis of the Council of Europe, its four appendices include two which list protected species of wildlife, with those species on Appendix II (including 19 species of cetaceans) being offered the greatest protection. At its annual meeting in 1989, the convention agreed to set up an informal small cetaceans specialist group and to establish a working group on the protection of the Mediterranean.

Convention on the Conservation of Migratory Species of Wild Animal (Bonn Convention, CMS, or Migratory Species Convention)

The first meeting of this convention was held in 1984; the next (third) meeting will be in 1991. It encourages countries (which need not be signatories) to protect shared wildlife species by developing regional 'agreements'; one such is a draft Agreement on Small Cetaceans in the Baltic and North Seas. However, none of the proposed agreements are as yet in place. There are seven species of small cetacean listed on Appendix II of the Convention. Appendix I, which requires strict protection for those species included, contains no small cetaceans.

Convention on International Trade in Endangered Species (CITES)

CITES seeks to regulate and, when necessary, prohibit trade in endangered species and their by-products. Appendix I (all trade prohibited) contains 18 of the cetacean species. Appendix II (which allows some trade, but on a restricted level) contains all the others. Countries can escape such restrictions by entering reservations on the listing of particular species in either appendix.

Convention on the Protection of the Mediterranean Sea from Pollution (Barcelona Convention)

This convention has four protocols, of which the most relevant for cetaceans is the Protocol Concerning Mediterranean Specially Protected Areas (adopted in 1982 and brought into force in 1986) which regulates dumping, discharges, fishing, hunting and tourism, and includes a special provision restricting traditional activities if they 'cause the extinction of, or any substantial reduction in, the number of individuals making up a species . . . particularly migratory species and rare, endangered or endemic species.'

Inter-American Tropical Tuna Convention (IATTC)

This is the basis for the Inter-American Tropical Tuna Commission, mandated to achieve the Maximum Sustainable Yield of tuna populations in the Eastern Tropical Pacific. The commission conducts a tuna-dolphin programme to monitor dolphin mortality in the purse-seine fishery for large yellowfin, and investigates possible alternative fishing methods which might reduce that mortality.

International Convention for the Regulation of Whaling (ICRW)

This is the convention on which the International Whaling Commission (IWC) is based. Many member governments feel strongly that the IWC should formally take on responsibility for the directed catching of all small cetaceans as well as the large whales, but all attempted moves in this direction have so far been blocked by the exploiting nations.

Marine Mammal Protection Act (MMPA)

First adopted in 1972, this US Act is considered a landmark in national marine mammal legislation. It has to be re-authorized every few years; at the last re-authorization, in 1988, it was revised to include lengthy new measures against the killing of dolphins by yellowfin tuna fleets in the ETP.

North Sea Ministers' Conference

This meeting of environment ministers from all North Sea states is held once every three years. The most recent (third) conference, which took place in The Hague in March 1990, adopted a memorandum of understanding on small cetaceans in the North Sea. In theory, all North Sea states must now enact national legislation to implement its requirements.

United Nations Convention on the Law of the Sea (UNCLOS)

UNCLOS legitimized the concept of the 200-mile Exclusive Economic Zone (EEZ) and provided distinct management regimes for EEZs, for the High Seas, and for 'highly migratory species', including all marine cetaceans. Coastal states or international organizations may also 'prohibit, limit or regulate' the exploitation of marine mammals more strictly than that of other living resources such as fish. Disputes over the provisions relating to mineral exploitation have prevented UNCLOS from being signed by enough nations for it to come into force.

C E T A C E A

A Classification of the Living Members of this Illustrious Order of Marine Mammals.

SUBORDER ODONTOCETI
Superfamily Platanistoidea
Family Platanistidae
    Platanista gangetica — Ganges river dolphin or susu
    Platanista minor — Indus river dolphin or susu
Family Pontoporiidae
  Subfamily Lipotinae
    Lipotes vexillifer — baiji or Yangtze river dolphin
  Subfamily Pontoporiinae
    Pontoporia blainvillei — franciscana, cachimbo, La Plata dolphin
Family Iniidae
    Inia geoffrensis — boto or Amazon river dolphin
Superfamily Delphinoidea
Family Monodontidae
  Subfamily Delphinapterinae
    Delphinapterus leucas — white whale, beluga
  Subfamily Monodontinae
    Monodon monoceros — narwhal
Family Phocoenidae
  Subfamily Phocoeninae
    Phocoena phocoena — harbor porpoise
    Phocoena spinipinnis — Burmeister's porpoise
    Phocoena sinus — vaquita or Gulf of California harbor porpoise
    Neophocaena phocaenoides — finless porpoise
  Subfamily Phocoenoidinae
    Australophocaena dioptrica — spectacled porpoise
    Phocoenoides dalli — Dall's porpoise
Family Delphinidae
  Subfamily Steninae
    Steno bredanensis — rough-toothed dolphin
    Sousa chinensis — Indopacific hump-backed dolphin
    Sousa teuszii — Atlantic hump-backed dolphin
    Sotalia fluviatilis — tucuxi
  Subfamily Delphininae
    Lagenorhynchus albirostris — white-beaked dolphin
    Lagenorhynchus acutus — Atlantic white-sided dolphin
    Lagenorhynchus obscurus — dusky dolphin
    Lagenorhynchus obliquidens — Pacific white-sided dolphin
    Lagenorhynchus cruciger — hourglass dolphin
    Lagenorhynchus australis — Peale's dolphin
    Grampus griseus — Risso's dolphin
    Tursiops truncatus — bottlenose dolphin
    Stenella frontalis — Atlantic spotted dolphin
    Stenella attenuata — pantropical spotted dolphin
    Stenella longirostris — spinner dolphin
    Stenella clymene — clymene dolphin
    Stenella coeruleoalba — striped dolphin
    Delphinus delphis — common dolphin
    Lagenodelphis hosei — Fraser's dolphin
  Subfamily Lissodelphinae
    Lissodelphis borealis — northern right whale dolphin
    Lissodelphis peronii — southern right whale dolphin
  Subfamily Orcaellinae
    Orcaella brevirostris — Irrawaddy dolphin, pesut
  Subfamily Cephalorhynchinae
    Cephalorhynchus commersonii — Commerson's dolphin
    Cephalorhynchus eutropia — black, or Chilean dolphin
    Cephalorhynchus heavisidii — Heaviside's dolphin
    Cephalorhynchus hectori — Hector's dolphin

  Subfamily Globicephalinae
    Peponocephala electra — melon-headed whale, or electra dolphin
    Feresa attenuata — pygmy killer whale
    Pseudorca crassidens — false killer whale
    Orcinus orca — killer whale
    Globicephala melas — long-finned pilot whale
    Globicephala macrorhynchus — short-finned pilot whale

Superfamily Ziphioidea
Family Ziphiidae
    Tasmacetus shepherdi — Shepherd's beaked whale
    Berardius bairdii — Baird's beaked whale
    Berardius arnuxii — Arnoux's beaked whale
    Mesoplodon pacificus — Longman's beaked whale
    Mesoplodon bidens — Sowerby's beaked whale
    Mesoplodon densirostris — Blainville's beaked whale
    Mesoplodon europaeus — Gervais' beaked whale
    Mesoplodon layardii — strap-toothed whale
    Mesoplodon hectori — Hector's beaked whale
    Mesoplodon grayi — Gray's beaked whale
    Mesoplodon stejnegeri — Stejneger's beaked whale
    Mesoplodon bowdoini — Andrew's beaked whale
    Mesoplodon mirus — True's beaked whale
    Mesoplodon ginkgodens — ginkgo-toothed beaked whale
    Mesoplodon carlhubbsi — Hubbs' beaked whale
    Ziphius cavirostris — Cuvier's beaked whale
    Hyperoodon ampullatus — northern bottlenose whale
    Hyperoodon planifrons — southern bottlenose whale
Superfamily Physeteroidea
Family Physeteridae
  Subfamily Physeterinae
    Physeter macrocephalus — sperm whale
Family Kogiidae
    Kogia breviceps — pygmy sperm whale
    Kogia simus — dwarf sperm whale

SUBORDER MYSTICETI
Family Balaenidae
    Balaena mysticetus — bowhead whale
    Eubalaena australis — southern right whale
    Eubalaena glacialis — northern right whale
Family Neobalaenidae
    Caperea marginata — pygmy right whale
Family Eschrichtiidae
    Eschrichtius robustus — gray whale
Family Balaenopteridae
  Subfamily Balaenopterinae
    Balaenoptera acutorostrata — minke whale
    Balaenoptera borealis — sei whale
    Balaenoptera edeni — Bryde's whale
    Balaenoptera musculus — blue whale
    Balaenoptera physalus — fin whale, finback
  Subfamily Megapterinae
    Megaptera novaengliae — humpback whale

This book includes all members of the Odontocete Superfamilies Platanistoidea and Delphinoidea. We have not included the Superfamilies Ziphioidea or Physeteroidea, or the members of the Suborder Mysticeti (baleen whales), all of which are considered to be whales and not dolphins.

S O U R C E S

GENERAL

Alpers, Anthony. 1961. *Dolphins: the myth and the mammal.* Houghton-Mifflin, London.

Bonner, Nigel. 1989. *Whales of the World.* Blandford Press, London.

Brownell, R.L. and C.P. Donovan (Eds). 1988. *Biology of the genus Cephalorbynchus.* Rep. IWC (Special Issue 9).

Cousteau, Jacques and Yves Paccalet. 1988. *Whales.* Harry N. Abrams, New York.

Ellis, Richard. 1982. *Dolphins and Porpoises.* Alfred Knopf, New York.

Evans, Peter G.H. 1987. *The Natural History of Whales and Dolphins.* Christopher Helm, London.

Fraser, F.C. 1952. *Handbook of R.H. Burne's Cetacean Dissections.* British Museum (Natural History), London.

Gaskin, David. 1982. *The Ecology of Whales and Dolphins.* Heinemann, London.

Haley, Delphine (ed.). 1978. *Marine Mammals of the Eastern North Pacific and Arctic Waters.* Pacific Search Press, Seattle.

Harrison, Richard (Ed). *Functional Anatomy of Marine Mammals.* Vol. 1, 1972 and vol. 2, 1974. Academic Press, London.

Harrison, Sir Richard and M.M. Bryden (eds). 1988. *Whales, Dolphins and Porpoises.* Merehurst Press, London.

Hoyt, Erich. 1984. *The Whale-Watcher's Handbook.* Doubleday, New York/Penguin, Markham, Ontario.

Klinowska, Margaret. (In press). *Dolphins, Porpoises and Whales of the World.* The IUCN Cetacean Red Data Book. IUCN, Gland, Switzerland.

Leatherwood, Stephen and Randall R. Reeves, 1983. *The Sierra Club Handbook of Whales and Dolphins.* Sierra Club Books, San Francisco.

Leatherwood, Stephen et al. 1988. *Whales, Dolphins and Porpoises of the Eastern North Pacific and Adjacent Arctic Waters: a guide to their identification.* Dover Publications, New York.

McNally, Robert. 1981. *So Remorseless a Havoc: Of Dolphins, Whales and Men.* Little, Brown and Co., Boston.

Norris, Kenneth S. 1974. *The Porpoise Watcher.* John Murray, London.

Perrin, W.F. and A.C. Myerick (Eds). 1980. *Age Determination in Toothed Whales and Sirenians.* Rep. IWC (Special Issue 3). ·

Perrin, W.F., R.L. Brownell and D.P. De Master (Eds). 1984. *Reproduction in Whales, Dolphins and Porpoises.* Rep. IWC (Special Issue 6).

Stenuit, Robert. 1971. *The Dolphin: Cousin to Man.* Pelican Books, Harmondsworth, England.

Stonehouse, Bernard. 1985. *Sea Mammals of the World.* Penguin Books, Harmondsworth, England.

Watson, Lyall. 1981. *Sea Guide to Whales of the World.* Hutchinson, London.

Whither the Whales? Various articles. **Oceanus**, Volume 32, No. 1, Spring 1989.

THE NATURE OF DOLPHINS

Barnes, Lawrence G. 1984. *Search for the First Whale: Retracing the Ancestry of Cetaceans.* Oceans, no. 17 (2), March.

Barnes, Lawrence G. et al. 1985. *Status of Studies on Fossil Marine Mammals.* **Marine Mammal Science**, 1 (1).

Bryden, M.M. and R. Harrison (eds). 1986. *Research on Dolphins.* Clarendon Press, Oxford.

Geraci, J.R. and D.J. St. Aubin (Eds). 1979. *Biology of Marine Mammals: Insights Through Strandings.* Marine Mammal Commission Rep. NTIS no. PB-293 890.

Goodson A.D., M. Klinowska and R. Morris. 1988. *Interpreting the Acoustic Pulse Emissions of a Wild Bottlenose Dolphin (Tursiops truncatus).* In **Aquatic Mammals**, vol. 14, no. 1.

Herman, L.M. (Ed) 1980. *Cetacean Behaviour.* Wiley Interscience, New York.

Holmes, Brian. 1990. *Dorad an Daingin. The Dingle Dolphin.* **Sonar** 3.

Klinowska, Margaret. 1988. *Cetacean 'Navigation' and the Geomagnetic Field.* **Journal of Navigation** 41 (1).

Klinowska, M. 1989. *Whales, Dolphins and Porpoises – Survival and Distribution in a Warmer World.* Paper presented at symposium Problems of Dispersion in Populations of Mammals, Brussels, 27 May.

Leatherwood, Stephen and Randall Reeves (Eds). 1990. *The Bottlenose Dolphin.* Academic Press, London.

Marten K.L. et al. Long Marine Lab., University of California. 1989. *Big Bang Theory Update: Debilitating Fish With Sound.* Paper presented at 8th Biennial Conference on the Biology of Marine Mammals, 7-11 December.

Norris, K.S. (Ed). 1966. *Whales, Dolphins and Porpoises.* University of California Press, Berkeley and Los Angeles.

Ridgway, Sam H. and Sir Richard Harrison (Eds). 1989. *Handbook of Marine Mammals Vol. 4. River Dolphins and the Larger Toothed Whales.* Academic Press, London.

Ridgway, Sam H. and Sir Richard Harrison (Eds). (In press). *Handbook of Marine Mammals Vol. 5.* Academic Press, London.

Schusterman, Ronald J., Jeanette A. Thomas and Forrest G. Wood (eds). 1986. *Dolphin Cognition and Behaviour: a comparative approach.* Lawrence Erlbaum Associates, Hilldale.

Thomas, Joanette and Ronald Kastelein (Eds). (In press). *Sensory Abilities of Dolphins.* Plenum Press, New York.

Tyack, Peter. 1986. *Population Biology, Social Behaviour and Communication in Whales and Dolphins.* TREE, vol.1, no.6, December.

Kanwisher, John W. and S.H. Ridgeway. 1983. *The Physiological Ecology of Whales and Porpoises.* **Scientific American**, June.

Würsig, Bernd. 1979. *Dolphins.* **Scientific American**, March.

THE WORLD OF DOLPHINS

Borobia, Monica and Nelio B. Barros. 1989. *Notes on the diet of marine Sotalia fluviatilis.* **Marine Mammal Science** 5 (4) 395-399.

Brownell, Robert L. Jr., Lloyd T. Finley, Omar Vidal, Alejandro Robles and Silvia Manzanilla N. 1987. *External morphology and pigmentation of the vaquita, Phocoena sinus (cetacea: mammalia).* **Marine Mammal Science** 3 (1) 22-30.

Goulding, Michael. 1989. *The Flooded Forest.* BBC Books, London.

Hoyt, Erich. 1984. *Orca: the whale called killer.* Camden House, Ontario.

Kirkevold, Barbara C. and Joan S. Lockhard. 1986. *Behavioral Biology of Killer Whales.* Alan R. Liss Inc., New York.

Perrin, W.F. , R.L. Brownell Jr., Zhou Kaiya and Liu Jianking. 1989. *Biology and Conservation of the River Dolphins.* Occasional Papers of the IUCN Species Survival Commission (SSC), No.3, IUCN, Gland.

Pilleri, Giorgio. 1980. *Secrets of the Blind Dolphins.* Sind Wildlife Management Board, Karachi.

Sigurjonsson, J. and S. Leatherwood (Eds). 1988. *North Atlantic Killer Whales.* **Journal of the Marine Research Institute**, Reykjavik, vol. 11.

Winn, H.E. and B.L. Olla (Eds), 1979. *Behaviour of Marine Animals.* Cetaceans, vol.3, Plenum Press, New York.

THE HUMAN THREAT: GENERAL

Greenpeace. 1989. *The Status of Small Cetaceans in the North Sea.* Submission to the Standing Committee of the Convention on the Conservation of European Wildlife and Natural Habitats, and to the International Meeting of Senior Officials of the Fourth North Sea Ministers Conference. Greenpeace International, Amsterdam.

Kayes, Roger J. 1985. *The Decline of Porpoises and Dolphins in the Southern North Sea: a current status report.* Political Ecology Research Group, Oxford.

Meith, Nikki. 1984. *Saving the small cetaceans.* **Ambio** 13 (1), 2-13.

Mitchell, Edward D. 1975. *Porpoise, Dolphin and Small Whale Fisheries of the World.* IUCN Monograph No. 3. IUCN, Morges.

Northridge, Simon P. 1984. *World Review of Interactions Between Marine Mammals and Fisheries.* FAO Fisheries Technical Paper 251, Rome.

Northridge, S. and G. Pilleri. 1986. *A review of human impact on small cetaceans.* **Investigations on Cetacea** Vol. XVIII, 222-261.

Tonnessen, J.N. and A.D. Johnson. 1982. *The History of Modern Whaling.* University of California Press, Berkeley.

THE HUMAN THREAT: HUNTING AND FISHING

Arctic Species

Brodie P.F., J.L. Parsons and D.E. Sergeant. 1981. *Present status of the white whale (Delphinapterus leucas) in Cumberland Sound, Baffin Island.* Rep. int. IWC. 31 579-582.

Boulva, Jean. 1981. *Catch statistics of beluga (Delphinapterus leucas) in northern Quebec: 1974 to 1976, final; 1977 to 1978, preliminary.* Rep. IWC 31 531.

Davis, Rolph A., W. John Richardson, Stephen R. Johnson and Wayne E. Renaud. 1978. *Status of the Lancaster Sound narwhal population in 1976.* Rep. IWC 28 209-215.

Finley, K.J., G.W. Miller, M. Allard, R.A. Davis and C.R. Evans. 1981. *The white whales (Delphinapterus leucas) of northern Quebec: distribution, abundance, stock identity and catch history.* Paper SC/33/SM9. Presented to the Scientific Committee of the IWC.

Gaskin, D.E. 1984. *The harbour porpoise Phocoena phocoena (L.): regional populations, status and information on direct and indirect catches.* Rep. IWC 34 569-586.

Ivashin, M.V., and V.M. Mineev. 1981. *Notes on the distribution and whaling for white whales (Delphinapterus leucas Pallas, 1776).* Rep. IWC 31 589-90.

Kapel, Finn O. 1983. *Revised statistical data on the catch of harbour porpoise (Phocoena phocoena) in Greenland.* Paper SC/35/SM19. Presented to Scientific Committee of the International Whaling Commission.

Kemper, J. Bryan. 1980. *History of use of narwhal and beluga by Inuit in the Canadian Eastern Arctic including changes in hunting methods and regulations.* Rep. IWC 30 481-492.

Marine Mammals and the Inuit. Special Issue of the **Journal of the Vancouver Aquarium**, Vol.10, 1987.

Sergeant, D.E. 1979. *Summary of knowledge on populations of white whales (Delphinapterus leucas Pallas) and narwhals (Monodon monoceros L.) in*

Canadian waters. Paper IWC/31/SM5. Presented to the Scientific Committee of the IWC.

Faroes

Joenson, J.S. and P. Zachariassen. 1986. *Statistics for pilot whale catches in the Faroe Islands 1584-1640 and 1709-1970*. Document SC/38/SM20, submitted to the Scientific Committee of the IWC.

Thornton, Alan. 1985. *Death in the Faroes*. **Defenders** Nov/Dec, 13-19.

Various Authors. *Pilot whaling in the Faroe Islands*. Four reports. Environmental Investigation Agency, London.

Williamson, K. 1948. *The Atlantic Islands: a study of Faroese life and scene*. Cullins, London.

Japan

Boreal Institute for Northern Studies. 1988. *Small-type coastal whaling in Japan*. Report of an International Workshop. Occasional Publication No. 27, Edmonton, Canada.

Kasuya, T. 1985. *Fishery-dolphin conflict in the Iki Island area of Japan*. In Marine Mammals and Fisheries (J.R. Beddington, R.J.H. Beverton, D.M. Lavigne eds.) George Allen and Unwin, London, 253-272.

Miyazaki, Nobuyuki. 1983. *Catch Statistics of Small Cetaceans Taken in Japanese Waters*. Rep. IWC 33, 621-631.

Ono, Tamichi and Masumi Iwama. 1989. *Dolphin Fishing*. **Asahi Shinbun** 28 February (Translation: Michi Mathias)

Vaquita

Brownell, Robert L. 1988. *The vaquita: can it survive?* **Whale News** 38, 1-2.

Marx, Wesley. 1988. *Vanishing vaquitas*. **Oceans**, October, 52-58.

Tuna/dolphin

Allen, R.L. 1985. *Dolphins and the purse-seine fishery for yellowfin tuna*. In Marine Mammals and Fisheries (J.R. Beddington, R.J.H. Beverton, D.M. Lavigne eds). George Allen & Unwin, London 236-252.

Brower, Kenneth. 1989. *The destruction of dolphins*. **The Atlantic Monthly**. July, 35-58.

La Budde, Sam. 1988. *Net-death: net loss*. **Earth Island Journal** 3 (2) Spring, 27-30.

Latin America

Best, Robin C, and Vera M.F. da Silva, 1986. *Yangtze perspective on Amazon dolphins*. **BBC Wildlife** October. 502-3.

Gaskin, D.E. and A.J. Read. 1987. *Preliminary results of studies in 1984-87 of the small cetacean fisheries in Peru*. Paper SC/39/SM10. Presented to the Scientific Committee of the IWC.

Helton, David. 1985. *River dolphin loses lucky charm*. **BBC Wildlife** December, 572-3.

Read, Andrew J., Koen van Waerebeek, Julio C. Reyes, Jeff S. McKinnon and Lynda C. Lehman. 1988. *The exploitation of small cetaceans in coastal Peru*. **Biological Conservation** 46, 53-70.

da Silva, Vera M. F, and Robin C. Best. 1984. *Freshwater dolphin-fisheries interactions in the Amazon region (Brazil)*. Paper SC/36/SM20. Presented to the Scientific Committee of the IWC.

Stone, Gregory S., Juan Carlos Cardenas and Miguel Sutzin. 1987. *Notes on cetacean conservation: issues in Chile*. **Whalewatcher** Summer, 17-18.

van Waerebeek, Koen. In Press. *Preliminary notes on the existence of a dolphin by-catch off French Guiana*. **Aquatic Mammals**.

van Waerebeek, Koen. 1989. *Uncertain future for Peru's small cetaceans*. **Sonar** 2 (Autumn) 16-17.

Sri Lanka

Leatherwood, S. and R.R. Reeves (editors). 1989. *Marine Mammal Research and Conservation in Sri Lanka, 1985-1986*. Nairobi, Kenya. United Nations Environment Programme, Marine Mammal Technical Report Number 1. vi + 138pp.

Rest of the World

Bannister, J.L. 1977. *Incidental Catches of Small Cetaceans Off Australia*. Rep. IWC 27.

Clarke, Robert. 1981. *Whales and dolphins of the Azores and their exploitation*. Rep. IWC 31, 607-615.

Collet, Anne. 1983. *Directed and incidental catch of small cetaceans by French fishing vessels in the North Atlantic and Mediterranean*. Rep. IWC 33, 169.

Hoyt, Erich. 1989. *New England's harried harbour porpoise*. **Defenders**, Jan/Feb, 10-17.

Notarbartolo di Sciara, Giuseppe. 1989. *Operation Cetacea*. Greenpeace, Rome.

Perrin, William F. 1985. *The former dolphin fishery at St. Helena*. Rep. IWC 35, 423-8.

Price, W.S. 1985. *Whaling in the Caribbean: historical perspective and update*. Rep. IWC 35.

Read, Andrew. 1989. *Harbour porpoises and gillnets in the Bay of Fundy*. **Whalewatcher** Fall, 8-9.

Reeves, R.R. 1988. *Exploitation of Cetaceans in St. Lucia, Lesser Antilles, January 1987*. Rep. IWC 38.

THE HUMAN THREAT: ENVIRONMENTAL DISRUPTION

General

Aguilar, Alex. 1987. *Using organochlorine pollutants to discriminate marine mammal populations: a review and critique of methods*. **Marine Mammal Science** 3 (3).

Alzieu, C. and R. Duguy. 1981. *Nouvelles données sur la contamination des cetaces par les organochlores*. **Cons. Int. l'Explor. Mer., Doc. C.M.** 1981/N:8.

Gaskin, D.E., M. Holdrinet and R. Frank. 1982. *DDT residues in blubber of harbour porpoises, Phocoena phocoena (L.) from eastern Canadian waters during the five-year period 1969-1973*. **FAO Fish. Ser.,** [**Mammals in the Seas**] 4. 135-43.

O'Shea, T., R.L. Brownell Jr., D.R. Clark, W.A. Walker, M.L. Gay and T.G. Lamont. 1980. *Organochlorine pollutants in small cetaceans from the Pacific and South Atlantic Oceans, Nov 1968-June 1976*. **Pesticides Monitoring Journal** 14. 35-46.

Viale, D. 1978. *Evidence of metal pollution in Cetacea of the western Mediterranean*. **Ann. Inst. oceanogr., Paris** 54. 5-16.

River dolphins

Perrin, W.F., R.L. Brownell Jr., Zhou Kaiya and Liu Jianking (Eds). 1989. *Biology and Conservation of the River Dolphins*. Occasional Papers of the IUCN Species Survival Commission, No.3, IUCN, Gland, Switzerland.

Belugas in the St Lawrence

Béland, Pierre. 1988. *Witness for the prosecution*. **Nature Canada**, Fall, 28-36.

Boychuk, Rick. 1985. *Why are the St. Lawrence whales dying?* **Montreal Gazette**, August 31.

Boychuk, Rick. 1988. *St. Lawrence blues*. **Harrowsmith** May/June, 36-45.

Martineau, D., P. Béland, C. Desjardins and A. Lagace. 1987. *Levels of Organochlorine chemicals in tissues of beluga whales Delphinapterus leucas 1985*. **Canadian Veterinary Journal** 26, 297-302.

Dolphin Die-Off

Geraci, J.R. 1989. *Clinical Investigation of the 1987-88 Mass Mortality of Bottlenose Dolphins along the U.S.*

Central and South Atlantic Coast. Final report to the National Marine Fisheries Service, U.S. Navy Office of Naval Research and Marine Mammal Commission. University of Guelph, Ontario.

Greenpeace. 1989. *Critique of the National Oceanic and Atmospheric Administration's Final Report on the Clinical Investigation of the 1987-1988 Mass Mortality of Bottlenose Dolphins Along the U.S. Central and South Atlantic Coast*. Washington D.C.

Johnston, Paul and Mark Simmonds. 1988. *A heritage of pollution*. **Environment Now** July, 28-9.

McKay, Bruce. 1989. *Fish story*. **Greenpeace Magazine** July/August, 12-13.

Martineau, Daniel. 1989. *Mass Mortality of Bottlenose Dolphins: review of the final report of Dr. Geraci*. Cornell University, Ithaca, New York.

Tanabe, Shinsuke. 1988. *PCB problems in the future: foresight from current knowledge*. **Environmental Pollution** 50, 5-28.

CONTROVERSY: MILITARY

Barton, Charles. July 1977. *The Navy's Natural Divers*. **Oceans**

Burnett, Lieutenant Commander Douglas R. September 1981. *Dolphins, Naval Warfare and International Law*. US Naval Institute Proceedings.

Butcher, Lee. November 1981. *The Navy's Underwater Allies*. **Oceans**.

Chapple, Steve. June 1977. *The Pentagon's Deadly Pets*. **Penthouse.**

Holing, Dwight. October 1988. *Dolphin Defense*. **Discover.**

Pryor, Karen. 1989. *Lads Before the Wind: Diary of a Dolphin Trainer*. (2nd Edition) Sunshine Books, Washington D.C.

Ridgway, Sam H. 1988. *The Dolphin Doctor*. Fawcett Books.

Trout, Rick. December 1988. *Tursi Ops: Exploiting A Gentle Intelligence*. (Testimony)

Wood, Forrest G. 1973. *Marine Mammals and Man: The Navy's Porpoises and Sea Lions*. Robert B. Luce, Inc.

CONTROVERSY: CAPTIVITY

Bigg, M.A., G.M. Ellis, J.K.B. Ford, and K.C. Balcomb. 1987. *Killer Whales: A Study of Their Identification, Genealogy and Natural History in British Columbia and Washington State*. Nanaimo, BC: Phantom Press & Publishers.

De Master, D.P. and J.K. Drevenak. 1988. *Survivorship Patterns in Three Species of Captive Cetaceans*. **Marine Mammal Science**. Vol. 4, No. 4.

Duffield, D.A. and K.W. Miller. *Demographic Features of Killer Whales in Oceanaria in the United States and Canada, 1965-1987*. **Rit Fiskideildar**, Vol. 11.

Easton, N. August 9, 1987. *The Death of Marineland*. **Los Angeles Times Magazine**. pp. 6-10, 23-26.

Greenwood, A.G. and D.C. Taylor. 1985. *Captive Killer Whales in Europe*. **Aquatic Mammals**, Vol. 11, No. 1.

Hohn, Aleta A. et al. 1989. *Growth layers in teeth from known-age free-ranging bottlenose dolphins*. **Marine Mammal Science** 5 (4).

Hoyt, E. 1990. *Orca: The Whale Called Killer*. (3rd edition) London: Robert Hale Ltd. and Toronto: Firefly/Camden House.

Reinhold, R. April 4, 1988. *At Sea World, Stress Tests Whale and Man*. **The New York Times** .

Sigurjonsson, J. and S. Leatherwood. 1988. *The Icelandic Live-Capture Fishery for Killer Whales, 1976-1988*. **Rit Fiskideildar**, Vol. 11.

CREDITS AND ACKNOWLEDGEMENTS

A special word about the credits. The collaborative way in which this book was assembled has made assigning individual credits a complex task. It should be made clear that the consultants listed have all been involved with different areas of the book but none has been involved with all the sections.

This is an important point to emphasize because there are many contradictory scientific theories and differing political and cultural perspectives regarding this subject matter. We have tried to present a balanced picture based on the best available evidence and to present the issues in their full complexity. It remains to be said that any mistakes there may be are the responsibility of the editor.

Strenuous efforts have been made by the editor to ensure that proper accreditation has been given and that copyright clearances have been obtained. We will happily amend any omissions in future editions.

We would like to acknowledge the assistance of Pierre Béland, Vera da Silva, Giuseppe Notarbartolo di Sciara, Andrew Dizon (NMFS), Kim Dodd (Ocean Images), Sidney Holt, Saneeya Hussain (Journalists' Resource Centre for the Environment, Karachi), Xhou Kiaya (Nanjing Normal University), Elizabeth Kempf, Anne McGhie, Diana R. McIntyre (Marine Mammal Images), Mike Marten and Rosemary Taylor (Science Photo Library), Robert Michaux, Stan Minasian (EarthViews Photo Library), Chen Peixun (Institute of Hydrobiology, Wuhan), Giorgio Pilleri, Julio Reyes, Rosamond Rowe, Bob Schoelkopf (Marine Mammal Stranding Center), Greg Silber, Paul Spong, Allan Thornton and Lorna Mackinnon (Environmental Investigation Agency), Peter Tyack (Woods Hole Oceanographic Institute), Koen van Waerebeek, Sean Whyte (Whale and Dolphin Conservation Society).

We would like to thank the following people within Greenpeace for their help, encouragement and advice during the production of this book:

Tani Adams, Yuri Blanco-Castillo, Andy Booth, Helene Bours, Leslie Busby, Juan Carlos Cardenas, Duncan Currie, Damien Durrant, Fabrizio Fabbri, Matthew Gianni, Mike Hagler, Sergio Lopez, Michael Manolson, Joan Martocello, Julie Miles, Kate O'Connell, Blair Palese, Xavier Pastor, Alan Pickaver, Diana Pipke, Alan Reichman, Trudy Richards, Nicole Rioux, Tracy Romine, Kalyani Sandrapragas, Claudio Serangeli, Mark Simmonds, Ruth Smitkin, Liz Somerville, Jay Townsend.

Our particular thanks to Lisa Beale, James Carr, Bruce McKay and Lesley Scheele, who took on a huge amount of extra work in order to help make this book happen and did so with unfailing enthusiasm and good humour.

Once more we acknowledge the continuing help and support of Martin Leeburn, Elke Martin and Dawn Carey at Greenpeace Communications. The unflagging faith of Steve Sawyer, David McTaggart and many others in the value of our enterprise is also much appreciated.

We would also like to extend our thanks to Sarah Wallace, Cindy Richards, Sally Welford and the rest of the team at Century Hutchinson for their patience and encouragement during the long and painstaking production of this book.

Kieran Mulvaney would, in addition, like to thank the following people for their help and understanding: Abigail Costelloe, Lesley Hunter, Paul Isham and Michael Knowles.

John May: This book is dedicated to the memory of Oliver Caldecott, who published the first book I ever worked on, *An Index of Possibilities*, which gave me and my colleagues our first real chance in publishing. He was also the one who provided the introduction to our current publishers, which led directly to the making of this book. He was a constant and true champion of new ideas and we are all indebted to him.

The sonograms on page 31 are reproduced from *Aquatic Mammals*, Vol. 14, no. 1 (1988), with kind permission of the editor, Victor Manton.

This book is printed on a low-chlorine paper called Silk-Art, produced by the Swedish paper manufacturers Papyrus Nymölla AB. At the time of buying, this represented the least environmentally-damaging option, given our requirements. An increasing number of paper mills are now producing chlorine-free paper, and it is to be hoped that such paper will become available in an increasingly wide range of weights in the future.